HISTORY OF EDUCATION

THE WOBURN EDUCATION SERIES

General Series Editor: Professor Peter Gordon

The Victorian School Manager   *by Peter Gordon*

Selection for Secondary Education   *by Peter Gordon*

The Study of Education
A Collection of Inaugural Lectures   *edited by Peter Gordon*

Volume I   Early and Modern
Volume II   The Last Decade
Volume III The Changing Scene

The Education of Gifted Children   *by David Hopkinson*

Games and Simulations in Action
by Alec Davison and Peter Gordon

Slow Learners – A Break in the Circle
A Practical Guide for Teachers in Secondary Schools   *by Diane Griffin*

The Middle School – High Road or Dead End?   *by John Burrows*

Music in Education   *by Malcolm Carlton*

Teaching and Learning Mathematics   *by Peter Dean*

Unequal Educational Provision in England and
Wales: The Nineteenth-Century Roots
by William E. Marsden

Dictionary of British Educationists
by Richard Aldrich and Peter Gordon

History of Education: The Making of a Discipline
edited by Peter Gordon and Richard Szreter

Educational Policy in England in the Twentieth Century
by Peter Gordon, Richard Aldrich and Dennis Dean

Teaching the Humanities
edited by Peter Gordon

HISTORY OF EDUCATION
The Making of a Discipline

Edited by
PETER GORDON
University of London Institute of Education

and
RICHARD SZRETER
University of Birmingham

THE WOBURN PRESS

First published 1989 in Great Britain by
THE WOBURN PRESS
Gainsborough House, 11 Gainsborough Road,
London E11 1RS, England

and in the United States of America by
THE WOBURN PRESS
c/o Biblio Distribution Centre
8705 Bollman Place, Savage, MD 20763

This collection copyright © 1989 The Woburn Press

British Library Cataloguing in Publication Data

History of education : the making of a discipline. –
(Woburn education series)
1. Education. British historiology
I. Gordon, Peter, *1927–*   II. Szreter, R.
370'9

ISBN 0-7130-0183-6

Library of Congress Cataloging-in-Publication Data

History of education : the making of a discipline / edited by Peter
Gordon and Richard Szreter.
    p. cm. — (The Woburn education series)
ISBN 0-7130-0183-6.
    1. Education—Historiography. I. Gordon, Peter, 1927–
II. Szreter, Richard. III. Series.
LA9.H53 1989
370'.9—dc19   89-5494
                                        CIP

Printed and bound in Great Britain by
BPCC Wheatons Ltd, Exeter

CONTENTS

Acknowledgements   vii

*Peter Gordon and
Richard Szreter*   Introduction   1

1. *Foster Watson*   The Study of the History of
                        Education (*Contemporary
                        Review*, cv, 1914)   19

2. *H.M. Beatty*   The History of Education (*History*,
                        ii, 1917)   30

3. *J.W. Adamson*   A Plea for the Historical Study of
                        English Education (in *The Illiterate
                        Anglo-Saxon and Other
                        Essays*, 1946)   39

4. *W.H.G. Armytage*   The Place of the History of
                        Education in Training Courses for
                        Teachers (*British Journal of
                        Educational Studies*, i, 1953)   47

5. *B. Simon*   The History of Education (in J.W.
                        Tibble, ed., *The Study of
                        Education*, 1966)   55

6. *G. Sutherland*   The Study of the History of
                        Education (*History*, lix, 1969)   73

7. *R. Szreter*   History and the Sociological
                        Perspective in Educational Studies
                        (*University of Birmingham
                        Historical Journal*, xii, 1969)   85

8. *H.C. Barnard*   The Historiography of Education
                        (in R.J.W. Selleck, ed.,
                        *Melbourne Studies in
                        Education*, 1970)   105

9. *A.C.F. Beales*   The Place of the History of
                       Education in the Training of
                       Teachers (in J.H. Higginson, ed.,
                       *Gleanings for Tomorrow's
                       Teachers*, 1971)   131

10. *J.E. Talbott*   The History of Education
                       (*Daedalus*, c, 1971)   143

11. *A. Briggs*   The Study of the History of
                       Education (*History of Education*,
                       1, 1972)   160

12. *C. Webster*   Changing Perspectives in the
                       History of Education (*Oxford
                       Review of Education*, ii, 1976)   176

13. *H. Silver*   Aspects of Neglect: The Strange
                       Case of Victorian Popular
                       Education (*Oxford Review of
                       Education*, iii, 1977)   194

14. *L. O'Boyle*   A Possible Model for the Study of
                       Nineteenth-Century Secondary
                       Education in Europe (*Journal of
                       Social History*, xii, 1978)   211

15. *R. Lowe*   History as Propaganda: The
                       Strange Uses of the History of
                       Education (in *Trends in the Study
                       and Teaching of the History of
                       Education*, 1983, History of
                       Education Society)   225

ACKNOWLEDGEMENTS

The editors and publishers gratefully acknowledge the following for permission to reprint the articles and chapters appearing in this volume:

The Historical Association for the articles by H.M. Beatty and Gillian Sutherland in *History*. Cambridge University Press for the chapter from J.W. Adamson's *The Illiterate Anglo-Saxon and Other Essays*. Basil Blackwell and Mott for the article by W.H.G. Armytage in the *British Journal of Educational Studies*. Routledge for Brian Simon's chapter from J.W. Tibble ed., *The Study of Education*. Melbourne University Press for H.C. Barnard's article in *Melbourne Studies in Education 1970*. J.H. Higginson for A.C.F. Beales' article in *Gleanings for Tomorrow's Teachers*, Christ Church College, Canterbury. The American Academy of Arts and Sciences for J.E. Talbott's article in *Daedalus*. Taylor and Francis for the article by Asa Briggs in *History of Education*. Carfax Publishing Company for Harold Silver's and Charles Webster's articles in *Oxford Review of Education*. Carnegie–Mellon University Press for Lenore O'Boyle's article in *Journal of Social History*. History of Education Society for Roy Lowe's article in the *History of Education Society Bulletin*.

The editors would also like to thank the contributors to this volume for their kind permission to reproduce their work.

INTRODUCTION

The present volume brings together a number of significant studies about rather than in the history of education. Its concern is thus historiographical rather than historical, and we believe it fills a major gap. For while public and professional interest in education runs high today and while the recognition of the value of the historical perspective to the understanding of today's and tomorrow's educational questions is growing, there is relatively little appreciation of the nature, of the why and how, of the transformation that the historical study of education in this country has undergone in the last twenty years or so. There is certainly no single book charting the progress of that change, from its antecedents earlier in the century, through the great innovative phase beginning in the early 1960s, to some new orthodoxies and their questioners today. In the United States, where the debate on the study of education had begun some ten years earlier,[1] a volume devoted to the historiography of education appeared in the early 1980s[2] but its content and tone are very different from this one; and the admirable small-scale study of *The History of Education Today* published in 1985 under the auspices of Unesco is very heavily French-oriented.[3] There are, however, in our predominantly British collection two contributions from American scholars (Nos. 10 and 14). One represents the closeness of the links, indeed the special relationship, between British and American historians of education and was written at a crucial moment as far as the consolidation of the 'new' history of education was concerned; the other hints at the greater readiness of American scholars to consider theoretical models as well as at their strength in comparative history. The other thirteen contributions take the story of the history of education in this country from the eve of World War One to the 1980s, relating them to both cognitive and institutional developments in history and in the study of education in universities and in the world of teacher education.

There were several possible ways of organizing this introductory essay. One obvious and tempting way of investing it with some shape and pattern would have been to enlarge upon and update the discussion of the six dimensions of recent change in the study of history which

1

Professor Asa Briggs delineates in his paper of 1972 (No. 11). These were: more sophisticated work on local history, considering structures and processes in addition to personalities and institutions; advances in comparative history, moving from local and regional sub-cultures to national societies and cross-national studies; more quantitative studies by historians, spreading from demographic and economic to wider social history; social historical studies 'from below'; a more analytical approach to political history, with 'less concentration on "landmarks" and more on the interplay of people and problems'; and, finally, better cultural and intellectual historical work, with less emphasis on 'great thinkers'.

This impressive sixfold scheme, in so far as it refers to the specialism of educational researches, has been helpful to us and will not be lost sight of in the following pages. But to adopt it as the framework for the present Introduction would be imitative, possibly to the point of plagiarism. The updating would prove an exceedingly difficult task and, full as the list appears to be, it is by now less than comprehensive: witness, for example, the recent revival of interest in studying informal education and quasi-educational agencies, from boys' comics to the Scout movement, and the growing interest in women and children in former times.

Another way of organizing this Introduction, which some readers might prefer, would be to follow the tag that 'history is what historians do', and to hang an extensive consideration of recent trends in educational history on the pegs of the major works, or thematic groups of works, of the last quarter century, or locate them in the most cultivated fields or most debated issues in the history of education. However, the principle we have just quoted is epistemologically highly suspect; the approach would make our Introduction into a vast multiple essay-review and this is not our intention. Thirdly, a skeleton plan for the present essay might be arrived at from a more theoretical (or pseudo-theoretical) examination and exemplification of novel questions and interests; of new methods *sensu stricto* (including sources) or perspectives; of changing emphases and biases as well as underlying, often ideological, assumptions; and of new organizing concepts. This way may smack more of social science than of history; the dangers of confusion and aridity of this approach are considerable and the sheer cerebral difficulty quite daunting.

Yet another possibility is afforded by bearing in mind the fact that in order to establish itself, a new discipline, or in this instance a sub-discipline or specialism, needs both a cognitive identity and a professional identity,[4] the latter being at the core of its institutionalization.

This duality might readily have guided our efforts. In so far as the principal interest of the present volume is cognitive, we could have proceeded by contrasting the 'old' and the 'new' history of education, while also paying some attention to the institutional interest which demands that we contrast the practice of the history of education in establishments devoted to the academic study of history with those concerned with professional teacher education. Such a schematic plan would certainly be too restrictive to cope with the rich variety of work to be considered and with the many exceptions and special cases we are likely to encounter.

We accept, of course, that all the approaches we have briefly considered are valuable, and in the present Introduction we shall seek to interweave, and, to some extent, to integrate them. There is one further possible principle of organization which we have not so far mentioned: it is certainly the simplest and arguably the most historical one, namely chronological. It would indeed be relatively easy and quite legitimate in this Introduction to survey the 120 years of educational historical endeavour from R.H. Quick to the present time. In the event, whilst the order we have adopted for the contributions in this collection is chronological, the Introduction is primarily analytical and thematic and deals largely with developments in the last quarter of a century.

In his little-known and somewhat unsophisticated 1917 article (No. 2), H.M. Beatty contends that following Quick's *Essays on Educational Reformers*, published in 1868, very little progress was made in the history of education in this country until the opening years of the present century. This is not entirely correct. In fact in the decade from 1868, valuable work was done by, for example, Oscar Browning in Cambridge or S.S. Laurie in Edinburgh; classical antiquity was well served by the slim volume by A.S. Wilkins, *National Education in Greece*, 1873, the Middle Ages by Sister A. Theodor Drane's *Christian Schools and Scholars – or sketches of education from the Christian era to the Council of Trent*, 1867, a two-volume work published anonymously, while Joseph Payne taught his course encompassing developments from ancient Egypt to his contemporaries at the College of Preceptors, with much of his work published in the 1880s. This was an age of forerunners, though; there were no followers until the beginning of the twentieth century and the second generation of historians of education. This latter period may be called the heroic age of the discipline, with the appearance of such outstanding scholars as Foster Watson, J.W. Adamson, W.H. Woodward, and slightly earlier, A.F. Leach.

3

Of these four, the first two are represented in the present collection (Nos. 1 and 3), albeit by pieces separated by over three decades and two World Wars. Foster Watson, who was head of the training department of Aberystwyth University College, Wales, 1894–5, was probably the finest mind of the four and certainly the most encyclopaedic. His 1914 article is still of great interest, particularly his subtle analysis of how the progress of the 'hard' sciences in the later nineteenth century promoted the historical study of knowledge. Watson's emphasis on a reasonably equal balance of context knowledge, especially historical, and of technical skills in teachers, was novel at the time. His insistence that all those involved in education should be concerned about 'the price paid for the neglect of the study of the history of education by teachers being *the tendency* to achieve an . . . egotism . . . without reference to other standards than those of the existing environment' presages Brian Simon's (No. 5) 1966 insistence on the liberating effect of studying the past of education. J.W. Adamson, the holder (at King's College, London, 1903–24) of the only chair of Education in this country that was to be specifically linked with history, produced a volume in 1930 entitled *English Education, 1789–1902*, which has yet to be superseded. His article in the present collection is perhaps less impressive (No. 3). He argues well for the historical stand against the dominance of psychology in educational studies, but he appears traditional in emphasising the study of educational institutions and thinkers, confining himself only to English thinkers. His piece is curiously nationalistic, a reminder that he was born in 1857 and was a product of the Victorian age. The title of his contribution is significant for our purpose: *A Plea for the Historical Study of English Education*. It was just that. The same may be said for Foster Watson's article and the contemporaneous one (No. 2) by Beatty who, by profession, was an Inspector of Schools in Ireland. So too, in the main, is the contribution (No. 4) by W.H.G. Armytage, Professor of Education at Sheffield University, 1954–82. It is instructive to compare Armytage's article, which was addressed specifically to the community of teacher-trainers, with that of A.C.F. Beales (No. 9),[5] written almost twenty years later. The area of higher education had changed out of all recognition during the intervening period, including the nature of the subject Education, a matter to which we shall return later.

We have, regretfully, included no contribution by Michael Sadler, as none appeared historiographical in character. But his importance must not be overlooked, and his relevance to our theme is twofold. First, he carefully planned his history of education syllabus at Manchester University, and the interested reader will find it reproduced in J.H.

Higginson, 'Establishing a History of Education Course: the Work of Professor Michael Sadler, 1903–1911', *History of Education*, 9 (3), 1980; secondly, he was the first historian of education in this country to acknowledge the value of sociology, both in his writings and by becoming in 1903 one of the earliest members of the Sociological Society.[6] Sadler's Inaugural lecture *National Ideals in Education* of the same date is included in a collection of such lectures published earlier in this decade.[7]

Among earlier holders of chairs in Education, several had written historical works, including Laurie and Payne whom we have already mentioned; the former's chair, established in 1876, was in Scotland and the latter's at the non-university institution of the College of Preceptors in London. The progress in the academic institutionalization of the study of education in England was relatively slow, the first chair being established at Durham College of Science (later, King's College, Newcastle), in 1895. It was in the 1890s that there developed, to quote Barnard (No. 8), 'a movement for the extension and deepening of teacher training, especially that of secondary teachers. The development of university day training colleges led to the growth of university departments of education . . . [and] in practically every case a study of educational history was required'.[8] It was, consequently, in the first decade of this century, largely through the efforts of Sadler, Foster Watson and Adamson, that the historical study of education became truly established at university level. That it was located in the departments of teacher training rather than in history departments may in the long run have threatened to isolate and weaken the sub-discipline. It would be several decades before mainstream historians began to show any interest in education, though their interest in studying their own university milieu had been in evidence already in the 1870s.[9] In the present collection, five of the fifteen contributors are historians unconnected with teacher training.

To conclude this section, it can be said that during the first half of the twentieth century a sizeable body of historical literature on education was built up, consisting of monographs, textbooks, collections of sources and articles in periodicals, though scattered for want of a specialist journal. The authors of the papers Nos. 1 to 4, however, were in the main making a case for a larger historical component in educational studies, but they were scarcely critical of the history of education as it was practised in the first half of this century. Yet a little over ten years after the publication of the Armytage article, Brian Simon in his powerful programmatic article on 'The History of Education' (No. 5),[10] called for a 'wind of change' in the discipline to ensure its rightful place among the other disciplines of education. What had happened since the mid-1950s to bring this about? It is time for us to consider in some more detail the emergence of the 'new' history of education.

The question of what was wrong with the 'old' history of education is an important one, for criticisms of it were both a precondition and part-and-parcel of the emergence of the 'new'. This emergence was, very interestingly, virtually a world-wide phenomenon;[11] it was first, admittedly, in evidence in the United States, though we shall here confine ourselves for the most part to developments in Britain.

There were, in the main, three substantive aspects of the writing on the history of education which engendered dissatisfaction and attracted criticism from the mid-1950s. For one thing, the excessive emphasis by traditional historians of education on thinkers and writers was noted. This criticism focused partly on the biographical–intellectual manner of studying them, often with little reference to the period and the social environment in which they wrote. Perhaps more importantly, this approach failed to appreciate the gap between their noble and elevated schemes and the actual educational realities of the day. Secondly, there was overmuch concern with educational legislation, detailed provisions of Acts of Parliament and of the personalities involved in their promotion, rather than dealing with important questions arising out of legislation such as its timing, adequacy or ideological hue. It was symptomatic of the nascent revolution in historical educational thinking that Eric Midwinter in 1966 should scathingly refer to 'the history of English education [that] is too often viewed as a list of legislative provisions, which the students pursue, like mountain goats, jumping from peak to peak'.[12] Thirdly, too much emphasis was laid upon the study of institutions. This deflected attention from other areas, such as informal education effected through the educative agencies of the family, the public library, or the eighteenth-century Grand Tour (Webster, No. 12, is critical of this tendency, though also of the other extreme of an over-inclusive view of education). It also suffered from two inherent faults: most of the works were about elite institutions like the Oxbridge colleges or great public schools, and many were uncritical and even eulogistic.

This was by no means all. For, linked with the above doubts, three further accusations, requiring more subtle epistemological analysis, were levelled against the traditional history of education, gathering strength as the discipline became increasingly associated with social history at large. There was dissatisfaction with its tone; a great deal of

6

writing, textbooks in particular, was descriptive to the point of being 'factographic' rather than analytical. It thus lacked sophistication, the power of stimulation and breadth of perspective. This can be demonstrated by comparing the standard textbooks of the immediate post-war decade and of the period a quarter of a century later, J.S. Curtis, *The History of Education in Great Britain*, first published in 1948, and J. Lawson and H. Silver, *A Social History of Education in England*, 1973. As a work of reference and a mine of information, Curtis is still of use today, but it is inclined to be overdetailed and dull and also tends to neglect wider social influences. Lawson and Silver has its imperfections, but it is livelier and more analytical, and the use of the word 'social' in its title is highly significant.

The second of the present trio of criticisms (relating to all three substantive ones) of the 'old' history of education is that it considered education as a closed world, operating apart from the wider society, the writers scarcely acknowledging economic, political and ideological pressures from without. Their blinkered perspective meant, too, if only by implication, that change in education tended to be ascribed to endogenous factors to the exclusion of the exogenous. This was not, of course, a wholly new criticism. In particular, the influential education-ist Sir Fred Clarke, historian by training and sociologist by inclination, whose impact, notably in his *Education and Social Change*, 1940, is repeatedly acknowledged by Professor Simon (No. 5), castigated this major shortcoming of historical and other writings on education. Probably more influential here was the small classic, *Education in the Forming of American Society*, 1960, by Bernard Bailyn. His insistence that education be studied 'in its elaborate, intricate involvement with the rest of society' was both salutary and seminal. However, it led John E. Talbott by 1971 (No. 10) to express concern that the field had become so broad as to be ill-defined, while another half-decade on, Charles Webster, Reader in the History of Medicine, University of Oxford, suggested that in some hands the history of education was becoming 'an encyclopaedia of social and intellectual history, in which it is almost impossible to obtain any clear focus on the educational experiences of childhood and adolescence' (No. 12).

It is clear that there were two works which were seminal to the 'new' history of education, both written outside this country. One was Bailyn's book, the other, the stimulating volume by the Frenchman, Philippe Ariès, translated into English under the title *Centuries of Childhood*, which appeared in 1962. Ariès not only directs students' attention to children in history but employs novel and not universally approved materials and methods, notably the iconographic approach.

7

And to move ahead of our story, the creative period in educational historiography of the 1960s and 1970s was exemplified by two large volumes published in 1979, both comparative in their perspective and, significantly, again neither written by a British historian of education: the sociologist Margaret Archer's *Social Origins of Educational Systems*[13] and the German-American historian Fritz Ringer's *Education and Society in Modern Europe*.

To return to the second group of criticisms of the 'old' history of education, perhaps the most intensive and prolonged attack on its ideological assumptions was launched in the 1960s in the United States. It was accused of adopting a celebratory 'Whiggist' approach that depicted past developments in education, especially public education, as continuous progress, beneficial to all: its historiography was being accused of class bias, racism, sexism and, all in all, rank elitism. The former charge was linked by Talbott (No. 10), himself no revisionist, with 'educational history becoming a weapon against adversaries living and dead, [and] a vindication of their own efforts and ideas in the struggle for public schooling'. It was also associated with 'presentism' which Léon defines as 'the projection on the past of currently topical themes . . . [in] the process of recovering history with a view to supporting or justifying certain theories or actions'.[14] The attack on such characteristics of the 'old' history of education as class-bias, while often tenable, indicated that the revisionists also were tainted with 'presentism'. Indeed, the powerful movement elicited a fair amount of reaction, by the mid-1970s, both to its frequent neo-Marxist stance and to its predilection for the conceptual apparatus and quantitative methodologies of the social sciences which yielded somewhat uneven results.[15] As R. H. Tawney had stated in his Inaugural lecture in 1933 of another branch of history, 'serious economic history, whether Marxian or not, is inevitably post-Marxian',[16] so, whether revisionist or not, today's educational history cannot help being post-revisionist. At the very least, this applies to the selection of research areas, as witnessed by the recent popularity of studies of girls' education or the social distribution of literacy; and it applies to some terminology, too, notably 'schooling'. There has been no revisionism as such in British educational historiography, but often, quite independently of the American currents, similar doubts regarding the 'old' approach were formulated by a number of writers. They are represented in the present collection by Harold Silver and by Roy Lowe of the University of Birmingham (Nos. 13 and 15 respectively).

Silver, who sees the revisionist movement as a dimension of 'the radicalization of American politics and intellectual life in the 1960s', reacts against 'presentism' in one British version thus: 'Only those structures, events, ideas . . . in Victorian education and society that have meaning in twentieth-century terms have been admitted to the definition of the history of education'. His theme of 'neglect', that is, his concern with the negative side of historical selection, which he explains in another publication as 'interest in the phenomenon of historical silence: what historians omit, evade, reject',[17] is, at bottom, revisionist. Lowe's contribution closes our volume not only for chronological reasons, but because with him our selection comes a full circle in that he brings his critique to bear upon some Whig historians-as-propagandists, including Foster Watson and Adamson with whom our volume opens. His neat threefold division adds to the motivating interests of teacher-trainers and administrators the self-interest of 'participant historians', that is active educationists 'cementing their own niche in history'.

In concluding this section, however, it seems worthwhile to point out that the faults of the 'old' history of education are not necessarily irremediable. This applies particularly to the substantive ones of overemphasis on educational thinkers, on legislation and on institutions. Thus, in a recent article, K.H. Jarausch, a critic of the benefits of the 'new' ways, wrote, 'The question of how to write history of education will not be decided by programmatic claims and counter-claims, but rather by convincing research results'.[18] It is consequently arguable that, despite the overall validity of the first three criticisms, the works of great educational thinkers and theorists should not simply be disregarded but re-examined. It has rightly been pointed out that 'ideas are not outdated because they are old',[19] and old thoughts can often be fruitfully re-thought in new contexts. Again, Talbott (No.10) referred favourably to Sheldon Rothblatt's *The Revolution of the Dons*, 1968, as 'new institutional history'. Less than two years after Midwinter's disparaging remarks about major legislative measures, P.W. Musgrave produced a stimulating work on *Society and Education in England since 1800*, basing much of his argument on a sociological interpretation of Acts of Parliaments as 'definitions of the situation'.[20] But to refer to the impact of sociology in the late 1960s upon the history of education in this country indicates that it is necessary to turn from the criticism of the 'old' history of education to a consideration of the novel and positive features of the 'new'.

Most of the work in the history of education has usually taken place in establishments concerned primarily with the training of teachers. The Robbins Report of 1963 recommended the substitution of the term 'teacher training' by 'teacher education'; this new nomenclature was appropriate in view of the changes which were occurring in the ethos and standards of those institutions and was readily accepted by them. Of particular interest here was the subsequent move away from studying education as a unitary subject in favour of an assortment of discipline-based courses in, for example, philosophy of education or history of education.[21] Hencefore it became rare for the history of education to be taught by other than specialists as had formerly been the case. The overall change also involved an increasing emphasis on research and publication in university departments of education and in the colleges; the drive towards an all-graduate teaching profession provided further motivation. This was paralleled by a shift in direction in the other parent discipline of the history of education, that is in history at large. Interest in social and economic history increased at the expense of political and constitutional history (the long-term impact of the French periodical *Annales*, launched in 1929, was important here). Some 'pure' historians now acknowledged that there were educational problems worthy of investigation, although the specialism still suffered because of its old association with the less than prestigious teacher-training establishments.

The expansion of social and economic history may be seen as a pre-condition of the emergence of the 'new' history of education, both because of its location within the ambit of social history and because of its association with the booming social sciences. Simon's insistence (No. 5) on viewing education as a social function was significant in this context. But as regards particular social sciences, their impact upon educational history was uneven, and this is reflected in our collection.

Two of the social sciences may, we believe, be discounted here: politics and psychology. The former has long been the centre of the historical study of education, although the works of the 1960s and later, notably Brian Simon's trilogy,[22] are a far cry from the writings of two or three generations ago. Psychology of course still forms the central pillar of the study of education as teaching-and-learning processes. It has lately enjoyed some prominence within the history of education because of the important advances in the study of the growth of psychometrics in association with eugenics, notably G. Sutherland, *Ability, Merit and Measurement*, 1984 (psycho-history has not as yet been taken up by British historians of education). Anthropological perspectives and methods have not so far received serious attention within the historical study of education in this country. This was pointed out by Lawrence Stenhouse in 1978 in his 'Case Study and Case Records: towards a contemporary history of education', *British Educa-*

tion Research Journal, 4(2), but his call apparently fell on deaf ears, as had Joan Simon's 1971 anthropology-flavoured work on *The Social Origins of English Education*. Also, although geography has few of the characteristics of a social science, we might mention the appearance in the 1980s of some valuable works on the spatial rather than social distribution of educational opportunity and attainment.[23]

It is surprising, however, that there are few British studies concerned with the value of the economic perspective it the history of education. Both articles included in this collection which demonstrate such an awareness are by American writers. Lenore O'Boyle of Cleveland State University suggests (No. 14) that the professions as occupational groups 'bringing together individual motive and social needs' are particularly useful for the purpose of making cross-national generalizations in analysing nineteenth-century relations between economic and educational expansion. Nevertheless there are several British historical works on education in which economic influences and determinants figure large: R.H. Tawney's pamphlet, *Some Thoughts on the Economics of Public Education*, 1938, John Vaizey's *The Costs of Education*, 1958,[24] and the controversial E.G. West's *Education and the State*, 1965, to mention but a few. Moreover, in recent years at least three areas of educational history have benefited from the active interest of economic historians and the use of economic perspectives. They are the debate on the 1862 Revised Code, defended largely on economic grounds by John Hurt in his *Education in Evolution*, 1970; the quest to elucidate the quadruple relationship between the Industrial Revolution, the provision of education, the spread of literacy and so-called social control;[25] and the debate on the elitism and classics-orientation of the public schools and the older universities versus industrial and economic progress, an issue popularized by M. Wiener, *English Culture and the Decline of the Industrial Spirit, 1850–1980*, 1981.

We are thus left with sociology, whose connection with the history of education is explicitly represented in this volume by Szreter (No. 7).[26] It is certainly arguable that sociology has affected the practice of the history of education, even if the results do not add up to a significant body of sociological history of education. There have, however, been some such works employing sociological concepts by authors who are primarily sociologists. These range from C.M. Turner's 'Sociological approaches to the history of education', *British Journal of Educational Studies*, 17(2), 1969, on the Mechanics' Institutes, to Margaret Archer's book to which reference has already been made. Secondly, and perhaps most pervasively, there have been many works of high quality in the last two decades by historians of education who have acquired a penchant for and skill in sociologising their work. This is scarcely surprising, for as P.J. Harrigan remarked, it took 'sociologists ... equipped with the tools of their discipline to ask questions few historians had posed: about elites, social advantage, reproduction of dominant class values, and structural relationships of schools to other social and political institutions'.[27] Last but not least, we should mention a negative impact of sociology of education upon history of education, which nevertheless resulted in important positive developments.

When sociology of education was introduced into teacher-education courses in the mid-1960s, it was largely at the expense of history of education. The resultant anxiety of the teachers of the latter specialism was a major factor in the formation in 1967 of the History of Education Society. The Society's achievements have been considerable. Through its conferences, its *Bulletin*, established in 1969, and its journal, *History of Education*, founded three years later, it has done much to maintain the standing of the history of education in this country. If in its other activities the Society has enjoyed limited success in bringing together historians employed in education and other historians specialising in educational issues, both parties have been well represented in the pages of its major journal. It should also be noted that several other countries publish specialist journals in this field,[28] and that valuable annual international meetings of historians of education have been promoted in recent years by the International Standing Conference for the History of Education.

Two other historical periodicals deserve a mention here. In some ways, as the *Annales* has been a moving force in promoting the widening scope of the study of history in France and on the Continent generally, so has in Britain the periodical *Past and Present*, established in 1952. This 'journal of historical studies' was almost from the outset espousing the causes of social and economic history, including anthropological and cultural perspectives. Marxist in its *Weltanschauung* for its first ten years and decreasingly so thereafter, the journal has always encouraged writers who presented novel themes. Education has featured in the pages of *Past and Present* more frequently than in the typical historical periodical. Joan Simon, in an article that was somewhat critical of its contribution to history of education,[29] admits that it 'has done more than most to put the subject on the map since its inception in 1952'. This, coincidentally, was the year in which the first issue of the *British Journal of Educational Studies* appeared. Conceived as a major scholarly journal for educationists other than those specialising in psychology, it was unrivalled for twenty years in attracting contributions from historians of and in education in this country.

The other historical periodical which is of importance in this connection is the *Journal of Contemporary History*, founded in 1965. Its title at first irritated many traditionalists as a contradiction in terms, but it soon acquired a sound reputation. Also, Szreter argues (No. 7) that history and sociology may be seen as natural partners rather than as rivals in educational studies: 'Since the sociologist's "present" is virtually always, in fact, the very recent past, and since historians now consider this as a part of their demesne, the *rapprochement* of the two studies has been advanced'. Like *Past and Present*, the *Journal of Contemporary History* has always been generous in the space it has devoted to educational topics, regarding education as a major, perhaps the major, component of the historical process. In 1967, the *Journal* published a special issue, entitled 'Education and Social Structure', vol. 2(3). While its thirteen contributors did not include a single British academic specialist, it marked 'the arrival of history of education as a respectable, even fashionable, subject for study'. These words were written by Gillian Sutherland, Fellow of Newnham College, Cambridge University, and her contribution to this volume (No. 6) is a widely conceived and perceptive essay-review on 'Education and Social Structure'.

Within the last decade, the proliferation of articles on educational themes in history and other humanities periodicals has been striking, as has been their increasing sophistication. A bibliography published in 1986 and covering nearly fifty non-education periodicals over a period of nearly fifty years,[30] testified to a fast-growing active research interest in education among a wide variety of scholars engaged in disciplines other than education.

If the 1960s and the 1970s saw the exciting rise of the 'new' history of education and much debate on the nature and desiderata of both the 'old' and the 'new', it is difficult as yet to discern any pattern and direction about the 1980s, let alone attempt to forecast future developments. Institutionally, there is little doubt that within the last decade the history of education has been on the retreat.[31] It has been losing ground, admittedly slowly, in the institutions of teacher education and gaining none, as far as is known, in history courses in other institutions of higher education. Yet, as has been demonstrated here, the writing and research in the field have been flourishing. There was some truth in Charles Webster's remark (No. 12) made in 1976 that 'Paradoxically, the decline in importance of the history of education in vocational training . . . has coincided with a revival of interest in the subject among scholars of widely different training and interest'. A decade later, Harold Silver asserted, in a similar vein, that 'there is, in fact, a vigorous output of high quality dissertations and theses in the history of education',[32] though he did not feel sanguine about their authors' professional prospects in the field. Even so, Silver's 1977 list of the discipline's 'items of neglect' (No. 13) has still much validity, and it is not difficult to point to some uncultivated or undercultivated patches in the field.

Judging by the number of recent publications, the history of education in antiquity and in the Middle Ages is sadly neglected in Britain. Nevertheless, the fascination of classical Greece is endless ('except for the blind forces of nature, nothing moves in this world which is not Greek in origin', to quote from Sir Henry Maine's 1875 Rede Lecture), and Rome and the Middle Ages also throw much light upon the fundamental and perennial questions in education:[33] those of ends and means, or of individual adjustment to the needs of the community. The historical heresy that only the recent can be relevant needs to be resisted.

Secondly, notwithstanding that some individual scholars in this country are still producing major historical works on education in particular foreign countries, such as L. W. B. Brockliss, *Higher Education in France in the Seventeenth and Eighteenth Centuries*, 1987, and that the quintet of slim volumes by Professor Armytage on the influences of selected foreign countries upon education in Britain retain their value,[34] there is a distinct shortage of writings showing the true comparative expertise in our literature of the history of education. Brian Simon's remark in his article that 'the comparative study is . . . an important adjunct to the historical' seems worth recalling here.

Next, although its importance has been increasingly recognised for some years, informal, out-of-school education has not so far attracted many scholars. It is a field as difficult as it ought to be rewarding. The processes and the agencies of informal education – youth organisations, juvenile literature, educational travel – all clamour for more historical attention. Above all, there is the educative work and influence of the family; perhaps more progress in this area will follow the current burgeoning of historical demography in conjunction with the waxing historical interest in childhood. Here, Webster (No. 12) offers some interesting analytical remarks on the value to the historian of an 'outlook involving reference to all means employed by the community for the socialization of the younger generation'.

In the field of institutionalised education, more studies are needed of the evolution of the various school subjects, including textbooks and their values as well as the time-lags between the emergence and

14

acceptance of new knowledge at higher levels and the incorporation of that knowledge in school manuals. The basic subjects have attracted some researchers, for instance, I. Michael on *The Teaching of English from the Sixteenth Century to 1870*, 1987, or A.G. Howson, *A History of Mathematics Education in England*, 1982. The process of curriculum change and its wider context of various kinds of social, economic and political change has been explored by P. Gordon and D. Lawton in *Curriculum Change in the Nineteenth and Twentieth Centuries* (1978); and there are some interesting if basically sociological works by I. Goodson, such as *School Subjects and Curriculum Change: Studies in the Social History of the Curriculum*, 1982. Most subjects, however, including, surprisingly, history itself, have yet to be investigated.

With the curriculum of maintained schools in England about to be dictated by the central authority, it is pertinent to note the scope for more research on the evolution of central government policy in the twentieth century. Two authoritative works, P.H.J.H. Gosden's *Education in the Second World War* (1976) and G. Sherington's *English Education, Social Change and War 1911–1920* (1981), parallel the studies on the nineteenth-century development and structure of the central authority and its part in policy-making by A.S. Bishop and G. Sutherland respectively.[35] There are no major studies of the rise and vicissitudes of the study of education in its several aspects in this century. It might be speculated that the 'new' educational history's reaction against the study of thinkers has been partly responsible for the neglect of this theme. It is surprising too, considering the public and professional interest in the area of late, that there are few publications on the provision for the handicapped. Some scattered periodical articles apart, the main representative in this field is still D.G. Pritchard's *The Education of the Handicapped, 1760–1960*, 1963. Sound and thorough as it is, the work is now dated in some respects; and as compared with the American volume by Sarason and Doris entitled *Educational Handicap, Public Policy and Social History: a broadening perspective on mental retardation* (1979), its scope is wider but its treatment is narrower.[36]

In his 1960 study, *Education in the Forming of American Society*, Bernard Bailyn rightly suggested that 'education not only reflects and adjusts to society; once formed, it turns back upon it and acts upon it'. Similarly, historical studies prompt and provoke historiographical reflections which then act upon the 'real' historical work of research and writing. If the present collection acts as a stimulus to fresh endeavours, its publication will have been well justified.

NOTES

1. See L.A. Cremin, 'The Recent Developments of the History of Education as a Field of Study in the United States', *History of Education Quarterly*, 7 (1), 1955, and following issues.
2. W.W. Brickman, *Educational Historiography: Tradition, Theory and Technique*, Cherry Hill, NJ, 1982.
3. A. Léon, *The History of Education Today*, Unesco, Paris, 1985.
4. See, for instance, A.W. Thackray and R.K. Merton, 'On discipline-building: the paradoxes of George Sarton', *Isis*, 63, 1972.
5. A.C.F. Beales, 1905–74, holder of the chair of the History of Education at King's College, University of London, 1964–72, was the editor of the *British Journal of Educational Studies* from its inception in 1952 until his death.
6. See R. Szreter, 'Some forerunners of sociology of education in Britain: an account of the literature and influences c. 1900–1950', *Westminster Studies in Education*, 7, 1984; for a list of Sadler's 631 publications in their entirety, see O. Pickering, *Sir Michael Sadler – a bibliography of his published works*, Leeds, 1982.
7. See P. Gordon, ed., *The Study of Education: A Collection of Inaugural Lectures*, volume I: *Early and Modern*, London, Woburn Press, 1980.
8. Barnard's contribution here differs from the others in being less a cognitive analysis than a vast annotated international bibliography. It is especially valuable for the period prior to rise of the 'new' history of education, as befitted a scholar whose life spanned the years 1894 to 1985.
9. J. Bass Mullinger, *A History of the University of Cambridge*, better known in its later single volume edition, was originally published in three volumes between 1873 and 1884.
10. Brian Simon, Professor of Education in the University of Leicester, 1966–80, published three other historiographical papers: 'Research in the History of Education', in W. Taylor, ed., *Research Perspectives in Education*, London, 1973; 'History of Education in the 1980s', *British Journal of Educational Studies*, 30 (1), 1982; and 'The History of Education', in P.H. Hirst, ed., *Educational Theory and Its Foundation Disciplines*, London, 1983.
11. See J. Herbst, 'The New History of Education in Europe', *History of Education Quarterly*, 27 (1), 1987; it mentions the Soviet Union, however, as standing apart.
12. E. Midwinter, 'Non-events in the history of education', *Education for Teaching*, 71, 1966.
13. A shortened student's edition appeared in 1984. For a valuable historical discussion of Archer's work see R.D. Anderson, 'Sociology and History: Margaret Archer's *Social Origins of Educational Systems*', *Archives Européennes de Sociologie*, 27 (1), 1986.
14. A. Léon, op. cit. See also B. Lewis, *History: Remembered, Recovered and Invented*, Princeton, 1975.
15. See D. Ravitch, *The Revisionists Revised: Studies in the Historiography of American Education*, Washington D.C., 1977.
16. R.H. Tawney, 'The Study of Economic History' (London School of Economics, Inaugural lecture), *Economica*, 13, 1933.
17. H. Silver, 'Nothing but the present or nothing but the past?', Inaugural lecture, 1977, at Chelsea College, University of London. The title Silver took was unusual, 'Professor of Education (Social History)', and the title of his lecture is from the economist J.M. Keynes. Several of Silver's studies may be classed as historiographical, particularly his 'Historiography of Education', in T. Husen and T.N. Postlethwaite, eds., *The International Encyclopaedia of Education*, Oxford, 1985, vol. 4.
18. K.H. Jarausch, 'The Old and "New" History of Education: a German Reconsideration', *History of Education Quarterly*, 26 (2), 1986.

19. E.B. Castle, *Ancient Education and Today*, Harmondsworth, 1961.
20. The authorship of this concept is credited to W.I. Thomas of the famous interwar Chicago school of sociology.
21. The distinguished economic historian Peter Mathias has stated that 'one can usually tell what kind of intellectual animal a person is by the discipline studied for a first degree: it sets an intellectual style and approach for the future in ways which one can rarely escape', 'Theory and the economic historian', in P. Maunder and R. Ryba, eds., *Economics and Reality*, Economics Association, 1975. Interestingly, several leading British historians of education did not read history for their first degree. For evidence of successful late discipline transfers by academics, see G. Lemaine et al., eds., *Perspectives on the Emergence of Scientific Disciplines*, The Hague, 1976.
22. B. Simon, *Studies in the History of Education*, London, 1960, *Education and the Labour Movement*, London, 1965, and *Politics of Educational Reform, 1920–1940*, London, 1974. A more recent work that is political in its conception, though subtitled 'a social history', is R.A. Lowe, *Education in the Post-war Years*, London, 1988.
23. See in particular W.E. Marsden, *Unequal Educational Provision in England and Wales: the Nineteenth-Century Roots*, London, Woburn Press, 1987. For French works see references in Chapter VI of A. Léon, op. cit.
24. Vaizey's work appeared in an updated and reorganised version as J.E. Vaizey and J. Sheehan, *Resources for Education: an economic study of education in the United Kingdom, 1920–1965*, London, 1968.
25. Of the many works on this theme, two are curiously little-known: M.W. Flinn, 'Social Theory and the Industrial Revolution', in T. Burns and S.B. Saul, eds., *Social Theory and Economic Change*, London, 1967, and Chaps. 4 and 5 in S. Pollard, *The Genesis of Modern Management: A Study of the Industrial Revolution in Great Britain*, London, 1965.
26. See also P.W. Musgrave, 'A Model for the Analysis of the Development of the English Educational System from 1860', *Transactions of the Sixth World Congress of Sociology*, 1966, vol. 4 (reprinted in his 'reader', *Sociology, History and Education*, London, 1970), and G. Bernbaum, 'Sociological Techniques and Historical Study', in History of Education Society, *History, Sociology and Education*, London, 1971.
27. P.J. Harrigan, 'A comparative perspective on recent trends in the history of education in Canada', *History of Education Quarterly*, 26 (1), 1986.
28. For the international *Paedagogica Historica*, the British *History of Education*, the French *Histoire de l'éducation* and the Italian *Studi di storia dell'educazione*, see R.J. Wolff, 'European perspectives on the history of education: a review of four journals', *History of Education Quarterly*, 26 (1), 1986. For Poland's *Rozprawy z dziejów oświaty*, see R. Szreter, 'Historical Studies of Education in Poland Today', *History of Education*, 8 (2), 1979. West Germany has *Informationen zur Erziehungs Bildungs historischen Forschung*, and Australia and New Zealand share the *History of Education Review*. Finally, the dual-scope *British Journal of Educational Administration and History* should be noted.
29. J. Simon, 'The History of Education in *Past and Present*', *Oxford Review of Education*, 3 (1), 1977.
30. R. Szreter, *The History of Education in non-Education Learned Journals 1939–84*, 1986; see also 'Supplement, 1985–86', *Bulletin of the History of Education Society*, 40, 1987.
31. See R. Aldrich, 'History of Education at the Crossroads', *The Historian*, 11, 1986.
32. H. Silver, 'The search for sources', *The Times Educational Supplement*, 9 October 1987.
33. Even W.B. Stephens, 'Recent trends in the history of education in England to 1900', *Educational Research and Perspectives*, 8 (1), 1981, offers the medieval period just two sentences of sympathy and a footnote.
34. W.H.G. Armytage, *The French Influences on English Education*, London, 1968;

The American Influences on English Education, London, 1967; *The German Influences on English Education*, London, 1968; *Looking North: Influences and Inference from Sweden in English Education*, Peterborough, 1969; and *The Russian Influences on English Education*, London, 1969. See also his perceptive if idiosyncratic 'Historiography of Education', in E. Blishen, ed., *Blond's Encyclopaedia of Education*, London, 1969.

35. P.H.J.H. Gosden, *Education in the Second World War*, London, 1976; G. Sherington, *English Education, Social Change and War 1911–1920*, Manchester, 1981; A.S. Bishop, *The Rise of a Central Authority for English Education*, Cambridge, 1971; G. Sutherland, *Policy-Making in Elementary Education, 1870–1895*, Oxford, 1973.

36. S.B. Sarason and J. Doris, *Educational Handicap, Public Policy and Social History: a broadening perspective on mental retardation*, New York, 1979. For a recent British work, see J.S. Hurt, *Outside the Main Stream: a History of Special Education*, London, 1988.

1

The Study of the
History of Education

FOSTER WATSON

I

In the time of the Renascence the appeal to the old writers of Greece
and of Rome on questions of education was as urgent as in all other
directions of literary studies and of practical arts. Erasmus seeks the
covering wing of Aristotle's *Politics* or of Quintilian's *Institutes*. Or to
cite an English example, Sir Thomas Elyot grounds his educational
studies on Quintilian and Plato. He requires his pupil to soak himself in
these authors, and is of opinion 'that those books be almost sufficient to
make a perfect and excellent governor.' In the time of Tudor absolut-
ism, the education of the governor was of crucial importance. Unless he
was trained to become noble, magnanimous, and the guardian of all the
highest, humanistic interest, the kingdom might readily become a spoil
for the despot, and a home-land of slaves. The best resource for the
tutor who had the responsible charge of training the budding princes
and governors, was to study and act upon the counsels of the old
educational writers. So, too, thought Ascham. His cry was: Back to the
aims of Cicero and the methods of Quintilian, if you wish the young
noble and gentleman to be trained liberally and for nobility. The
highest praise that could be given to the Father of modern pedagogy,
Juan Luis Vives, was to style him the 'second Quintilian'. It is needless
to go through the list of the illustrious writers on Education of the
sixteenth and seventeenth centuries. No one in recalling them would
fail to pause before the name of John Milton, whose devotion to the
ideas of the ancients constitutes one of the classical instances of the
appeal to educational history in English writers. 'To govern well is
to train up a nation in true wisdom and virtue, and that which springs
from thence, magnanimity (take heed of that!).' It is the plea for

19

magnanimity that draws Elyot, Ascham, and Milton to the old writers, or in other words leads them to commend the study of the great educationists. How could they show the regard due to the teacher better than by citing the ancient letter written by King Philip to Aristotle, to announce the birth of Alexander? Great as was his gladness in the birth of this son, Philip, he declared his joy was equally great that that son would have Aristotle as teacher. Thus was honoured in antiquity the function of the teacher. Thus educationists of the sixteenth, seventeenth, and part of the eighteenth centuries, gloried in recalling the *dicta* of the ancient writers, in magnifying the work of teachers, and in inspiring schoolmasters to the best efforts in accomplishing the task they had in hand of training noble youth.

It is true that such appeals to the history of education were largely by way of citation so as to point a moral or adorn a tale, educationally. The systematic treatment of educational history had not been developed, any more than the systematic treatment of any other kind of history. But the great solatium of the teacher when he suffered from the 'unthankfulness' of the parent and the pupil (of which Elyot, Ascham, and Brinsley most bitterly complain) was to fall back on the noble tradition of the schoolmaster's function, guaranteed by the 'schools of the prophets' of old, Plato, Aristotle, and Plutarch amongst the Greeks, and especially Quintilian amongst Romans. We may say that the best humanistic work has rarely been done in literature or in art without the conscious background of great previous achievements and inspirations. It is sufficient surely to point out that literature today looks back to a Dante, a Shakespeare, a Goethe, even when it has ceased to study Homer, the Greek dramatists, and Virgil and the classical models generally. Even if the classical models are disregarded, their influence is not thereby excluded. Many moderns prefer the ease of taking classical models second-hand. Yet the very greatest of modern writers, to whom the late generations owe unswerving allegiance, often themselves dipped deep into classical sources. The artists whether painters or musicians either look with reverential awe on 'the old masters', or at least study them before they superciliously pass them by. If the schoolmaster then wishes to regard his occupation as a 'fine art', is it not reasonable that he should carefully have examined 'the Galleries of old Masters' in the craft of education?

The way of approaching the study of the arts formerly was by precept-teaching. Precepts were given by old Galen and Hippocrates for medicine; farther back Solomon furnished his precepts for the practical life, so we should not be surprised that in the history of education earlier teaching of principles was by precepts, and that later educationists, in following the older thinkers, availed themselves of the method of citation of the precept-teaching educationists. Systematic educational theory in modern times was founded by Juan Luis Vives and by John Amos Comenius.

II

But alongside of the development of systematic educational theory proceeded the differentiation of the natural sciences, and for the same reason; since with Vives and Bacon set in the employment of the methods of observation and experiment, and the use of the inductive method in both the natural sciences and in education, Comenius then seized upon these methods as the basis of this theoretical treatment of education. The various natural sciences developed in every direction, especially after the formation of the Royal Society, until the time of Locke, when we find that as an educationist Locke trusts largely to 'common sense', and it is difficult to make out whether he had given any study to previous educationists at all. Locke strikes the modern key-note of the adverse critics of the study of educational history. 'The extent of knowledge of things knowable is so vast, our duration here so short, and the entrance by which the knowledge of things gets into our understanding so narrow, that the whole time of our life is not enough to acquaint us with all those things, I will not say which we are capable of knowing, but which it would not only be convenient but very advantageous to know.'

The modern teacher, subjected to the constantly increasing demands of the governors, Local Authorities, the Board of Education, parents and public opinion, is *a fortiori* of Locke's opinion, and outside pressure has increased in environmental power enormously since his time in the direction of limiting the teacher's attention to present conditions only. Moreover, after Locke came Rousseau, and after Rousseau, the French Revolution. After the French Revolution, the whole emphasis of educational activity changed. The old classical ideals were broken up. The main educational stream flowed through the meadow-land of democracy. The methods and even the ideals were framed with a keen outlook towards the quantitative factor. The education of the masses became the absorbing theme in politics as well as in education. The old educationists were out of court. They had treated of high qualitative curricula and aims for the nobility. Elyot, Ascham, Milton and the rest were aristocrats in education. After the French Revolution, Lancaster, Bell, Robert Owen, Pestalozzi and the rest are keen democrats. The classics were doomed. The classical and even the historical spirit and atmosphere were, from the point of view of public educational leaders, obsolete. The appeal was not to the past, either to classical antiquity or to the Renascence educationists. The nineteenth century was an age of individualism, and as politics and religion came often to be regarded from the point of view of individualistic rationalism, so education developed along those lines, and reference to the historical side came to smack somewhat of an anachronism.

But philosophical radicalism might ignore all kinds of history, and regard all values as determined by the relation of the individual to his environment, easily ascertained by a process of trained visualisation or intuition; yet the advance of science increasingly pressed upon the notice of students the importance of the genetic method of the treatment of subjects. Geology, of itself, proved the necessity of the study of history on large and massive lines. 'The history of a piece of coal' showed the necessity of a wide reach of imagination to cover the meaning of the word 'environment'. Consequently, largely from the very development of scientific conceptions, which formed the main sphere of intellectual energy in the earlier and middle parts of the nineteenth century, there arose the new scientific demand for the study of the historical side of humanistic subjects.

III

History has, therefore, come back again into the curricula of the universities and schools. It is realised in the outer world of nature that the slightest attempt to analyse the present state of an organism leads us to the past – for what is the past but the antecedent states of the parts which in their organised form now constitute the present? Thus there sprang up the idea that all human experience, in common with physical and biological phenomena generally, is accumulative, organic, continuous.

The late Professor Maitland said in 1901 that the attempt to teach history as a leading university study was 'very new – some of those who watched its cradle are still amongst us, are still active, and still hopeful.' It is not necessary here to detail the origin and progress of the university teaching of ancient history, of ecclesiastical history, of modern history, of economic history, of constitutional history, and of the history of political philosophy. Nor is it necessary to more than mention the lately established university teaching of Palæography and Diplomatic. The History Schools in the Universities are firmly established, though so surprisingly new. The influence of the historical aspect of studies is much wider than the provision of facilities for the direct study of all the defined branches of historical science. Such new sciences as those of anthropology and sociology make appeal to historical researches. Comparative and historical Law have been illumined by the profound investigations of Professor Maitland and others, who have not only made many discoveries, and added to the body of knowledge of legal history, but have also developed new legal aims, new methods of legal study, and raised the subject still higher as a mental discipline. Slowly, too, the history of medicine is being developed, and a worker like the late Dr F.J. Payne has done much to prove the value of historical research in this direction. In the field of comparative and historical religion there is no need to elaborate illustrations. The publication of over sixty of the Sacred Books of the Religions of the East is a sufficient indication of the enormous erudition that is being brought to bear on the historical side of the study of Religion.

IV

The fact is that in all humanistic studies the search for knowledge has become strenuous on new historical lines to the point of making a new Renascence in all historical learning. It is recognised that truth, founded upon knowledge, is like a mountain-peak, accessible from many sides, and he knows the mountain best who has ascended it from many starting points. Historical studies, then, have won their way at the instigation of the permeating idea of evolution in all branches of science, as well as from their own inherent impetus. They have already served to elucidate not only the old humanistic subjects, where they have always been in evidence, but new whole tracts have developed into differentiated provinces of study: anthropology, sociology, economics, where the triumphs of the historical method are creating new sciences almost alongside natural sciences in rigour of aim and method.

What, then, is to be said of Education? Is it likely to be the only humanistic subject of study to stand outside of the historical treatment? Already we have seen that formerly it fell into rank with other subjects and made the usual citatory appeal to the ancients. Other subjects now have progressed, and enlarged their borders by other methods, and yet fall back upon the genetic, evolutionary, comparative, historical methods for complementary treatment, to their incalculable advantage. The whole round of methods has proved insufficient without the effort to collect and interpret systematically the accumulated experiences of the past. Is it probable on the face of things, or in view of the idea of the continuity of knowledge is it possible, that education stands in an entirely isolated position, and what was once a cherished method for its guidance, and what is now a most successful method in all other humanistic studies, is, for education, a superfluity and a pitfall? And, again, since the time of the French Revolution, having lost the habit of glancing its eye over the past – has not education exercised sufficiently its absorption in its immediate environment until it now needs the stimulus of historical study, so as to enlarge its vision and then to come back to itself, and duly recognise the perspective of its own achievements and prospects in the light of the past educational experience and progress of the ages? For the 'eye sees not itself'.

V

It is argued that the training for a profession should concern itself with increasing technical skill, not with historical studies. Let us take the case of architecture. It may be suggested that there is no relevancy between the effective planning of an out-house at a minimum of expenditure, and the understanding by the designer of the way in which the builders of antiquity produced the massive works of engineering which are still a marvel of the world, or how the mediaeval builders built the great Cathedrals and Castles. The expenditure of time on the study of styles of architecture by the student who is to practise as an architect on a small scale and in common surroundings may seem wasted. But on the other hand the cultivation of knowledge by the articled pupil in architecture of the designs of the greatest masters of the craft, might, in time, lead not merely to the carrying out of humble commissions as a provincial architect, so as to suit the ignorance of conceptions on the part of his *clientèle*, but the architect might contribute to the gradual uplifting of architectural design in its humblest applications amongst the public at large. It is desirable, therefore, in the public interest, that there should be professors of, and advanced research students in, architecture, who study past styles and stages of the development of architecture, and organise their knowledge as an art, in its relation to other arts, as well as to literature and to science. In fact, an excellent index of the position of architecture as a profession is afforded by the degree in which the general practitioner shares in the ascertained body of knowledge of his subject, and by the degree in which he performs his work in the light of this extended knowledge. Such skilled practitioners not only execute their work after 'inner' standards but also tend to raise the architectural tone of the community.

24

Similarly, whilst the professors and other investigators into the history of education have a distinct work to perform, the school teacher may reasonably be expected to emulate the professional eagerness of the architect by learning how to profit by the study of the 'old masters', and not only to teach his individual lessons or perform his other tasks by those rationalized methods which his theoretical and practical studies suggest to him, but also to realise that his professional *status* will be dependent largely upon the extent of the interest he has in the organized knowledge underlying the work, present and past, of education, over and above what he requires directly for application to the individual lessons. Actual individual power in any ordinary professional act is measured by the amount of knowledge and power *in reserve*. Hence the knowledge of the history of education contributes to the reserve-forces of the teacher. The acquisition of such knowledge is a mental discipline, as well as an addition to the storage of knowledge available for application at a given moment. It is, of course, too much to expect the teacher to take an active, strenuous part in the investigation and research into the history of education. But the national organisation of education is clearly defective, if provision is not made somewhere in the national system, for the building up of a thorough body of knowledge of the history of education. This is an essential task, not only for the teachers, and for students of education, but also for the knowledge of history in general.

VI

Let me give an instance of the light thrown on general history by the study of educational history. King Henry VIII is often represented as a sort of escaped Oriental, absorbed in sensual self-seeking, whose intellectual outlook was casual and feeble. On this estimate, his discussions on Erasmus's *Free-will*, and particularly his own answer to Luther in the *Assertion of the Seven Sacraments* can only be regarded as accidental, and Pope Leo X's conferment of the title of *Defensor Fidei* must be regarded as a blatant piece of partisan recognition. But let us realise the fact that as King Henry VII trained his elder son Arthur with the humanistic learning such as Sir Thomas Elyot desiderated for the youth who was to become a 'governor', so the student age of Henry VIII was occupied in the preparation for 'the mitre'. He was destined, we are told, to the Archbishopric of Canterbury, and the possible eventual dignity of the Cardinalate, and who could tell? perchance the thoroughly ecclesiastically trained youth might reach the papal chair. Who does not see that the history of education in supplying the facts of the central idea of Henry VIII's early training also provides the key to Henry VIII's specialistic knowledge of theology, his insight into the disputes of Lutheranism, and a familiarity with conditions of the ecclesiastical hierarchy which, in the circumstances of later history, paved the way for himself to the Royal Supremacy over the English Church; since his accession to the royal throne put out of court his assumption of the papal chair?

Then, again, the question will be raised: Granting the necessity of the study of the history of education as a part of general history – what is 'the good' of its study to the teacher? It will be objected that the subject-matter is unsuitable for the curriculum of a school, though on this point it may be recalled to mind that Milton advised the reading of an old book on education even by schoolboys. Innumerable hints and suggestions certainly are to be found in the past which might afford educational lessons for the present. Educational history, however, does not call for study because of the 'tips' to be obtained from it from application to present-day needs, either of the nation or the class-room.

VII

Yet in all questions of broad, decisive educational policy, the historical aspect is not a literary luxury; it is the categorical demand of a sound judgment. If we are to understand the so-called 'religious' question in connection with English primary education, we shall find that it is chiefly an historical question, emerging from the voluntary supply of many hundreds of primary 'charity' schools at the end of the seventeenth and throughout the eighteenth centuries, chiefly by the Church of England. This supply was suddenly confronted, after the Industrial Revolution, with the demand for filling up by State organization the gaps in the national system. Finally, the different kinds of schools which have been found necessary for England – as supplied by the Church, by Undenominationalists, and by the State and other agencies – are so miscellaneous and satisfy such diverse needs that it is said, not without some ground for the statement, that the real solution of the educational problem can only be met by recognizing that there is no *one* system of education adaptable for England. Whether such a statement be true or not, and what the educational policy should be in view of English conditions, can only be determinable by careful study of the antecedent conditions which have been developing for several hundred years. The real depth of the citizen's judgment on educational questons to-day can be gauged by the attention he has given to the origins and development of the various movements in evidence in the present education of England. So, too, we must realize that 'each nation has to solve its educational problems in many directions in its own way'. But we must add 'in accordance with its own history'. When we realize that France enters into the heritage of Romance traditions, founded upon the old Roman disciplines, language and civilisation, we see that the instinct of her best writers for refined, accurate style is no mere accident, but the outcome of countless generations of profound study of the classics, ingrained in the scholarship of generation after generation amid all the changes and development of language. The educational problems, therefore, of France or of Italy in relation to, say, the classics, are different from those of Germany or other Teutonic nations, because the national history is different. It is true such studies may not aid directly the individual class-lesson. But they will make the teacher a citizen of the great world whilst in his own province where, after all, it is a little disconcerting, if not humiliating, for him not to be at home.

We urge then that all educationists – the Minister of Education, the officials of the Board of Education, Inspectors of the Board, Directors of Education, administrators of every form of Education – as well as teachers, and that important body of persons who should be educationists, the parents, and the large portion of the public who assert bold decisive views on education, should study the history of education so that, with judgments intelligently and carefully formed, they may enter into the discussions affecting the continuity of national educational progress, and that they may have the necessary material before them for comparison and judgment as to the different present-day ends, as to human ends generally, and as to their due educational co-ordination.

VIII

But for the teacher the necessity is still greater than for the citizen interested in educational progress. It cannot be well for each individual teacher to wrap himself up in his own thoughts, and in those of his own generation, and to refuse to go out on the highway of humanity, to learn from past experience and the counsels of the greatest thinkers. Educational history presents numerous points of contact with the whole current of the history of humanity and human interests, and necessarily develops a broad outlook. The price paid for the neglect of the study of the history of education by teachers is *the tendency* to achieve an insufferable egotism, priding itself on examinational or other subjectively measured results, and on the glories of present-day educational progress, so-called, without reference to other standards than those of the existing environment. In other words, the risk is run of developing a professional Sir Willoughby Patterne spirit, ready to drink in the awaited homage of the future, and to let sink into oblivion the obligations of the past, in the absorbing concentration on present self-expansion.

For the educationist to go back to the study of the history of education is not decadence. For all students the final justifying reason for this extra study is that education has a humanistic end, and to accomplish it, those actively engaged in it must ever keep alive within them the brightly burning lamp of humanism. Each good teacher must have been at some time transfigured with something of the nobility of aim and endeavour which has characterized the efforts of the best educators in all ages and in all climes. We are seriously told to-day by Professor J.J. Findlay in his able book *The School*, 'that the school and its teachers are the creation of the community; the teachers spring from "the people", and the people control the schooling; hence the ethics of the school, its standards and ideals, are such as its creators fashion'. This surely means that bread-and-butter subjects, bread-and-butter methods, bread-and-butter aims of the teachers, being the primary necessities, are in control of the situation. 'If teachers', we are further told by the same writer, 'think more of ideal service than of the rate of payment, that *is not in the bond*'. If this is a true diagnosis of present-day education, well, all the more need for the true teacher to look backward into history; to 'estrange himself' from absorption in the present atmosphere; to take refuge with Plato, with Quintilian, with Vittorino; and in the thought of the great national civilizations and the part education has played in them hitherto, to cultivate a confidence that the old educational spirit will preserve its continuity, and perform its beneficent part in the more complicated problems of the present and the future, as it has done in the past. Government has passed from the hands of the 'nobility' for whom Elyot wrote, into the hands of the democracy, but this does not mean that the present age can dispense with nobility of life and conduct in the new governors. That the democracy is so numerous makes the claim all the stronger that the new 'governors' should also be distinguished by gentleness of manners and refinement of mind and heart. The teachers, of all men, then, must throw themselves into the task of teaching the future governors, the democracy, not as a trade for profit but as an heritage from a noble ancestry, whose aims they cherish and express in their work. If they live in a utilitarian environment, all the more they must be permeated with the old belief in the greatness and privilege of their task. The real ground for the study of the history of education is the sense of entering into the large-heartedness, the high visions, and the unconquerable hopefulness for the noblest aims hitherto put forward for the development of humanity through the young. We must let the history of education keep before us the idea, in the words of Milton, that 'to educate well' means 'to train the nation in true wisdom and virtue, and that which springs from these – magnanimity (*take heed of that!*).'

2

The History of Education

H.M. BEATTY

'History is natural, civil, ecclesiastical, and literary; whereof the three first I allow as extant, the fourth I note as deficient. For no man hath propounded to himself the general state of learning to be described and represented ... without the which the history of the world seemeth to me to be as the statua of Polyphemus with his eye out; that part being wanting which doth most show the spirit and life of the person ... For it is not St. Augustine's nor Saint Ambrose' works that will make so wise a divine, as ecclesiastical history, throughly read and observed; and the same reason is of learning'.

When Francis Bacon penned this encomium of the history of learning, or what we might call intellectual development, it does not appear that he had any prevision of specific histories of education; nor, when two centuries and a quarter later (1830) Carlyle wrote his essay on 'History', did he find a place for them beside the histories 'of medicine, of mathematics, of astronomy, commerce, chivalry, monkery', although two general histories of the subject (those of Mangelsdorf and of Schwarz) had already been published in his beloved German; and although as early as 1695 England had possessed what might pass for a history of education in the translation of Claude Fleury's *Traité des Choix et de la Méthode des Études*, published in that year by S. Keble. Shortly after the year of Carlyle's essay, the stream of histories in many languages began to flow freely. France has its old-fashioned but interesting Viriville, to which Matthew Arnold acknowledged his obligations; followed among others by Paroz and the *History of Pedagogy* of Compayré, familiar to us in its English translation. Germany produced an array of volumes of characteristic 'Gründlichkeit' – Von Raumer, with his sixteen hundred pages of a quite un-Teutonic geniality, which commended him to the author of our well-known *Educational Reformers*; amazing Schmidt, with the three thousand closely packed pages of his *Geschichte der Pädagogik*, and the six hundred pages of his less amazing but still formidable *Geschichte der Erziehung*; the equally amazing Schmid; Dittes, Schiller, Ziegler, and very many others. Italy also has in Cerruti's sketch of Italian education what is almost a general history, as well as the more recent Giuffrida, and, I think, one or two others. Switzerland has Niemeyer, Martig, and the very readable Guex; Belgium has Damseaux, and so on.

In English, the first survey appears to have been published in 1842 by H.I. Smith, a teacher of German at that Gettysburg which is familiar wherever the name of Lincoln and 'government of the people, by the people, and for the people' are known. Since then there have been many more – Graves in three volumes; Monroe's 'Big Book' and Monroe's 'Little Book' (to adopt J.R. Green's phraseology); Painter, Davidson, Seeley, Kemp, Aspinwall, and others, not to mention Barnard's *American Journal of Education*, a 'great treasury of material', as Graves terms it, which in its thirty-one mighty volumes 'includes every phase of the history of education from the earliest times'.

So England has produced her fair share of histories of education? Far from it. The truth is that the British Isles are in this respect simply a statua of Polyphemus with his eye out. They have *no* general history of education; those enumerated are all American. Even Thomas Davidson, though a Scot by birth, spent the greater part of his wandering life in America and dated his preface from New York. All that the British Isles have to show are Joseph Payne's *Lectures*, delivered at the College of Preceptors half a century ago; which, whether they deserve the unkind epithets of 'fragmentary and unmethodical' which have been applied to them – and a history which assigns to Jacotot seven times as much space as to Locke or to Herbert Spencer does offer special difficulties in the choice of epithets – at any rate supply, not a history of education, but a series of monographs on educators. It is almost fifty years since Quick complained that not only *good* books, but *all* books on the history of education were in some foreign language; and it is still as true as then that our histories must be imported. Even a comprehensive history of British education on an adequate or any scale is still to seek.

This is a humiliating confession. What is the explanation? The most obvious and practical explanation is that there is no demand. The story of Quick's *Educational Reformers* is so illuminative in this respect that it well deserves narrating. But, before coming to that, it may be mentioned as a significant fact that a quarter of a century ago both

Principal Donaldson and Mr. Bass Mullinger were credited with the intention of publishing histories. Neither of these has appeared.[1]

The *Educational Reformers* is undoubtedly and deservedly the most popular of all the books on this subject which have been published in Britain; and not merely in its native country. Parmentier in France and Guex in Switzerland have spoken of it in as flattering terms as Quick's countrymen. The history of the book, as gathered from his own account and from Storr's interesting *Life* of the author, is as follows. The *Reformers*, after being offered to, and rejected by, Macmillan, on the ground that 'books on education don't pay', was published in 1868 by Longmans at 7s. 6d., and required, even with a reduction in price to 3s. 6d., about five years to clear off its five hundred copies, after which it remained twenty years out of print. But in the meantime three different publishers in the United States had reprinted it without Quick's consent; and from one of these pirated editions he imported copies which he sold at cost price to English readers. These editions, it must be remembered, were quite apart from the authorised and fourth edition which was issued subsequently in America by Messrs. Appleton. The first volume of Joseph Payne's *Lectures on Education* had, as appears from the preface to the second volume, a somewhat similar fortune.[2]

These instances suggest that there is no demand; but the question remains – Why is there none? In general history Britain has played no ignoble part. From from it; Gibbon, Grote, Carlyle, and Green are masters in their several domains, and four of the greatest historians of Lord Acton's time unanimously pronounced Macaulay to be the greatest historian of all time. Our natural bent towards compromise and tradition, rather than to speculation on principles, is indeed favourable to research and narrative. And here perhaps we may find a clue to guide us. This love of compromise has given to our histories what may be designated as a character of tentativeness. This is shown first in a weakness of architectonic construction. Take Macaulay and Buckle, for instance. No doubt they died prematurely; but that does not explain. A centenarian in full vigour could hardly have completed their tasks, as they were planned. Lecky and Symonds wrote, as it were, piecemeal; and Lord Acton did not even begin his *History of Liberty*. This defect is, however, rather English than British; it is less marked in Scottish historians, and Lecky seems to have degenerated in constructive power in an English atmosphere. This characteristic is, of course, not confined to our histories; the symmetry of Greek and French tragedy and the numerical homologies of the Divine Comedy seem to us unreal and mechanical. Accordingly, except in the case of the cosmopolitan Gibbon, œcumenical surveys, such as the history of education demands, have not been congenial. But this tentativeness has the further effect of directing the historian's attention to the concrete in preference to what Bacon calls 'a just story of learning, containing the antiquities and originals of knowledges and their sects'; of leading Freeman, as Mr. Gooch phrases it, to 'believe action alone to be history', and Seeley, as Lord Acton said, to 'discern no Whiggism but only Whigs'. The history of education, on the other hand, must deal largely with speculation; it not merely narrates the lives and fortunes of educators and of educational institutions, but also expounds and discusses the theories explicit or implicit which animated them. The history of education trenches on the histories of civilisation, of psychology, and even of philosophy. But in these departments England has never been pre-eminent. Our general histories of civilization are merely translations; when Professor Baldwin (an American, be it observed) was writing his short history of Psychology some years ago, he was unable to find one of any kind in book form in the English language; and the book which served as our large-scale history of philosophy till recent years was avowedly written to discredit metaphysical speculation. One admirable pendant to the history of education has been supplied recently by Sir John Sandys in his learned and felicitous *History of Classical Scholarship*; but this work, though it throws light on the progress of education does not deal with its psychological development.

These defects in our historical equipment may no doubt be largely due to that 'intellectual apathy', that absence of 'the sacred thirst for investigation', for which we have been lately upbraided, and to an incapacity for abstract speculation. But they may be, if not derived, at least reinforced from a nobler source. Histories of the development of thought are, as a rule, written with a bias towards some particular form of thought − are written to support a thesis. The English mind has a robust and healthy objection to theories, and regards a Rousseau or a Hegel as little better than a degenerate. The theorist, unless he is one of the rare spirits of supreme and unerring perspicacity, must, if an honest man, have in the course of a long work his hours of disillusionment and doubt: 'tasks in hours of insight will'd', to use Matthew Arnold's words, must be 'through hours of gloom fulfill'd' − such doubts as, we have been recently told, fell on Carlyle in the middle of his *Friedrich* as to the nobility of his hero. Possibly to men of other stock the symmetry and coherence of the design may appear as *prima facie* evidence of the truth of the thesis. If the English mind, rooted in compromise and 'fair play', spurns that solace, the self-denial is not altogether ignoble.

Instances of such theories pushed to extremes are not difficult to find in some of the histories of education which we import. In the *Educational Ideal* of James P. Munro we read at p.231: 'The school and the schoolmaster are still necessary factors in education, but they are no longer primary ones. They are adjunct only in the holy work that must rest supremely upon the father and mother'. If this be so, all previous views of education have been so completely revolutionized as to render historical treatment of educational ideals a waste of time: education from this point of view loses all the features which have been associated with the name and defies all treatment of a fruitful kind. One quarter of Davidson's History is devoted to savage and barbarian education, of which, as he expresses it, we can only 'divine the nature', and which in any case can hardly be brought into useful correlation with the education of more civilized peoples. But the horizon of these writers is contracted compared with that of Letourneau, who, in his very interesting *L'Evolution de l'éducation*, devotes more space to the education of elephants, chimpanzees, and other animals than to the education of man during the last five hundred years. In such company, Professor Adams's *Evolution of Educational Theory* must seem hopelessly anthropocentric.

There are, however, other reasons to regret the want of native histories. No doubt it is wholesome 'to see oursels as others see us', and therefore when Graves (iii, 95) casually informs us that 'as a whole the English occupation of New York would seem to have set public education back about one hundred years', or when Paul Monroe (p.668) tells us that 'Through England came much of the Pestalozzian influence exerted on the United States, and to this is largely due the formal and even superficial character of much of it, relating as it does or did to petty methods', we can only be grateful for their bracing frankness and resolve to profit by it. But a large part of the chapters in Graves's book on modern education, dealing as they do with American life, are for us too exotic to be either interesting or useful in a general history. The space devoted to American education is, naturally enough from his point of view, about five times as great as that given to Britain. To this objection Monroe's books are not open; as digests of information punctiliously apportioned, they are irreproachable. But, to speak frankly, they are deadly dull, and written in a laboured style which is at times scarcely intelligible and is little better than broken English. It is hard to believe that on either side of the Atlantic expressions like the following are idiomatically correct: 'In numerous ones of these treatises', for many of these treatises; 'great Renaissance leaders who exerted any wide reputation'; 'grammatical texts which were impossible of any mastery save a verbal one', by which is apparently meant that they were learned by rote. It would be deeply regrettable if this standard of English expression were accepted by our future school-teachers on the authority of the Professor of the History of Education in Columbia University.[3]

At any rate, there is no reason why this history should be dull. Mahaffy's book on Greek education and Leach's on the schools of mediæval England are not wanting in human interest nor Mullinger's history of the University of Cambridge in descriptive powers. Quick's *Educational Reformers*, Matthew Arnold's sketch of popular education in France, and Newman's of the rise of universities are models of easy, lucid grace. The story of Vittorino de Feltre in his 'Joyous Gard' at Mantua is an idyll; the life of Comenius is a romance of tragic adventure; Pestalozzi, Rabelais, Rousseau, and the Jesuits are fascinating psychological enigmas; Germany, the older, nobler Germany, has stirring tales of educational uprisings in the days of Luther and Napoleon; Plato, Aristotle, Locke, Herbart, and Herbert Spencer supply the philosophical framework.

This story, one might think, would have appealed to British power of narrative. But is it of any practical use to learn that story? Sir Frederick Pollock in claiming a place for political science, of which he had written a history, urged that his science must and does exist, if it were only for the refutation of absurd political theories and projects. In the same way, I would plead that at the lowest estimate the history of education is useful for the refutation of the daily papers. At a time when our education is being reconstructed, and erroneous deductions from imaginary facts are offered as pleas for questionable projects, this is no small merit. For instance, some protagonists of science, exhilarated by their victorious progress in the war against the Humanities, have recently abandoned their powerful positions in order to raid the neutral territories of history. One distinguished scientist has lately announced that, in the first quarter of the seventeenth century, Latin was taught because all available treatises on history, among other subjects, were in Latin; he has again announced that the restriction of the word Humanism to a literary connotation is a recent abuse of the term, which has no sanction from English literature or from the historians of the Renaissance. These two statements simply reverse the facts, as, to go no farther, the bibliography of Tudor translations in the Cambridge History of English Literature or a reference to the Oxford Dictionary would show.

Here again are other instances. For some time, utterances on educational reform have ended with the refrain: No Germanising of our schools. Of that there need be no fear, however efficient and thorough may be the teaching of the Huns:

Quidquid id est, timeo Danaos et dona ferentes.

But in order to avoid Germanism, the first thing is to learn what it is; and that is exactly what many of our monitors have not learned. Within the past few months I have seen the three following statements, two of them at least made by men whose words carry the greatest weight: that in German higher schools Science has ousted the Classics; that in German schools religious instruction is minimized, if not ignored; that in Germany there is a startling uniformity of teaching method and of educational administration, the whole system being completely under the control of the State. These three statements reverse the facts. But as Professor Gilbert Murray has demolished the first and Professor Alison Phillips the second, my intrusion is uncalled for; although, with regard to the second, it is a proof how completely Matthew Arnold is forgotten, that such a statement should be promulgated as indisputable fact, in face of the striking passage in his last Special Report of 1886, where Arnold contrasts the 'energy and seriousness' of the religious teaching and the 'intelligence and interest' of the children – 'No one could watch the faces of the children, of the girls particularly, without feeling that something in their nature responded to what they were repeating, and was moved by it' – with the detachment of the adult working classes in Germany from the received religion. The third statement mentioned above is, to say the least, extremely misleading to an English reader. There is *no* control by the State in Germany, such as there is in France and England, because there is no central Department; each State has its own independent Education Department. The diversity of organization, programme, and even nomenclature in the Mittelschülen is simply bewildering; and, in the stages of education below the Gymnasien, there is local initiative, finance, building, and even inspection. The similarity, by no means uniformity, which prevails is due not to centralized administration, but to unanimity of national aspirations and docility of national character.

The history of education can, however, confer other benefits than the revision of unwarranted statements of fact. It corrects the tendency to deduce the effects of various studies and methods from psychological premises, which do not take account of such things as the force of inertia, the energy of illogical impulses, and the nature of the social and political environment. The psychologist is slow to recognize that for the educationist it is more important to learn what is the actual effect of certain studies in the complexity of life than what it ought to be according to the laws of his still imperfect science. Instances of this will easily be found in the discussions in our educational papers. There are many problems in education which cannot as yet be solved by the application of scientific methods. The results of experiments cannot be ascertained for at least a generation, and are complicated with the problems of sociology. Therefore it is well to call in the aid of those who have discussed and attempted similar experiments in the past. Comenius will throw light on the question between the classicists and the scientists; and the study of Rousseau, Pestalozzi, and Froebel would help us to view Dr. Montessori's work in due perspective. None the less, like all other history, that of education is psychological both in itself and in its action on ourselves. Below the varying lights of victory and defeat, success and failure which play along the surface, it enables us to plumb and measure the current of ideas, which have been the motive force; and to our own minds it lends flexibility of judgment and provides a suitable atmosphere, that will not refract our vision, in contemplating educational problems, which must be solved as such.

NOTES

1. In Will S. Monroe's *Bibliography of Education*, and in Sonnenschein's *Best Books* (new edition), a history of education by Donaldson is recorded as having been published by Murray in 1895, even the size and price being added. Being unable to find any such book in the catalogue of the British Museum or of the London Library, I wrote to Mr Murray, who informed me that it had never been written. As I have referred above to Will S. Monroe, it may not be superfluous to note that, as there are three historians of education called Smith, Schmidt and Schmid (the two latter of whom were, I remember, confused in the catalogue of the old official Education Library in South Kensington), there are also three called Paul Monroe, Editor of the *Cyclopedia of Education*) Will S. Monroe, the Associate Editor; and James Monro, author of *The Educational Ideal*.
2. Even my own humble experience furnishes corroborative evidence. Almost the entire edition of a volume, illustrative of educational history, which I was foolish enough to publish some years ago, would have returned to its native dust-heap, but for a timely demand from some 'idiotic Yankees'.
3. As I have above spoken strongly in regard to the jargon which some educational writers, especially in Germany, choose to employ, I will quote in justification a continuous passage from Monroe (Text book, p.336): 'It has been noticed, previously, that while Plato defined the aim of education in terms of knowledge, and Cicero in terms of eloquence, meaning knowledge of content and of form of literature, much more was indicated by these terms than is now connoted. Both terms which now would indicate for the most part the receptive or even formal side of education then included the expression side as well. During the early Renaissance period this expression side was even wider than that indicated by efficiency in writing or speaking, since at that time these powers stood for that effective participation in the affairs of the times that is now represented by the differentiated activities of all of our learned professions and by the public press'.

The tendency which this passage exemplifies, especially in the use of terms such as 'expression side', to introduce into history that symbolical or algebraical use of language, which is no doubt unavoidable in the treatment of exact science, is one to be resisted, as destructive of the finer shades and associations of words and paralyzing to their natural growth.

3

A Plea for the Historical Study
of English Education

J. W. ADAMSON

Surely, if very slowly, the field of History is being enlarged, so that it now includes ground which the older school of constitutional and political historians regarded as either outside their province or non-existent. Economic history, social history, literary history, are familiar subjects of study. Attempts have been made to write histories of 'civilization' and of 'culture'; handbooks on the history of different branches of art are as numerous as tourists' guide books. The line between history and archaeology cannot be drawn with precision; and there are those who talk and write of 'primitive man' as though the evidence concerning him were complete and unquestionable.

From one point of view the history of education is the history of mankind; but the landscape being so broad and so deep and in places so obscure, it is very doubtful whether this particular point of vantage really helps the would-be observer. Even if we limit the survey to civilization or to culture, the breadth and the obscurities remain, and the student is tempted to confide in vague generalities which too often rest upon most unsteady foundations. But a time comes in the history of a people when it embodies its educational ideals and practice in schools, universities and the like. In Western Europe, our own country included, institutions of this kind have a very long history, in the course of which they have undergone marked development, keeping pace more or less with the development through which the several nations have themselves passed. The schools and colleges of an age, in so far as they are alive, are closely related to some phase or phases of the life of that age. They are part effect, part cause of that life – a fact which becomes more evident when education is studied, not as a thing apart, or in the void, but as it is connected with the nation's life, in a word, as history.

The growth of the historical spirit and its wider and ever wider application might therefore be expected to bring within its scope the subject of national education. Histories of national education nevertheless are few and the British contributions to them are of the fewest. Yet 'Education' (with a capital letter) has played a serious, even a prominent part, in English *political* and social life during the last hundred years.

English neglect to study the history of English education is the more to be regretted since England, perhaps more than other countries, would be helped by an understanding of her educational past. Although, as that past shows, English education is not without principles of its own, and although England has made notable contributions to educational theory on the great scale, many English 'educationists' and some English teachers are for ever pursuing some scheme or device of foreign origin, making it the fashion of the hour until it is thrown aside for something else equally alien. In the meantime they never look within, and in consequence miss the clues which might lead to stability.

A study of educational history would show that such foreign conceptions as can be applied with profit to English practice have often been anticipated in forms more intelligible to Englishmen by native thinkers and practitioners. Yet the native ideas have been forgotten long before the appearance of the foreigner. When in the mid-nineteenth century Froebel was first made known to Great Britain, and Dickens was enthusiastically booming the Kindergarten in 'Household Words', the educational work of the Edgeworths had long been forgotten. Yet in *Practical Education*, published nearly sixty years earlier, father and daughter had virtually formulated the essential principles of the Kindergarten, so far as those principles have practical value. Moreover, the two Irish writers were free from that metaphysical fog which perhaps commended the German to some of his admirers. *Omne ignotum pro magnifico*.

Even within the limits of English education a general ignorance of its history hides from us some of the lessons which might be learned from experience. It is often assumed that to Arnold of Rugby may ultimately be traced the modernization of the studies of the English secondary school and the introduction of a system of government which assigns extensive disciplinary powers to the senior pupils. In point of fact the prefect system was old when it figured in the first statutes of Winchester, the oldest of our public schools and the place of Arnold's own school education. To credit him alone with the changes which in the end broke the monopoly of Latin and Greek in the school-room is to ignore the earlier labours of Samuel Butler at Shrewsbury and of others now forgotten. For in truth that reform was due neither to Arnold or Butler, nor to any Public School master. The modernization of studies was first effected in the private schools of the eighteenth and early nineteenth centuries largely in response to the demands of middle-class parents, partly as a consequence of the fact that the teachers in many private schools had been denied a share in the traditional education then established in grammar-schools and universities. As long as the part played by private schools at that period is not appreciated, so long shall we fail to realize how salutary an influence such schools, when good, may exercise in a national scheme. In our own day, when the bureaucrat threatens to dominate all grades of education up to the universities themselves, the history of private enterprise in schools has many important lessons to teach. Failing the knowledge of that history, we base our opinion upon Squeers and Dotheboys Hall, which tell but one part of the story. We ignore the Hills and their book, *Public Education: Plans for the Government and Liberal Instruction of Boys in Large Numbers, as Practized at Hazelwood School* (1822), published some six years before Arnold went to Rugby. In this work a public-spirited family told how they revolutionized the studies of the school, and how they introduced a mode of self-government amongst their pupils, which was far more thorough-going than some forms of it now much advocated, which follow American models.

The lack of a philosophical grasp of English education as a whole, the want of the steadying influence afforded by the study of history, allow our 'educationists' and their disciples in the school-room to accept for truth the fallacy that from the particular principles, rules, practices and 'system' of a single thinker there may be evolved an education fully suited to all places at all times. But education, if it is effective in any real sense, is part of the national life, a reflexion of its most characteristic features, a development which has proceeded along lines parallel with those of the national evolution. Consequently education must be of its age as well as of its nation. A 'system' which proclaims itself to be 'of Paul' or 'of Apollos' is merely sectarian, ill-founded and doomed to sterility and disappearance. So far as such sectarianism gets translated into practice, so far may it hinder the natural development of national education.

The essential thing in educational theory, as in ethical theory, is the formulation of the end, or ends, to which the process itself is directed. Broadly, no doubt, the master of the medieval grammar-school, his Elizabethan successor and the master of the modern 'secondary school' may be said to pursue the same great end. But the mode of attaining it and the subordinate purposes which the three practitioners cherished, are very different. And a like set of differences marks the art of, say, the English public school master or the teacher in an English elementary school, and the American school teacher (very rarely a man) and the *professeur* in a *lycée*.

The controversies of the last hundred and especially of the last seventy years have been, and still are, due to the neglect of any profound consideration of the ultimate end, the master-purpose of education, irrespective of the age or social position of those to be educated. At its beginning (1833–39) English public administration of instruction addressed itself to political or social aims, sometimes to charitable endowment or even to measures of policy. The aim was limited by the desire to instruct those children *only* whose school-life, under the conditions then existing, could be but brief, ending at the age of ten or eleven. Even to-day, most proposed schemes deal with pupils under sixteen. The resultant 'system', which some public authorities greatly admire, is purely empirical, based on the presumed needs and restricted to the social circumstances of a class. An empirical system easily gives itself to controversy. The 'religious difficulty', a burning question in 1870, remains unsolved to-day. Failing a general agreement as to the end of education, whether of school *or university*, the problem will remain insoluble.

At the present time students of educational theory, perhaps the majority of them, ignore ends and devote their attention exclusively to processes. Psycho-analysis, the writings of Freud and Jung, 'intelligence-tests' and similar psychological material, from which much guidance in method may be extracted, fill their thoughts and their books; but they are silent as to the ultimate ends to which method itself is merely auxiliary.

A less numerous school, which mingles biological conceptions with psychological and greatly favours theories of American birth, states the educational end without reference to time or place and with scant recognition of existing institutions. Thus their philosophy of the educational end is either so generally and so vaguely expressed as to be a nose of wax rather than a finger-post, or else it is summarized in a catch-word. Some of these alien phrases are full of menace to education as hitherto understood in these islands. One such catch-phrase states that *the* end of education is the development of 'self-expression' in the individual pupil; but no objective standard of this self is laid down. Hence such words as 'higher', 'lower', 'good', 'bad', 'right', 'wrong', are meaningless in this connexion, so far at least as any normal connotation belongs to them. They may be relevant in an aesthetic sense, in so far as the self-expression attained is more or less harmonious or complete. But even so, no criterion is vouchsafed for our guidance.

Education on these lines is equally satisfied whether the outcome is saint or sinner, Alfred the Great or Adolf Hitler, Kit Marlowe or John Milton. The princes and scholars of the Cinquecento who made their one object in life personal distinction or, failing that, notoriety, are an historical protest against making self-expression an educational end of high rank, until a conception of the kind of self which is worthy of expression is clearly formed.

It is significant that this school of writers attaches great importance to the study of instinct, and is apt to get impatient when the claims of reason are pressed. Nevertheless it must be insisted that human advance has been conditioned by making instinct obey the behest of reason; and to education has been traditionally assigned the task of ensuring this subordination. Of course, a time impatient of discipline accepts with avidity so congenial a doctrine as the supremacy of instinct amongst all human qualities. To that extent the doctrine may claim to be the product of our own day. A similar reaction against theological dogma has given a new lease of life to Rousseau's dogma of original righteousness. 'All children are born good' is cheerfully accepted by the optimists who are proof against the experience which might have been gained in the domestic nursery and in the bigger world beyond it.

But in order to set any particular doctrine in its due place, we need the perspective, the criticism, the 'control' which history furnishes. Without such a guide it is difficult, in some cases impossible, to say whether we are wise, or the reverse, in acting upon catch-words, or whether their importance is simply trivial.

What may without offence be called the unhistorical study of education seems to have its origin in the belief that education is, or may be made, a science, using that word in its commonly accepted meaning. Hence the disregard of 'ends', with which natural science has nothing to do.

The difficulty in accepting this idea of educational theory is that in practice we find ourselves compelled to attempt a synthesis of principles derived from many branches of enquiry. Ethics, aesthetics, logic, psychology, and other divisions of philosophy, political theory, all have their bearing upon education, to say nothing of biology, physiology and the results of trial and error through the centuries. A body of doctrine so composite is not what is commonly understood by the term 'science'. The exponents of 'education as a science' can only retain the phrase by ignoring the synthetic character of educational theory.

Again, all experience goes to show that the personality of the teacher, or educator, is a very potent factor in the education of the individual. Even a method which is logically, psychologically correct cannot be applied with the precision of a mathematical formula, but will vary in its results with the individual pupil and teacher. A process so dependent on human personality can only be described as an art. Of course, the more the principles and processes employed are in accord with the nature of the mind and body operated upon or, to put it briefly, the more scientific the principles upon which the educator works, the more efficient will the education be. But this does not remove education from the arts or place it among the sciences. Psychology, logic, biology, all have their importance for the teacher; but these alone will not yield a true theory of education, since the latter must take into account ends even more than means. The artist should be a scientific thinker; but artist he remains.

'Education a science' has been a will-o'-the-wisp for more than a century in British history. It was an idea propounded by James Mill; but he was too good a philosopher to forget the teleological aspect of education. Had he read history with a less prejudiced eye, he might have given valuable teaching on educational ends. As it was, he did little more than sketch the outline of a theory based upon utilitarianism and the associationist psychology. When John Stuart Mill published his *Logic* in 1843 he suggested a new branch of enquiry which he called ethology; education he conceived as the practical application of the first principles revealed by ethology, the science of character. But Mill did not pursue the subject; when he addressed the St Andrews students as their Lord Rector in 1867, education as a science, or as based on a science, found no place in his address, which was a purely empirical presentation of his own extraordinary education, with certain additions and criticisms suggested by his experience as youth and man. A few years later Alexander Bain wrote a book with the express title *Education as a Science*. It is chiefly an associationist's explanation of, or apology for, the then current schoolroom practice, much of which has since been largely discredited. All these presentations of the subject were alike in their neglect of history.

So long as the uncertain human factor forms so great a part in it, education cannot be a science in the sense that chemistry or biology or psychology may be rightly so called. If education ever becomes such a science, it will not be human education, but the education of the bee-hive or ant-hill, those ideal communities of the bureaucrat.

Still, the teacher's craft, to say nothing of education as a whole, is not such an empirical business that it is devoid of principles. And these are

44

not confined to pure practice. Philosophy and the mental sciences claim to be heard when those principles are being considered; and biology puts in no small claim. But to avoid a barren scholasticism, theoretic knowledge of this kind needs a concrete foundation, such as is furnished by an historical study of educational institutions.

English history of that kind extends at least over some thirteen hundred years. It has seen the rise and development of schools and universities, of courses of study and revolutions in text-books, in methods of teaching and ways of administering the economy of schools and colleges. These changes have sometimes come from within, stimulated by some powerful personality; more often they have been brought about by the pressure of external circumstance or the deliberate action of authority. But always these changes have had their counterpart in the national life; while a general idea of what education should accomplish has never been absent. England was markedly slower than her neighbours in building for herself a national administrative scheme; and there has been considerable action and re-action between the growth of that system and the political and social life of the people. From a study of this wealth of material it should be possible to discover the main as well as the subsidiary objects at which English education has aimed and aims. In particular, historical enquiry of this kind would reveal the nature and limits of administrative control, local and national, a matter which promises to become a burning question.

Subjects of study and methods of teaching would then be open to a saner criticism than can be furnished *a priori* or by a mere *ipse dixit*. Practice, like a living theory, can never be stereotyped; but based upon historical enquiry it may be relatively stabilized and above all freed from quacks and cranks, from whose mischievous activity education, both as theory and as practice, is notoriously liable to suffer. Individual opinion would then find its due place, and neither the teacher nor the administrator would believe he was bound to swear by the name of any one master. On the other hand, a popular writer would not undertake to place before the public a presentation of a great headmaster without first being careful to make a study of English education as it was in the great headmaster's day. Blind alleys and impassable barriers would be recognized for what they are, and time and zeal would be saved in consequence. Does anyone doubt the power for good or evil which education may wield over a nation's life; if not, why should this particular factor in that life lack its competent historian?

Here is work in plenty for some of the many men and women now being trained in the universities to understand and to employ the historical method. We need more carefully documented histories of particular schools and colleges, more especially as these relate to purely educational activities. The *Alumni Cantabrigiensis* makes it evident that in the sixteenth century schools and teachers capable of preparing the boys for the university existed in places where we should not expect to find them to-day. Can more be discovered about them, and what was their effect upon the England of their time? It is certain that sixteenth-century England before the Reformation was far less illiterate than its successors assumed. The evidence is to be found *passim* and is therefore cumulative. Can this not be 'assembled' and added to? The 'Ancient Correspondence' in the Public Record Office should be worth examining from this point of view alone. We need a scrutiny of memoirs, autobiographies, and correspondence to furnish the needful checks upon the good intentions expressed in school and college statutes. There is room for a study of reforms projected by *English* writers, setting forth their success, or failure, thus throwing light upon the problems of to-day. There is the great field of educational legislation; studied, either in whole or in part, in the historical way it would prove of the greatest assistance to those who direct administration.

These are but a few of the many topics, here set down at random, which await the historical student's investigation. But to whichever topic, or topics, of this kind he turns, he can hardly fail to render a service, not only useful but necessary, to the upbringing of England's youth.

4

The Place of the History of Education in Training Courses for Teachers

W.H.G. ARMYTAGE

'This subject is utterly despised by the University', lamented R.H. Quick after giving his first lecture on the History of Education to an audience of intending teachers at Cambridge in October 1879; 'people don't know anything about the history of Education and don't want to know'.[1] Now, nearly three-quarters of a century later, things have changed. Books on the history of education exfoliate, and the subject has become not only an integral part of the training course, but a field in which a great deal of research is being done by teachers themselves. The emergence of the history of education as a recognized subject of study and the results of the research reflect three closely related trends in society: the displacement of the clergyman by the schoolmaster, the enhancement of secular educational administration and the impact of science on a curriculum relatively unchanged for three hundred years. The mutual interaction of these three trends can be traced back before Quick's time, but we are concerned with the seventy-four years which separate his experience from our own. Throughout that period historians of education have been unconsciously evolving the philosophy for their times: their histories have become exercises in critical evaluation.[2] Like other historians they have adventured into the past to discover the present, and their insights have been affected by the three trends I have indicated. In short, they have become part of the process they have investigated.

I

The displacement of the clergyman by the schoolmaster, so presciently observed by Coleridge and Disraeli, was reflected in the increased attention devoted to educational, as opposed to ecclesiastical history.[3] And just as the Biblical critics who sapped the foundations of faith in the early nineteenth century were Germans, so too were the first real historians of education. The work of Karl von Raumer[4] and others, translated by Henry Barnard, influenced R.H. Quick's own book, *Essays on Educational Reformers*, published in 1868: the first English book on the subject to be published. 'I have found', he wrote just before he became a schoolmaster at Harrow, 'that in the history of education, not only good books, but *all* books are in German or some foreign language'.[5] And Quick's work was, in spite of the oblique influence of Henry Barnard (acknowledged by Quick when he dedicated the second edition to him in 1890), a distinctively English work: eclectic, free from bias, assessing each school on its method. Typical of the writer was his refusal to add, at Seeley's suggestion, a final chapter summing up the proposals of the various reformers.

Quick's labours were supplemented by those of the first professors of education at Edinburgh and Aberdeen: S.S. Laurie and J.M.D. Meiklejohn. Laurie, a philosopher of some distinction, published amongst other books *The Life and Educational Writings of John Amos Comenius* (1881) five years after his election to the chair: the first complete account of Comenius and his works in any language. It ran to six editions by 1898. It was followed by *Mediaeval Education and the Rise and Constitution of Universities* (1886), a *Historical Survey of Pre-Christian Education* (1895) and *Studies in the History of Educational Opinion from the Renaissance* (1903). Meiklejohn, on the other hand, translated Kant's *Critique of Pure Reason*, read papers on the heuristic method, and, in pious memory of the person from whom his chair took its name, wrote a *Life of Dr. Andrew Bell*.

Quick's successor at Cambridge, Oscar Browning, did much to popularize the subject. He wrote the article on the History of Education for the *Encyclopaedia Britannica*, and made current the work of distinguished continentals in the field. His own *History of Educational Theories* (1881) was derived from Schmidt's *Geschichte der Pädagogik* (1868) and Compayré's *Histoire Critique des Doctrines de l'Education* (1879), and was translated into Hungarian and Servian – an index perhaps of its soundness rather than of any innate brilliance.

As ordinands fell away, teachers increased, and in the last decade of the nineteenth century, as that falling off both in quality and quantity was being loudly lamented, Day Training Colleges for teachers were growing rapidly in the civic universities. They numbered six at their start in 1890, and by 1902 had increased to nineteen. These developed into Education Departments and soon commanded a respectable muster of students, some taking a four-year course, and others a one-year post-graduate course. Naturally the Professors at the heads of these departments attempted to sketch some kind of historical perspectives for their students. Foster Watson, who held the chair at Aberystwyth from 1894 to 1913, was especially active. An edition of Mulcaster in 1898 was followed by *English Grammar Schools to 1660: Their Curriculum and Practice* (1908), *The Beginnings of the Teaching of Modern Subjects in England* (1909), and two books on Vives. Smaller books and articles flowed from his pen. He was asked to contribute a bibliographical account of English books on Education for the U.S. Government. He also wrote the chapter on 'Scholars and Scholarship, 1600–1660' for the *Cambridge History of English Literature*, volume 7, in 1911, and crowned a lifetime's work by editing the *Encyclopaedia of Education* (1922), which made his name well known among teachers in the twenties of this century. His efforts were supplemented by those of E.T. Campagnac of Liverpool University, J.W. Adamson of King's College, London, M.W. Keatinge at Oxford and Michael Sadler at Manchester.

II

Michael Sadler also reflects the second trend in the last seventy-four years: the increasing impact of secular administration upon the organization and curricula of the schools. He gave perspective to the developments of his own day. His series of reports from the Board of Education as Director of Special Inquiries are excellent examples of the comparative method working to enlighten public opinion as to the issues at stake. They form a useful background for anyone wishing to understand the architectonics of the 1902 Act.

The need for a perspective of the past in framing a policy for the future can also be seen in the work of A.F. Leach, who, as a Charity Commissioner from 1884 to 1915, was brought into continuous contact with the endowed schools, whose trusts were being individually re-modelled by the Charity Commission. Leach, who had held a fellow-ship at All Souls from 1874 to 1881, was a great scholar. His *English Schools at the Reformation 1546–8* (1896), *History of Winchester College* (1899), *History of Bradfield College* (1900) were followed by *Early Yorkshire Schools* (1899, 1903) and a *History of Warwick School* (1904). Most valuable, perhaps, were the detailed histories of schools which he wrote for the *Victoria County Histories* of *Hampshire* (1903), *Surrey* (1904), *Lincoln* (1906), *Northamptonshire* (1906), *Berkshire, Derbyshire, Durham, Gloucester, Sussex, Yorkshire* and

Suffolk (1907), *Bedfordshire, Buckinghamshire, Hertfordshire, Lancashire* and *Warwickshire* (1908), *Nottinghamshire* (1910) and *Worcestershire* (1913). For the more general reader his articles in the *Encyclopaedia Britannica*, and in Paul Monroe's *Cyclopedia of Education*, are still attractive. *Educational Charters and Documents* (1911) and *The Schools of Mediaeval England* (1914) gave a magnificent synthesis of forty-two years' continuous research, and remain as standard works. For Leach had an asset denied to later workers: he was first in the field of documents at the Public Record Office.

Another administrator who sketched historical frameworks for official reports was R. Fitzgibbon Young, Secretary to the Consultative Committee of the Board of Education from 1920 to 1939. He wrote the historical introductions to the famous Government reports that mark the years between the wars. Models of their kind, these reports are still invaluable to the student: *The Differentiation of Curriculum for Boys and Girls in Secondary Schools* (1923), *The Education of the Adolescent* (1926), *Books in Public Elementary Schools* (1928), *The Primary School* (1931), *Infant and Nursery Schools* (1933) and *Secondary Education* (1938). The second and the last, the Hadow and the Spens Reports respectively, are in such great demand that they have been often reprinted.

Nor, in the elucidation of our educational tradition, should the work of the schoolmasters themselves be forgotten. Apart from the histories of individual schools (of which a great number have been recently appearing, owing to the coincidence of a number of quatercentenaries) there have been a number of able, imaginative expositions of the grammar school tradition. These, appearing at a time when the very nature of the grammar school is being criticized by the advocates of 'comprehensive' schools, inevitably draw a picture of the past in which the grammar school is shown to have responded to social needs. One might add for instance the writings of Mr. A.D.C. Peterson or Dr. Eric James. One of Dr. James' predecessors as High Master of Manchester Grammar School, Dr. Samuel Dill, devoted his vast erudition to describing the disintegration of the cultural framework of the Roman Empire. Dr. James marshals arguments from the history of the last hundred years to prevent the disintegration of our own.

III

Dr. Samuel Dill was a classicist, Dr. Eric James is a scientist. The difference between them epitomizes the third change that has come over the educational system: the withering away of the traditional classical hegemony of secondary and further education and the rise of science. This is the real educational revolution of our time, and one which is still imperfectly understood. Yet the historians of education have given their warnings, most notably Thomas Davidson, who advocated the abandonment of 'pedagogy' in its narrow sense, and the interpretation of the history of education in terms of the history of science and philosophy. 'Kant and Comte have done their work', he wrote, 'taken the sun out of life, and left men groping in darkness. Without metaphysics even physics is meaningless; that which *appears* also *is*; that beneath all seeming is that which seems'. Whether lecturing for Bronson Alcott, or arguing with William James at Harvard, or galvanizing the Fellowship of The New Life in London (the predecessor of the Fabian Society), or talking with Schliemann in Greece, he was pre-eminently inspirational. Havelock Ellis described him as 'the most remarkable man, the most intensely alive man I had ever met'.

Davidson was a wandering scholar, one of the twelve most learned men in the Europe of his day, who saw clearly that social development was far more important than socialism. He lamented that 'even to this day there is no philosophy of actual experience, no working theory or norm of life, based upon the results of carefully digested science'. He saw where such a philosophy should arise: 'you must avoid all one-sidedness', he wrote, 'all over-devotion to the past or the present. You must correct Karl Marx by Isaiah and vice versa'. Davidson's own attempt to express this was his own *History of Education*, published in 1900.[6]

The correction of Karl Marx by Isaiah and vice versa, the elaboration of a theory of life based on the results of carefully digested science, is a paramount duty of the historians of education at present, and those outside the Departments of Education see it most clearly. Lancelot Hogben, one of the leading contemporary scientific humanists (or correctors of Isaiah by Karl Marx) has declared that 'the Departments of Education in our universities have the power to lay the foundations of a new humanism with its roots in the scientific outlook'.[7] On the other hand, a Christian apologist like Sir Walter Moberly, commenting on the 'heavy responsibility which rests upon the universities for sifting and transmitting ideas', stressed the 'pre-eminent role' which Departments of Education would have to play as 'natural centres' and 'the key positions in which the greatest service can be rendered'.[8]

IV

Times of crisis invariably provoke an inquest on the past, a revaluation of tradition, a purging and enrichment of our knowledge of the past. When, a hundred and fifty years ago, Prussia was humiliated and disillusioned, Niebuhr and Vom Stein prescribed 'a drastic study of antiquity' rather than 'new theory'. And today, when social observers all around us diagnose a 'crisis' in our contemporary culture, it is interesting to observe that Sir Walter Moberly prescribes 'a re-discovery or re-invigoration' of our tradition, and its interpretation in terms of a large-scale mechanical civilization.

'The fact is', Nathaniel Hawthorne once wrote after a visit to the British Museum, 'the world is accumulating too many materials for knowledge. We do not recognize for rubbish what is really rubbish'.[9] In the discoveries of the last seventy-four years we have accumulated a great stock of knowledge, a lot of which is really rubbish. It is time for a bold, imaginative re-interpretation of our tradition. The significantly named *New Bearings, Revaluations, Explorations* and *Rehabilitations* produced by a certain school of literary critics are, in one sense, reactions in that direction. Mr. Bantock's recently published *Freedom and Authority in Education* is a product of this school.

Now the Education Departments of Universities have a great opportunity for similar work. Their student population is superior to that of the normal academic department in three important respects. They are relatively mature, they possess diverse academic interests, and they have not to face the rigours of a final examination. Their congregation in Education Departments offers a stimulating challenge to the imaginative presentation of our educational tradition, a presentation which will enable them to appreciate their subject as part of the *speculum mentis*, and win insights into other specialisms. True, great efforts are made to enable the graduate in the natural sciences to appreciate the cultural aspects of the arts, but few attempts are being made to enable the arts graduate to appreciate the cultural content of the sciences. It is not too much to say that the Education Departments have it in their power to discharge the functions of what Ortega y Gasset called a 'Faculty of Culture' to bring students 'up to the height of the times'.[10]

V

How is this to be done? Teachers of the history of education have, at the present, to lift their sights. The assignments in the base areas on antiquarian histories of particular schools and institutions serve well enough for the post-graduate degree, and there is no lack of such intellectual navvies.[11] The sharp end of the contemporary conflict is up in the no man's land of ideas, and we need a group of intellectual commandos of the Dilthey and Collingwood variety to essay a contemporary raid into the *Geisteswissenschaften*, and to plot a new *speculum mentis*. As those two have shown us, such essays will be inevitably affected by their contemporary situation (*zeitbedingt*), but, as they have also shown us, they will in turn influence the development of that situation. For man transforms himself, and if he is to continue to do so, his teachers must be aware of both Nature and History, must disturb them and be continuously aware of them.[12]

Since education is the process of the self-transformation of man, and since all the contemporary systems of government are based on appeals, not to the supernatural, but to experimental and documentary evidence, it is for teachers to realize this, and also to realize that even scientific theories have a historical setting. How much clearer would the nature of 'intelligence' become if the enormous vested interest of the bureaucracy in a reliable filter for the great capacity catching machine was realized? And how much more wholesome would the often barren techniques of educational measurement (so often misinterpreted as 'research') become if the measurers were aware of the general forces shaping such intelligence?

For too long, education departments have played on sections of the University periphery with bits and pieces of other studies, pejoratively labelled 'educational'. They have shrunk from the centre, from the union of Arts and Science (History and Nature) since their equipment is shabby and always deteriorating. They might start by jettisoning some of this equipment in their B. echelons: the literacy tests, the antiquarian catalogues of acts and reformers, and the pedagogic panoply of audio-visual aids; and then embark (as a first step) on experimental courses in the history and philosophy of science, conducted, not by some pretentious second rater, but by someone specially recruited for the task.

This is not to exalt what Jacques Maritain called the third, fourth and fifth misconceptions of education – Pragmatism, Sociologism and Intellectualism – but to restore the traditional liberality of the arts.[13] It is

53

no more (in its temporal context) than the medieval student enjoyed when he studied for his *licentia docendi*, or master's degree, when the mathematical sciences (arithmetic and geometry) and the physical sciences (astronomy and music) were the main arts of the quadrivium. His modern counterpart has to be made aware of the accumulated legacy of the physical, biological, philosophic and sociological legacy he is to inherit, and from which, through the personal transmission of gifted teachers (not all occupationally so classified) he will form his repertory of convictions. The account of the way in which this legacy has grown, and has been transmitted, will reflect the way it is being transmitted, and will become his story: the history of education.

NOTES

1. F. Storr, *Life and Remains of R.H. Quick* (Cambridge, 1909), 75–78.
2. Cf. C.S. Peirce (*Collected Papers*, ed. Hartshorne and Weiss, Harvard 1934, V, 297), 'it is the belief men *betray*, and not which they *parade*, which has to be studied'.
3. For a discussion of this trend see E. Halévy, *History of the English People* (Epilogue: 1895–1905, Book 2). (Pelican Books, 1939, 58–64.)
4. Karl von Raumer (1783–1865), author of a four-volume history dealing with education from Dante to Pestalozzi and the German Universities, which was attacked by the *Saturday Review*, a leading Anglican organ of the day. For Raumer was a geologist, and geologists were undermining the very foundations of faith.
5. *Essays on Educational Reformers* (London, 1929), viii.
6. For an appraisal of Davidson see *History of Education Journal* (Ann Arbor, Michigan, 1951, 74–79).
7. Lancelot Hogben, 'The Education of the Citizen' in *What Science Stands For* (London, 1937, 125).
8. *The Crisis in the University* (London, 1949, 252–4, 294).
9. Mark van Doren, *Nathaniel Hawthorne* (London, 1952, 208).
10. Ortega y Gasset, *Mission of the University* (translated by Howard Lee Nostrand), London, 1944, 80–92. See especially p.83:
    'There is always a system of live ideas which represents the superior level of the age, a system which is essentially characteristic of its times; and this system is the culture of the age. He who lives at a lower level, on archaic ideas, condemns himself to a lower life, more difficult, toilsome, unrefined. This is the plight of backward peoples – or individuals. They ride through life in an ox-cart while others speed by them in automobiles. Their concept of the world wants truth, it wants richness, and it wants acumen. The man who lives on a plane beneath the enlightened level of his time is condemned, relatively, to the life of an infra-man.'
11. Sir Fred Clarke (*Freedom in the Educative Society*, 1948, 83) once referred to 'the vicious habit of identifying education with formal schooling'; and the work of the Leach school of institutional historians has, in its way, contributed to this.
12. The difference between Dilthey and Collingwood is that Dilthey was much more optimistic as to the value of the human studies of history and the social sciences, as he well might be, since he wrote a generation earlier. For a stimulating discussion of the difference between them (which bears on the value of each for the contemporary historian of education) see H.A. Hodges, *The Philosophy of William Dilthey* (London, 1952, 315–360).
13. Jacques Maritain, *Education at the Cross Roads* (Oxford, 1943, 13–19, 71, n.3).

5

The History of Education

BRIAN SIMON

I

There is no need to make out a case for the study of the history of education as an essential aspect of the course offered to intending teachers. It has long been accepted as such in most colleges and universities and is almost universally taught, in its own right, as part of the education course. There is, however, considerable room for discussion about what is taught. It may well be that this subject could be better treated if it were more closely related to other educational studies and that in this way the real objective of historical study could be more fully realized.

It is the present tendency to review the past development of the English educational system, and of particular institutions within it, as if this took place by its own momentum rather than in relation to changing social pressure and needs. As a result, what is likely to emerge is a somewhat indigestible mass of dates and facts, orders and Acts. This is all the more likely in that educational ideas are usually treated separately as if they belonged to a separate world. To approach the matter in this way, it may be argued, is to miss the whole point of historical study.

Education is a social function, and one of primary importance in every society. It should be one of the main tasks of historical study to trace the development of education in this sense, to try to assess the function it has fulfilled at different stages of social development and so to reach a deeper understanding of the function it fulfils today. Not only have educational institutions been socially conditioned, but also the body of educational theory which lies behind the practical day to day business of teaching and school organization. This too has developed, not in isolation, but in dependence upon the practical possibilities for education, the demand for it at different times from various sections of

55

the community for various ends. It is necessary and important, therefore, to consider educational development as a whole, and not to relegate institutions and ideas to separate categories.

The historical approach should bring educational developments into perspective, and in so doing open the teacher's eyes to the real nature of his work. It is the most difficult thing in the world to view *objectively* a system in which one is immediately involved. Historical study can be a powerful means to this end. It enables the student to understand that educational 'principles' contain historical components, some of which may no longer be relevant – or, in the light of advancing knowledge, viable – and which are, therefore, open to reconsideration. The same applies to institutions which have often been changed in the past and will certainly be changed in the future. There is, perhaps, no more liberating influence than the knowledge that things have not always been as they are and need not remain so.

It is with the study of education as a social function, then, that historical study should be primarily concerned. But while it is clear that education has changed as society itself has changed – many examples from the nineteenth century spring to mind – it is also clear that these changes have often been slow, or only very partially accomplished. To recognize this, and inquire further into the matter, is to come up against the fact that society has not always been united in its educational demands, that the impulse for reform often comes from only one section while it is in the interests of another to maintain the *status quo*. It is often a great deal easier to keep things as they are than to change them, and here tradition makes its weight felt.

The older established schools and colleges tend to lay great emphasis on their traditions and these may have some very positive aspects. But the appeal to tradition can also be suspect, a matter of unexamined assumptions rather than based on solid historical fact. For instance, it has been argued that English grammar schools have traditionally been concerned with the clever child and have, in this sense, made a valuable contribution to English life through the centuries. But the briefest acquaintance with educational history is sufficient to question both these claims. No institutions stagnated more painfully in the late eighteenth and nineteenth centuries than the endowed grammar schools up to the time when they were rescued and set on a new footing by the Endowed School (and later the Charity) Commissioners. It is only since the Education Act of 1944, which provided for the abolition of fees, that entrance to many of these schools has been solely by selective examination. This is not to pass any judgment on their present effectiveness.

Mention of the selection examination at eleven-plus, and its relatively recent origin, brings to notice another major advantage of historical study, that it encourages a sceptical approach to ideas which may simply rationalize existing practice. It is a tendency among educationists, psychologists and philosophers of all ages, to advance theories as if these represented not the *present* level of social development, or of knowledge deriving from inquiries of various kinds, but ultimate, proven truths. The trend continues even in a scientific age. No theory was advanced with more certainty, for example, than that 'intelligence' is a fixed quality of the mind which can be measured accurately by means of intelligence tests. Psychologists no longer adhere to this theory; as knowledge has increased it has been replaced by others much less sweeping and more tentative. But the idea still lingers on in the schools, in the minds of many teachers, with immediate effect on their attitudes to children and methods of teaching. To study the history of education attentively, to discover just how and why the division between primary and secondary education became fixed at the age of eleven, to trace the course of development from the 'scholarship' examination first introduced in the 1890s to the eleven-plus of the post-1944 years, is to become aware that the main factors at work were often political and economic rather than educational and psychological. Awareness of this necessarily implies a critical approach to educational and psychological arguments advanced in support of this procedure long after it became established. There is the less tendency to accept such theories unquestioningly, only to face the painful process of growing out of them with all that this implies in terms of entering on an educational *cul-de-sac*.

One of the most enlightened educationists of recent times, the late Sir Fred Clarke, one-time director of the University of London Institute of Education, laid great stress on the need for 'critical self-awareness' in teachers and the place of historical study in promoting this kind of outlook. In *Education and Social Change* (1940) he argued that to live unquestioningly in the immediate present is to run the danger of developing a conditioned response to current practice: a set of attitudes unconsciously determined rather than consciously formed. The teacher in a particular type of school which goes about the business of education in a particular way, comes to believe that this procedure – and only this – is education. Faced with the suggestion that other methods might be possible and desirable he reacts not with interest and inquiries but impatience and annoyance. A recent example (1962) is the response by teachers in junior schools, in which children are streamed into A, B, C classes, to an inquiry as to whether it might not be better educationally to abolish streaming.[1] Many answers were given with an absolute assurance, as if it were ridiculous (or, as one teacher said, 'the height of professional irresponsibility') to entertain the idea of such a change. At the same time it seems clear that these teachers were unaware that streaming in junior schools was only generally introduced some thirty years ago, when a change to this practice took place. Nor did they know that this procedure is almost unique to England. Knowledge of either of these facts could have made the difference between an open or a closed mind.

Here it may be noted that comparative study of the educational systems of different countries is an important adjunct to historical study in the sense that has been outlined. The intrinsic interest of learning about other practices apart, this brings home the fact that educational development is not a preordained process which must follow particular lines, as in England, but that there is a great variety of possible lines of development. There are, indeed, examples on our doorstep in the school systems of Wales, and particularly Scotland, though all too little use has been made of them. Even more illuminating, perhaps, is study of the part played by education in societies of different levels of social development, particularly primitive societies of various kinds but also those more advanced. Such anthropological study brings out most strikingly differences in the role of education – of the family, peer groups, institutions – and can, therefore, fulfil the same educative or liberating function as comparative or historical studies.

Clarke looked at English education – in particular, social and educational distinctions between different kinds of school which have so often been taken for granted – with the sceptical eye of one who had spent twenty-five years in the Dominions. He noted that writers on the subject 'show little explicit awareness of the social presuppositions of their thought', pointing out that while 'highly generalized principles' of education figure largely in the textbooks, as the supposed determinants of educational practice, in fact both thought and practice 'are much more closely conditioned by social realities which are themselves the result of historical and economic forces'. This led him to insist on a new function for the educational historian, that of unravelling the social and historical influences which have played so potent a part in shaping both the schools and what is taught inside them; and, most important, of distinguishing the genuine educational theory from the rationalization which seeks to explain away rather than elucidate.

Seen in this light, the history of education takes on a new aspect, as a vital contribution to social history – rather than a flat record of acts and ordinances, punctuated by accounts of the theories of great educators

58

who entertained ideas 'in advance of their time'. Consideration of the social origins of these ideas brings to light the elements in society ready for change at different times, and leads on to inquiry into why changes of a particular kind were needed, what assisted or prevented their realization, what compromises were made, breakthroughs achieved, and with what effect. In the same way, to study legislation in its origins and development is to understand much more fully what this represented or failed to achieve. The 1870 Education Act, the Act of 1902, did not spring ready-made from the mind of a Forster or a Balfour but were the products of much controversy, the balancing of forces representing sectional interests, general political considerations and the like. If these acts have had a powerful effect in shaping the educational system, it cannot be accepted that the shaping has been solely in accordance with educational considerations; to see this is also to get a clearer view of what remains to be done and how to go about it.

The educational system is not, of course, merely an institution to be studied for its own sake – so many nursery, elementary, secondary schools, so many special services, colleges of various kinds which have come into being in a variety of ways. Education is, by its very nature, concerned with the formation of men. 'He who undertakes the education of a child undertakes the most important duty of society', wrote Thomas Day, author of the famous eighteenth-century treatise *Sandford and Merton*. He was writing at a time when the family took a far greater part in education than it now does and outlined a course of upbringing designed to develop the qualities he esteemed most highly, both in terms of the kind of knowledge to be acquired and traits of character. Many past reformers have epitomized their educational aims in this way, and the procession of models through the centuries tells us much about changing social and educational values – the medieval scholar, the Renaissance gentleman combining classical learning with active skills, the seventeenth-century virtuoso and amateur of science, through Locke, Chesterfield and others to the modern age. If the models come predominantly from the upper classes, there are interesting contradictions and variations even within this range. Just as, in the early seventeenth century, Peacham's *Complete Gentleman* was more polished and less puritan than Braithwaite's *English Gentleman*, so in the nineteenth century Thomas Arnold's ideal of the Christian gentleman combining 'godliness and good learning' gives place to the Kingsley–Maurice ideal of 'manliness'. This brings a spotlight to bear on differences between the 'public' school ethos of 1830 and that of 1880, for if ever schools set out to form their pupils, it was the public schools of this age.

This raises yet another point of great importance, the relation between educational aims and educational achievement. The body of theory with which the educationist operates is often anything but clearly organized and adequately validated, in the sense that other disciplines represent an ordered body of knowledge. But he has got a means of testing the viability of his ideas in terms of the end product of teaching. To return to the example of the late Victorian public school is to find that this did, to a noteworthy extent, successfully form its pupils according to the model desired. Whether or not the model was desirable, in social terms, is another matter, irrelevant in this connection. The point to be made is that education, as a social function, can be judged by its fruits, and often has been down the years. Today education draws much more than in the past on psychology and sociology for methods and theories and gains very much in the process. Not, perhaps, until psychology becomes a fully fledged science can education have a sound scientific basis – a goal towards which educational reformers of the modern age have looked, as history shows. But if this goal is to be reached there must be insistence, despite the debt to other disciplines, that education itself is a viable field of study going beyond all these, and so having its own points of reference. In other words, the present position of educational studies in this country must be seen as only a stage in the historical process.

These are some general examples of ways in which the historical approach can assist the study of education. If the emphasis has been on the practical applications of this study it is because the teacher in training is not a student of history but of the history of *education*. 'Truth as founded upon knowledge is like a mountain peak accessible from many sides', wrote Foster Watson, one of the pioneers of the historical study of education, 'and he knows the mountain best who has ascended it from many starting points.'[2] Education now makes use of many disciplines, of philosophy, as well as psychology, and sociology. History introduces an extra dimension which helps to bring all these into focus. It has, therefore, a vital coordinating role, the more necessary now that philosophy has abandoned its former generalizing function to concentrate on logical and conceptual analysis. At the same time it is one of the main functions of historical study to foster objectivity of mind, that 'critical self-awareness' which is the mark of the teacher who is both knowledgeable and ready to extend his knowledge and develop his practice. This is the educational justification for its place in the intending teacher's course.

II

In criticizing English social blindness and outlining a fresh approach to the historical study of education, Clarke provided some apt practical examples and suggestions. In the Report of the Consultative Committee to the Board of Education on secondary education published in 1938 (the Spens Report) there is no mention whatsoever of the public schools. This in itself is surprising enough, once thought is given to the matter. Still more astonishing to Clarke was the fact that no one remarked on the omission; it was regarded as entirely natural that an official committee investigating secondary education should leave out of account the only schools which, on their own estimation, are peculiarly national in character, the best fruits of British genius in education. This example is cited to illustrate how far it is taken for granted that there should be two systems of education – a fact so curious as to impress any outsider.

A closely allied question is that of different types of school within the public system of education; the underlying reasons for these divisions, Clarke was one of the first to note, 'are much less educational than they ought to be. They are rather social, historical and administrative.'[3] In fact, to examine secondary education in its origin and development is also to bring to light the changing nature of generalized statements about children's abilities over a comparatively brief period. If the Taunton Commission (1868) estimated that boys of 'exceptional talent' from the working classes, intellectually worthy of a secondary education, constituted well under 1 per cent of the child population, the Bryce Commission, nearly thirty years later conceded that the proportion was slightly larger. Forty years on the Spens Committee (1938) estimated 30 per cent as worthy of a selective education and, in 1959, the Crowther Committee raised this to 50 per cent – though here the idea is expressed in more modern terms, as the proportion capable of learning through grasping abstractions. This is but another way of indicating that the educational principles enunciated at different times may be less worthy of attention than the social and administrative considerations which remain unvoiced and must be sought out.

Once preconceptions are set aside, a host of questions arise for investigation. The age of transition from primary to secondary education has already been referred to, and is now under active discussion, but what concrete historical reasons determined that this age should be fixed at eleven and how far were the psychological and educational justifications advanced rationalizations covering existing practice?

The raising of the school leaving age also brings forward some fundamental questions on which historical inquiry can throw considerable light, in particular the relation of this matter to the use of adolescent labour by industry – still a very actual question as it concerns, for instance, the system of day release. This kind of inquiry, which links educational measures to the really determining factors in social life, has been singularly lacking.

There has been little effective historical study of the evolution of the curriculum, the changing content of education. Here again it is worth directing attention to Clarke's argument which relates this closely to the changing demands of different social classes. The British conception of education for culture, he says, is 'shot through with compromise', the uneasy resultant of two conflicting traditions – that of the aristocracy, clergy and gentry embodied in the classical tradition in the grammar schools and ancient universities, and that of puritanism and dissent, with its insistence on science and the 'relief of man's estate'. The latter outlook, that of modern studies, the teaching of science, found a home in the dissenting academies and later in those schools and colleges founded by the radical middle class in the nineteenth century. This is the background to problems which still weigh on the schools for when science was generally introduced in the nineteenth century it was simply tacked on to a traditional core, while the organization of 'sides', or later, of specialist studies merely reflected the two conceptions of culture which Clarke defined as the literary (or classical) and the scientific (or modern). J.D. Bernal has aptly described the kind of syllabus we present to pupils today as 'a kind of geological record of the education of the past in which stratum after stratum is laid down one after the other' – the classical, the mediaeval scholastic, the renaissance humanist, the eighteenth century enlightenment, the factual Gradgrind, with, 'rather unconsolidated at the top', various efforts at a child-centred project education.[4] Similarly, as new sciences develop, or as science itself advances, the tendency is simply to add to the existing syllabus without any attempt at a fundamental readjustment.

Steps are now being taken towards recasting courses as a whole, particularly in science and mathematics, but much remains to be done. Detailed inquiry into the way the subject matter of different disciplines has accumulated, the balance sought and achieved at different periods, the relation between special and general education and varying arguments in support of different proportions for each – all this leads to a deeper understanding. The student who has studied these developments will be in a better position to plan his own courses, recognize their relation to others, and perceive the educational programme as a whole, its sense and direction. He will also be forewarned against the tendency to justify existing practice on the grounds that it corresponds to certain innate qualities of the child's mind – such, for instance, as the Crowther Committee's claim that grammar schools rightly provide a highly specialized form of education in their sixth forms because children are essentially 'subject-minded'.

In the field of methodology and school organization, one of the major questions at issue is the role of class teaching (which bears on the question of streaming and setting), the place of individual work and the value of group projects. At the university and college level there is the lecture, a mediaeval survival, which may well not be the best method of imparting knowledge (or stimulating thought) in the 1960s. To study the evolution of teaching method is to find that it has closely depended on general pedagogic ideas, the availability of teachers and their standard of training, the kind of technical aids to be drawn upon, the nature of school buildings provided and so on. Class teaching (the 'Prussian' system, as it used to be known) appears as the product of a specific set of circumstances, particularly during the past century. All this is both full of interest and a material help to getting present problems and possibilities into perspective. Do we want schools with separate classrooms in the future, as in the past, or do the new technical aids now coming into use, the methods of teaching at our disposal, and indeed our whole approach to the educational process, suggest considerable changes in the arrangement and organization of the school? It is only if such questions are well thought out, and teachers press for the facilities necessary to engage in new methods of education, that it is possible to short-circuit, as it were, the tendency of educational institutions to be rooted in yesterday's needs. How great an influence on the progress of education has been exerted by the all too solid barracks erected by the Victorians who built to last!

This raises the question on what may be called educational archaeology. History is on the ground, particularly in the great cities of the industrial age, and more may be learned by a day's tour of school buildings of different periods than from a dozen lectures or books. The reactions of students when they first go into the schools to teach, their comments and criticisms, are sometimes a revelation to an older generation which has learned to accept things as they are. An integral understanding of the educational system in its origin and development can help to preserve this freshness of outlook.

Examinations are another matter which tends to be taken for granted and these, again, have often been justified by appeal to the intrinsic nature of the child; competition is the best, if not the only, motivation to learning, hence the constant use of mark sheets and form orders in certain types of school. Here it is instructive to compare, for instance, the attitude to competition of Wordsworth (*The Prelude*) and Bentham (*Chrestomathia*) at the outset of the period when competitive examinations began to enter on the educational scene. To what extent was the increasing use of competition as a motivational technique the product of growing individualism, what were the corresponding educational arguments and the relevant factors outside the schools in terms of a new development of the professions and the setting of minimum standards of entry? Or, to approach the matter from the opposite angle, there is a movement of opposition to be traced in some circles and some schools up to the progressive schools of today.

All this is, of course, closely linked with ideas about the learning process. As has already been noted it has been a prevailing tendency of recent years to interpret children's abilities in terms of available educational facilities, in particular the overall proportion of places in selective schools. But new light can be thrown on this matter by taking a long view of educational history. To do so is to find that at certain periods the emphasis has been on educability, on the potentialities of human beings and on educational policies and methods framed to realize these potentialities. In other words, failure to learn was not ascribed to some form of innate incapacity – rather to inadequacies in the methods of teaching used. The predominant attitude was one of optimism, belief in human powers and in the possibility of developing them by education. One might cite the educational ideas and projects of the humanists in the fifteenth and early sixteenth centuries, the age of the Commonwealth in England, the late eighteenth century in France (and among some circles in England), as times when the formative role of education was particularly stressed; a corollary was the attempt to develop a scientific approach to the psychology of learning, of education. This raises a key question, the extent to which educational ideas and aims are themselves socially conditioned, however unaware of the fact their authors may be. How far, for instance, has the tendency to stress the limitation of children's abilities in England been a product of the economic and social circumstances of the decades between 1900 and 1940? How far does the present movement away from this view depend on social and technological changes, the replacement of unemployment by full employment, of economic stagnation by the maintenance of a consistent, though small, rate of economic growth – all factors requiring a higher educational level among the population?

Study of the historiography of education can also be rewarding. Why has there been interest in this subject at some points in particular directions and none at others; what was it, for instance, about the turn of the century that gave rise to a new interest in study of the educational past? Foster Watson has provided one of the answers to this question, that it was the development of science that 'increasingly pressed upon the notice of students the importance of the genetic method of treatment of subjects. ... From the very development of scientific conceptions', he added, 'there arose the new scientific demand for the study of the historical side of humanistic subjects.' In other words, people were no longer satisfied with philosophic generalizations about education and the educational process; they wished to penetrate into the historical development of education itself. 'It is realized in the outer world of nature', continued Foster Watson, 'that the slightest attempt to analyse the present state of an organism leads us to the past – for what is the past but the antecedent states of the parts which in their organized form now constitute the present?'[5] Psychology was also making its own inroads on part of the philosophical field. It was again Foster Watson who drew attention to one of the pioneer psychologists, Juan Luis Vives, who was insisting that learning begins with sense impressions more than a century before Thomas Hobbes or John Locke. The idea that education could also become more scientific, and that one of the essential means to this end was a rigorous study of its history, was a particular stimulus to historical inquiry.

This was a time when W.H.Woodward brought educational developments at the Renaissance to attention, de Montmorency wrote on legal and administrative aspects of English education and J.W. Adamson began to make his major contribution to the writing of English educational history from early mediaeval times. A.F. Leach added further accounts of schools and of the development of mediaeval education to an earlier work which stemmed in large part from the findings of the Schools Inquiry Commission. There have been few names to set beside these since, though the situation is beginning to change again. Both Foster Watson and Adamson, though scholars of note, pursued their work particularly with the teacher in training in mind and were convinced of the vital importance of historical study to enlightened educational thinking. Adamson commented sadly towards the end of a long life on the fact that histories of English education are 'of the fewest', a neglect the more to be regretted 'since England, perhaps more than any other country, would be helped by an understanding of her educational past'.[6] This remains as true as ever it was but there are now fresh opportunities to close the gap.

In particular, the trend in historical studies away from predominantly political and constitutional matters towards economic and social developments with an accompanying interest in the people rather than peers is a material aid to the historian of education. If he plays his part, when history is rewritten education should take its proper place not merely as an adjunct to the historical process but as one of the chief factors conditioning men's outlook and aspirations, attitudes to which express clearly current beliefs about the human condition and the direction of social advance. So far as the history of education itself is concerned, this, too, will concentrate not so much on particular institutions or the eminent *alumni* of particular schools, but on those broad movements which have affected the majority of people, and essentially constitute the educational history of the nation.

III

Methods of studying the history of education in courses for the intending teacher have already been touched upon. The primary difficulty is the relative shortness of the time available by comparison with the vastness of the field as a whole. It is for this very telling reason that 'history of education' often takes the form of a concentrated course covering chiefly what might be called surface phenomena. Rarely does it extend back beyond the early nineteenth century, in the later decades of which the educational system begins to become complex and there is an unending mass of detail to outline. There remains too little time to give point to all these facts by filling in the background – the more general relations between church and state, for instance, other social factors influencing legislation, the politics and pressure groups operating when particular educational measures are under consideration, or, more fundamental, technological and industrial developments which necessitate an adaptation of education. What is likely to emerge so far as the student is concerned, is little more than an external description of events. Why these particular events took place and no other does not appear as a problem at all, though it is perhaps the question of most relevance and interest.

It is clear, from what has already been said, that to see the history of educational development as a simple linear process is to get an entirely false impression. This is so as much in the realm of ideas as in the field of practice. The remedy would seem to be that which has also been applied in the historical field generally; study in time of particular topics and study of particular periods in depth.

If the student of education suffers from the disadvantage of lack of historical training he. has the advantage of some knowledge of the educational system – a knowledge most historians tend to lack. Attitudes to education as well as educational provision may have varied widely down the ages but the fundamental educational issues remain essentially the same. It is ability to distinguish the important questions from the irrelevant that provides the key to fruitful historical investigation.

This is not the place to discuss the structuring of the main studies in education of the intending teacher. It may well be that the particular contribution of historical studies – or of the historical approach generally – can best be made to a carefully thought out integrated course on education based on a series of topics. The weight given to the historical approach in this situation would depend on its relevance in each case. This matter is referred to again later; in the meantime, even if the history of education is thought of in terms of a relatively self-contained study, there is much to be said for a first approach to the past through the present, by study of issues which are of particular moment in the educational scene today. By choosing interrelated topics on the one hand, and studying these also in the context of periods covering important 'moments' of change, it is possible to arrive at a course of study which is both internally consistent and meaningful, and which can be adequately supplemented by wider reading. Such a course might well constitute part of the basic course in education.

It might be accompanied by optional studies, for instance, study in depth of a particular period. The most illuminating periods are usually those of rapid social change when educational developments also are accelerated, so that a clear picture emerges of the nature and direction of change. It is often the advances made at such times that have left the most permanent mark on educational theory and practice, for instance, the new institutions and ideas of the period 1790–1830, of the decades 1640–60, or, going further back, at the time of the Reformation. There are equivalent periods of interest in the modern age in the decades 1850–70, or 1890–1910, study of which involves picking up earlier threads and looking ahead to future developments. The object would be to study the institutional structure of education – the relation between educational theory and practice – as aspects of the social, economic and intellectual history of the age. If the view can be extended to other countries, so much the better.

Limited research projects are a useful adjunct of study on these lines. There is an immense amount of local historical material in many districts, both in local record offices and in some of the schools, not to speak of the memories of those who have taught and learned in an earlier generation whose experiences rank as history for the student of today. No specialized historical knowledge is needed to get the most out of a school log book, a school board minute book, or from the reminiscences of a teacher and much may be gained in terms of bringing the past to life. Research projects of this kind can be carried out individually or, if more ambitious, as a group undertaking.

One of the main difficulties hitherto has been lack of the necessary materials to stimulate and inform a new approach to educational history. It is for this reason that there has of necessity been recourse to the lecture as the main means of imparting basic information, together with a heavy reliance on a limited group of textbooks. With additional aids there should be more scope for a variety of methods – the group discussion, individual research – though the lecture may still be the most suitable means of introducing periods or topics, of outlining methods of approach. In this matter education departments and colleges of education might well show others the way by discarding the traditional type of lecture which does little but follow the textbook and using the lecture to break new ground. There is also much scope for building up libraries and collections of other material – documents illustrating local education, photographs of schools and classrooms of different periods, prospectuses, examination papers, and anything else that throws light on what went on in the schools.

It is to be expected that courses for the B.Ed. degree will include an historical component and here there may be a place for a more extended course. More specialist and scholarly study of the history of education can find a place in diploma courses taken by practising teachers and in other courses leading to a higher degree. There is encouraging evidence of a fresh interest in historical research at this stage and it is on such researches that the rewriting of the history of education must in large part depend. Only in so far as teaching is combined with research on the part of those responsible for the subject in colleges of education and universities can there be a guarantee that it will itself be lively and forward-looking and ensure that educational history attains a new status.

Here the same considerations apply as have already been outlined. If we are to interpret the nature of education as a social function, then it is essential to study it in its origin and development as one aspect of a much wider social and economic scene. This must not mean, however, losing sight of the internal development of the educational system and its various parts, for established institutions do take on a life and develop an ethos of their own which then to a considerable extent shapes their further course; it may, indeed, be the dominant determining feature at a time when outside pressures are not very strong. At such times, it may be worth noting, established educational institutions tend to ossify, so that the concept that educational provision tends constantly to improve hardly accords with the facts. The great period of the grammar schools, for instance, was the century 1560–1660 when these were genuinely national schools – the opportunity of the ordinary local boy, farmer's or tradesman's son, reaching the university in the period 1620–40 was, certainly in Leicestershire, greater than it was to be at any future period until comparatively recently. The history of education records set-backs as well as advances; deprivation of educational facilities as well as their provision.

The problem here is to disentangle the strands which go to make up the very complex process of social change, and to assess their significance for education. At the root lie those technological developments which bring about changes in the structure of industry and the nature of production and in so doing change ways of life and work more or less fundamentally; the process is most clearly to be discerned, of course, at such periods as the 'industrial revolution' but is always operative to a greater or lesser extent. But whether or not latent potentialities are realized, to what extent and in what direction, depends on factors at the level of social organization; all industries do not share equally in, for instance, technological advance or commercial expansion, nor do these affect all classes in the same way – hence the varying programmes for, and resistances to, the corresponding educational changes, contradictory influences which also make themselves felt within the educational system itself.

Scientific and technological developments also influence the nature of education through transformation of its content. As knowledge increases, so new subjects enter the schools, though often not without a struggle sometimes extending over centuries: cosmography, splitting into history and geography; mathematics; natural philosophy, dividing into the various sciences; eventually technology itself, first developed 'on the job', becomes a subject of disciplined study in universities and, later, in technical colleges. Closely connected with the advance of knowledge are changing ideas as to the nature of learning which directly affect teaching methods and pedagogical ideas generally. If Vives was, perhaps, the first of the 'moderns' to teach towards a scientific psychology, this approach was developed by the English philosophers Hobbes and Locke, and, with the development of Hartley's associationism, profoundly influenced men's thinking about the nature of education. Thus the content and methods of education, as well as the general approach to the child and learning, are the resultant of a complex set of circumstances rooted in the social developments and intellectual movements of the time.

Also to be considered here are such factors as the pressures of increasing population and movements of population – which always have an immediate effect on educational institutions – and the varying structure of urban and rural society, down to the nature of the family and the part family life plays in education. Then there is what might be called the cultural environment, in a general sense; that is, not merely what the critic of literature or art passes as a worthy product of the age but the kind of pamphlets, broadsheets and newspapers which made up the reading matter of ordinary people at different social levels, and the kind of objects which helped to form their taste. This is to direct attention to the education which perpetually takes place in the course of daily social living, to which organized education is an adjunct.

This is a propitious time to make a new approach on these lines since such questions constantly arise for the working teacher, now that the whole child population is in school for at least ten years. In particular, perhaps, it has been forced on our attention that technological and scientific advances closely condition educational change. The controversy about the 'two cultures', the earlier efforts of an Eliot to arrive at a definition of culture, are but two examples of the rethinking that has been going on and the different forms it can take. But there is nothing intrinsically new about these discussions; rather, they reproduce in terms of today arguments that have been advanced in very similar form in the past. In other words, just as the fundamental educational issues have remained the same through the years – who should be educated, how, to what level or different levels in the service of what social or industrial needs? – so the conditioning social and economic factors continue to operate. Failure to recognize this results in mere enunciations about education rather than meaningful statements about what it is and does; these must essentially depend on knowledge of what education has been and has done, not merely in general but for different classes of the population.

In the age of Bacon, for instance, there was controversy about the relative value of liberal and scientific studies as there was also about the very nature of knowledge and so of the learning process; and new ideas on the subject (today generally accepted) were rejected out of hand in many quarters as an unwarranted challenge to current methods of education, indeed to all scholarship. The fear that entrance of 'the masses' on to the stage of politics or into the schools constitutes a threat to order, to culture, to all established standards, has been a recurring theme in history – at certain times voiced with acute anxiety, at others forgotten. All this throws light on present dilemmas and controversies and the factors which influence our thinking today.

In this connection, it was one of Clarke's suggestions that rather than outlining 'the educational outlook' of an age as if this were ever a uniform and generally accepted view, it would be fruitful to look into the educational ideologies of different social groupings: for instance, the very different attitude to education of Methodists, or Chartists, or country gentlemen in the nineteenth century. Again, there is the nature and effect of the training for different professions; if the clergy, schoolmasters, lawyers, physicians of this age showed 'a marked disposition to ally themselves with the ruling order', to what extent was this the outcome of an education on traditional 'clerkly' lines, more or less consciously designed to produce this attitude? To approach the same question from another angle is to investigate why the interests of the new manufacturing classes were ignored by the majority of established schools at this period, the kind of steps taken to provide an alternative, and the ultimate outcome both in terms of the educational system and adaptation of the curriculum in other schools. More ambitiously, Clarke proposed a general history of a new kind, under some such title as 'The Politics of Education', proclaiming the intention to interpret thought and practice since the Reformation in the light of conflicting social interests and their political expression. It is from this conflict of interests, as he consistently emphasized, that educational change has emerged – in a form tempered by the political settlement arrived at – and, too, compromises in terms of thought and practice. It is relevant to note here that this book, which still has so much to offer, was published at a time of much upheaval and heartsearching, in 1940.

If it is a main aim to make study of the history of education more rigorous – to eliminate both the lists of facts and the easy, unhistorical generalization – this should make it more stimulating and interesting. It is, after all, by entering into conflicts and controversies and seeing what they were all about – rather than leaving them aside to present educational change as a simple upward and onward movement – that those entering the field of education today are best equipped to take a positive part.

NOTES

Abridged by kind permission of the author.

1. Brian Jackson, *Streaming, an Education System in Miniature*, 1964, pp.31–47.
2. 'The Study of the History of Education', *Contemporary Review*, Vol. cv, 1914, p.86. See W.H.G. Armytage, 'Foster Watson 1860–1929', *British Journal of Educational Studies*, Vol. x, No. 1, Nov. 1961.
3. *Education and Social Change*, 1940, p.37.
4. *World without War*, 1958, p.197.
5. Foster Watson, loc. cit., p.85.
6. 'A Plea for the Historical Study of English Education' in *The Illiterate Anglo-Saxon*, 1946, pp.155–6. See No. 3 in this volume.

6

The Study of the History of Education

GILLIAN SUTHERLAND

The study of the history of education seems at last to be coming into its own. It has spent too long as an appendix either to studies of the philosophy and psychology of education, or to descriptions of contemporary educational institutions: as a kind of intellectual I-Spy – spotting the first appearance of a great idea – or as a last-ditch explanation for the more extraordinary anomalies of some particular complex of educational institutions. Now, however, more and more historians are coming to recognize the significance of Durkheim's classic definition:

Education is the influence exercised by adult generations on those that are not yet ready for social life. Its object is to arouse and to develop in the child a certain number of physical, intellectual and moral states which are demanded of him by both the political society as a whole and the special milieu for which he is specifically destined.[1]

The provision of education represents the most sustained and far-reaching attempt of a society, or sections within it, to re-produce itself, to shape its future; and it necessarily involves a degree of self-consciousness on the part of the providers about that society. The education system – or its absence – is thus of crucial importance in studying any society: and more and more historians are seeking to emulate M.G. Jones, who made her book, *The Charity School Movement in the Eighteenth Century* 'a study of a neglected aspect of social history'.[2] Work on education in sixteenth- and seventeenth-century England has benefited from the editorial encouragement of *Past and Present*.[3] There have been a number of studies which together throw light on ideas and policy on popular education in nineteenth-century England.[4] *The Cambridge Group for the History of Population and Social Structure* have begun to turn their attention to the problems of measuring literacy;[5] a *Society for the Study of the History of Edu-*

cation has been formed;[6] and the arrival of history of education as a respectable, even fashionable, subject for study may be said to have been well and truly signalized by the issue of a whole number of the *Journal of Contemporary History* devoted to *Education and Social Structure* in both Europe and America.[7]

This collection of essays brings into focus some of the problems to be faced in studying the history of education. In some cases recent work in this field has not matched the sophistication with which other aspects of social history are currently being treated. Two problems stand out in particular. The first involves a kind of hindsight, a marked tendency to write and analyse in terms of ideals and absolutes, good and evil, and struggles for progress. The second is a tendency to dignify a simple description of some aspect of an educational system with the label 'education-and-society', as if description of the one automatically invoked and even explained the other. The relationship between these two problems is rather that of frying-pan and fire: but between them they often deflect attention from the more serious problem of integrating evidence about the number of people experiencing a particular type of education with the highly personal assessments of that experience which have survived.

The first tendency often takes the form of the projection of current battles backwards onto an historical ground. The organization of explanations in terms of efforts to attain a particular ideal, not always explicit, but clearly determining the categories of the analysis, can be identified in two of the articles in the *Journal of Contemporary History*; in Dahrendorf's 'The Crisis in German Education', and Herbst's 'High School and Youth in America'.[8] Dahrendorf's short essay on recent changes in German education is primarily a manifesto for further reform, shaped entirely by the assumptions that equality of opportunity in education is intrinsically desirable, and is desired by the mass of opinion in West Germany. Herbst describes what he considers to be the failure, over a long period, of both American educational policy and schools to 'come to terms with the problem of youth', and to create 'adolescent-centred schools' – whatever these may be. It is clear he considers that there is a solution to the problem; but this is nowhere explicitly worked out.

The same tendency, however, in a much more subtle and elaborately worked-out form, can be identified in parts of Brian Simon's *Education and the Labour Movement 1870–1920*. Amongst other things, Simon is concerned to examine why the Labour movement failed to prevent the institutionalization of an 'educational ladder' by the 1902 Education Act, and thus the institutionalization of a degree of social mobility which tended to reinforce rather than cut across class structure in England.[9] He lays great stress on the role of the Fabians, and in particular the Webbs' links with Morant, making the 1902 Act seem like the product of a successful conspiracy. He fails to make it sufficiently clear that one of the reasons for the successful establishment of a system of secondary education based on selection, and qualitatively different from primary education, was the relative inadequacy and incoherence of the alternatives presented.[10] The 'broad highway', as the proposal for secondary education for all and its corollaries came to be called, did not command enough support, and was not worked out sufficiently clearly or forcefully to offer a serious challenge to the notion of the ladder. Some members of the Labour movement, besides the Fabians, were attracted by the ladder. Others, inspired perhaps by Morris's great vision in *News from Nowhere*, clung to the image of the 'broad highway', but failed to relate a concept which was essentially revolutionary to their social-democratic tactics. Yet others were prepared to be revolutionary; and Simon clearly wishes there had been more of them. But if he is seeking to establish a moment of 'betrayal', or rather, to look for the beginnings of the process whereby class and education became so firmly intertwined, then Sidney Webb, Morant and the rest cannot really be elevated to the importance of arch-villains. It is necessary to go further back into the nineteenth century. The important questions are not about the plottings, real or imagined, of the Fabians, but about the contrasts between the exuberance of those early radicals and Chartists to whom learning was a liberation and a delight, who believed literally in Ebenezer Elliot's assertion that

> Mind, mind alone
> Is light, and hope, and life and power;[11]

and the cringing servility of a Bradley Headstone, the frustrated bitterness of a Jude Fawley, or even the quiet dignity of the achievement of F.H. Spencer.[12] The origins of the inextricable interaction of class-structure and education must be sought not at a moment at the end of the nineteenth century, but in the early years of industrialization, in a complex set of experiences both political and social – in which it is difficult, not to say fruitless, to see who should be blamed, or for what. We may lament it, but that is a different question.

Of course, hindsight, his own commitments, are perennial problems for any historian. But historians of education seem peculiarly vulnerable to their distorting effects for several reasons. To some extent they are a legacy of the period when history of education was simply an appendix to studies of educational psychology, theory, etc.; and it is depressing to read that the Society for the Study of the History of Education spent part of its first meeting in 1967 discussing

What part should the study of the history of education play in general Education courses? ... How far should one try to escape from the traditional chronological treatment? Ought topics to be preferred rather than the study of set periods? Or should the approach be through 'practical' contemporary problems considered in the light of (presumably recent) history?[13]

It sounds as though the Society has yet to establish for itself the independent status and nature of historical enquiry. At a deeper level, however, the tendency may, in a curious way, be a reflection of the central importance of an educational system as both a conditioning and a dynamic force. For the education we ourselves experience is permeated with moral implications: the process itself is presented as intrinsically moral, both for teachers and taught; and we are given not only a vocational training but a set of moral absolutes, an image of a good society, a good citizen. We may reject these, but often substitute in their place alternative images of the good. Because we therefore consider education as a moral activity, it becomes especially difficult to consider a system of education in the past in any other terms, to achieve the degree of detachment necessary to see it primarily in terms of the demands made by this or that 'political society as a whole, and the special milieu for which the child is specifically destined'.

Nevertheless it can, and has been done. Clarence Karier, for example, in his article 'Élite Views in American Education',[14] begins to unravel the tangle of élitist practices and egalitarian professions which characterizes so much of American education. In the first part of the article he compares the slight practical impact of Dewey with the massive influence of William Thorndike's so-called scientific Test and Measurement Movement. Thorndike positively correlated morality, wealth, intelligence and social power, and announced his empirical finding that 'abler persons in the world in the long run, are more clean, decent, just and kind'.[15] There were other contrasting élitist schemes for American education, which never got as far as policy; but in discussing them Karier provides a salutary reminder that élitist is a large label which can cover everything from the fascist to the meritocratic.

All this serves to emphasize that any system of education can only be examined within the context of its own society, and that this implies as full a knowledge of that society as possible. Unfortunately the implication is often forgotten, and some of those who write about 'education and society' do little more than describe aspects of education, as if the links between an educational system and its social context were so plain to see that mere mention of some aspect of the educational system immediately conjured up the salient aspects of the social structure in which it was located. This is simply not so: and the attempt to unravel and delineate the relationship between the two is a most difficult and delicate task. Indeed, there are those who are doubtful whether it is worth attempting at all. Professor Donald Macrae has delivered a long and involved warning on the subject:

Every serious historian, whether he likes it or not, today possesses a set of tacit, *ad hoc* sociological assumptions of which very often he is only imperfectly aware. ... One of the premises of nearly every *ad hoc* sociology is the idea that at some level of reality there must be in principle – whether or not it is accessible – an organic connectivity between all the elements of social structure at a given time, so that, for example, the educational arrangements of a society will correspond to its economic and institutional structure and will also represent the needs of that society. These 'needs' are understood in very different and surprising ways: they may be the needs of the society's future (an odd prescience) or of its ruling élite or of its economic and technological culture, or of its ancient traditions, and so on. In fact, it is bad sociology, though it is better than none, and such assumptions are in the vicious sense, merely metaphysical. I do not mean by this that there are no systematic relationships between public education and social structure and that these relationships cannot be investigated: merely that these relationships are various, involve structural discontinuities and are singularly lacking in symmetry.[16]

There may well be those who practise the secret vice of functionalism among historians, as among sociologists, but altogether this luxuriant denunciation imputes a remarkable degree of simple-mindedness to historians.[17] Few would deny that the relationships between *any* institutions and the structure of the society in which they are to be found 'are various, involve structural discontinuities, and are singularly lacking in symmetry'. Nevertheless, historians of education cannot altogether abandon the notion of 'needs', since a great deal of their enquiry is directed towards finding out what definition of 'needs' is offered by those who construct an educational system and the extent to which the system constructed fulfils these. Nor can historians completely lose sight of the notion of 'total social structure'. Few of them would be silly enough to want to draw a flow-diagram of the shapes and relationships they saw in the society they were studying, or to want to suggest that these had an objective, immutable existence beyond their work. But they do need a rough notion of the whole, as a device for communication and explanation: if they are writing about the educational provision for a certain group in a society, this cannot be offered as a description located in a vacuum; they need to offer some clue to the relative position of this group – strategic, influential or menial. In addition historians have to deal with the notions of the whole society on which the educators act, if only to explain why cherished schemes did not produce the effects they were intended to produce.

The attempt therefore is difficult, but surely must be made – and Professor Macrae, indeed, has no alternatives to offer. It would be stupid to attempt to make guidelines, let alone rules: there could be as many as there are relationships to be traced. But both successful and unsuccessful attempts can at least be illustrated. One of the most important problems in the history of education is the relationship between élite groups and particular institutions, especially those of higher education. A number of recent writers, including a majority of the contributors to the *Journal of Contemporary History*, have chosen to look at this. Dr. Theodore Zeldin, in his 'Higher Education in France 1848–1940',[18] offers precisely the kind of meticulous, scholarly, institutional description which leaves one begging for more clues about the social location and implications of the institutions. The bibliography in the footnotes provides admirable guidance for those to whom the subject is entirely new; and the article is studded with such remarks as 'the faculties of law ... had long been looked upon as a kind of finishing school for gentlemen. ...'[19] Of the *École Normale* and *École Polytechnique* he writes

Both were residential and developed an unique esprit de corps. The result was that sizeable groups within the ruling class and among the most influential people in the country's economic and intellectual life were graduates of a few institutions.[20]

and in a concluding paragraph he suggests that the oligarchy of the *Grandes Écoles* in French education was matched by an oligarchy in society and politics.[21] All of these points invite extensive discussion. Zeldin himself goes on to qualify his comments about the *Normaliens'* esprit de corps by stressing the diversity of their subsequent political careers and opinions.[22] But then one cries, with a recent contributor to *Past and Present*, 'Léon Blum was a socialist; Édouard Heriot a Radical; both were *Normaliens* – what price this common experience?'[23]

A similar sense of description in a vacuum is conveyed by Professor McGrath's article on 'Student Radicalism in Vienna'[24] in the later nineteenth century, which at first sight looks as though it might be approaching the question of the educational experience of an élite from a different standpoint. But he offers simply an account of the involvement in the pan-German movement of Viennese students of the late 1870s, early 1880s, among them Freud, Viktor Adler, Friedjung and Herzl. That all these active and committed people were students is not much more than a coincidence, on the evidence McGrath presents. Perhaps it wasn't anyway: but if the target of the study is the relationship of the educational system to the structure of the society, then the significance of these men expressing these opinions *as students* ought at least to be discussed. What was the status of university education? Where did these students come from? Were they the leaders of their age group? Did the student community usually express, in an extreme form, a growing opinion in the community at large, or were they, more fashionably, 'alienated', and did this presage any kind of rift in Austrian society?

By contrast, Professor Fritz Ringer in his article 'Higher Education in Germany in the Nineteenth Century'[25] does have a thesis; although, unfortunately, it is one he fails to establish beyond doubt. The main burden of his argument is that experience of higher education in Germany did in itself create membership of an élite, rather than simply reinforce and extend a superiority based on wealth or birth. He suggests that its members 'thought and acted as a unique social group and developed their own characteristic sense of values',[26] and he quotes Friederich Paulsen to the effect that

The academically educated constitute a kind of intellectual and spiritual aristocracy in Germany. ... They form something like an official nobility as indeed they all participate in the government and administration of the state. ... Together they make up a homogeneous segment of society; they simply recognize each other as social equals on the basis of their academic cultivation. ... Conversely anyone in Germany who has no academic education lacks something which wealth or high birth cannot fully replace.[27]

But Ringer does not supply enough evidence that academic cultivation could, of itself, create status; nor does he show how this status might differ from that conferred by a classically-based public school education on the sons of landowners and industrialists in nineteenth-century England. He does not provide illustration of the unified thought and action of this unique group, or of its characteristic set of values, which have to be distinguished from the values of those who had the same social background, but not the education. He does give figures for the occupations of the fathers of Prussian university students, in particular the detailed break-down in percentage terms for 1902–3.[28] But these only indicate that the landowning and professional classes had a near-monopoly of university education, as in England. The figures for the business community he finds 'surprisingly low' (although to prove this he needs figures for the relative proportions of these occupational groups in the population as a whole, which he does not provide). But if this is so, it suggests that what Ringer calls 'the most progressive sector of the economy' did not agree with Paulsen that 'the acquisition of a university education had become a sort of social necessity'; as the English reformers thought,[29] they found their requirements supplied elsewhere; and it suggests, therefore, that the initial and fundamental distinctions of status were those of occupational interest, extensively reinforced and developed by education. The important questions would then seem to concern this cultural 'gap', its extent, duration and implications. While Ringer indicates this gap, he does not explore it.[30]

Some of these weaknesses stem from having only a small space within which to handle such large issues. However, some similar weaknesses are to be found in Sheldon Rothblatt's ambitiously-titled book *The Revolution of the Dons: Cambridge and Society in Victorian England*.[31] Professor Rothblatt sets out to examine Cambridge's changing consciousness of its role in nineteenth-century English society. In particular, he looks at the social composition of the undergraduate population, at the proclaimed objectives of some of the reformers, especially Seeley, and at the actual reorganization of teaching methods, in which Sidgwick, Jackson and Oscar Browning were, in their different ways, so influential. All these provide *prima facie* evidence of considerable shifts in opinion and self-consciousness; but the interactions between them are never clearly worked out, and one is left puzzling over what or who was really revolutionary.

On the other hand, David Ward, in his article 'The Public Schools and Industry after 1870',[32] shows how effectively history of education can be written. He sets out to examine the kind of education the second and third generations of English commercial families received: and he shows how successfully the old landed aristocratic élite rejected the notion of the entrepreneur and imposed the ideal of the gentleman on those who challenged their leadership with wealth newly acquired in trade and industry. He concludes:

the public schools facilitated the transmission of the culture of the landed and gentry classes to the industrial classes [*sic*], a culture which virtually ignored the economic life of the country; and by speeding up the transmission to a rate that would hitherto have been impossible, they produced a haemorrhage of talent, and perhaps of capital, in the older industries which could not be made good.[33]

In reaching these conclusions, Ward has to deal with the problem of *measuring* the impact of public school education, its success in establishing its ideal: he attempts this tentatively, but so far as he goes, convincingly. In describing the curriculum, and the cultural ethos of the schools, he has inevitably to rely heavily on what is usually called 'literary' evidence, varying in this case from school songs, and memoirs, to H.A. Vachell's novel *The Hill*. Then he goes on to sketch the links between these and the subsequent career patterns of the boys. His figures for the numbers of boys actually entering commercial and industrial occupations are too patchy and varied to indicate any trend,[34] but he does make the valid point that their education gave them little technical equipment to cope with such work. He is more effective when he sets out to look at the careers of those boys who came nearest to being the 'ideal-types' in their respective schools, the head-boys of Loretto and Sedbergh, in Wellington, the winners of the Queen's Medal. Only 1 of the 24 head-boys of Sedbergh 1875–1900, 6 of the 41 Loretto head-boys 1858–1900, had careers which could be described as commercial. Wellington, between 1860 and 1900, produced 2 stock-brokers (if these can be called commercial) out of 41 Queen's Medallists. A considerable number of the boys (10 Sedbergh, 10 Loretto, 6 Wellington) went on to become schoolmasters themselves, presumably preaching the values they had been taught.[35] Altogether, these figures, incomplete though they are, hint that the public schools achieved a considerable measure of success in exalting the ideal of the gentleman, at the expense of the entrepreneur.

Thus Ward begins to face up to a problem more fundamental than those of hindsight, or adequate location. For the problem of integrating evidence about quality and evidence about quantity is at least as acute for historians of education as for all those economic historians who have been arguing about the standard of living for years. So far, the only sustained attempts to deal with questions of this kind have been made by historians working on the sixteenth and seventeenth centuries. Professor Mark Curtis has tried, with some success, to see how much weight can be attached to Hobbes' assertion that 'The core of the rebellion ... are the universities'[36] and has established that there were, by the beginning of the seventeenth century, sufficient numbers of unemployed clerics to be a serious cause for concern, and a likely source of discontent. On a larger scale, Professor Lawrence Stone has tried to locate educational provision fully in its social, political and economic context in his massive study of the aristocracy 1558–1641; and any bald attempt at summary would do violence to the complexity of the interactions he traces and suggests.[37] But studies on the same scale have yet to be undertaken for much of nineteenth-century England.[38] For instance, historians have yet effectively to relate evidence about the spread of literacy with, on the one hand, Samuel Bamford's recollection that

When I first plunged, as it were, into the blessed habit of reading, faculties which had hitherto given but small intimation of existence, suddenly sprang into vigorous action. My mind was ever desiring more of the silent but exciting conversation with books, and of whatever was conveyed to it from that source, small was the portion that did not remain.[39]

and, on the other hand, Dickens' picture:

'Bitzer', said Thomas Gradgrind, 'Your definition of a horse.' 'Quadruped, graminivorous, forty teeth, namely twenty-four grinders, four eye-teeth, and twelve incisive. Sheds coat in the spring; in marshy countries, sheds hoofs too. Hoofs hard, but requiring to be shod with iron. Age known by marks in mouth.'[40]

Again, the map of literacy in England in the late 1830s which Dr. Roger Schofield has recently compiled from the Registrar-General's statistics, indicates that considerably more males than females were literate, that among the areas of highest male literacy were Dorset, the Northern Border counties and London, and that the males of East Anglia and Wales were least literate of all.[41] Apart from the immediate and enormous question why, there is also the question, crudely, so what? Does this mean they behaved differently? If so, how? How does it relate to areas of high employment, unemployment, Chartist activity, and so on. In general, how much does it matter that some people, more people, can read, go to school, go to university: how much does it matter that they read some books rather than others? These may sound banal and familiar questions, but for most societies at most periods they have yet to be adequately answered: and it may be that the answers are different for different societies at different times, with a variety and subtlety far beyond the simple division of societies into pre-industrial and industrial. Just because the relationships between education and social structure 'are various, involve structural discontinuities and are singularly lacking in symmetry', there is a whole new, important field for exploration in the history of education.

NOTES

1. In the collection of essays translated as *Education and Sociology* by Sherwood D. Fox (Glencoe, Illinois, 1956), p.71.
2. Cambridge, 1938.
3. e.g. *Past and Present* No. 23 (November, 1962), Mark H. Curtis: 'The Alienated Intellectuals of Early Stuart England'; No. 24 (April 1963), Lawrence Stone: 'Communication' – on Curtis's article; No. 26 (Nov. 1963), Joan Simon: 'The Social Origins of Cambridge Students 1603–40'; No. 28 (July 1964), Lawrence Stone: 'The Educational Revolution in England 1560–1640'. See also his *The Crisis of the Aristocracy 1558–1641* (Oxford, 1965) and Joan Simon: *Education and Society in Tudor England* (Cambridge, 1966).

G. SUTHERLAND

4. e.g. Brian Simon: *Education and the Labour Movement 1870–1920* (London, 1965); Harold Silver: *The Concept of Popular Education* (London, 1965); Mary Sturt: *The Education of the People* (London, 1967); and W.A.C. Stewart and W.P. McCann: *The Educational Innovators 1750–1880* (London, 1967).
5. On the methodological problems involved, see Roger Schofield: 'The Measurement of Literacy in Pre-Industrial England' in *Literacy in Traditional Societies*, ed. J. Goody (Cambridge, 1968).
6. *History of Education Society Bulletin* No. 2 (Spring, 1968).
7. *Journal of Contemporary History*, vol. 2, no. 3 (Summer, 1967), hereafter cited as *JCH*.
8. *JCH*, pp.139–47; 165–82.
9. Brian Simon, *op. cit.*, pp.165–235.
10. The details of this are examined in an admirable study by W.P. McCann: *Trade Unionist, Cooperative and Socialist Organisations in relation to Popular Education 1870–1902*. Manchester Ph.D. thesis 1960.
11. Quoted in R.D. Altick: *The English Common Reader* (Chicago, 1957), p.130; *cf.* also *ibid.* pp.240–60, and J.F.C. Harrison: *Learning and Living, 1760–1960* (London, 1961).
12. F.H. Spencer: *An Inspector's Testament* (London, 1938).
13. *Bulletin*, No. 1 (Spring, 1968), p.2; *cf. ibid.* p.5.
14. *JCH*, pp.149–63; much of this article provides, involuntarily, an ironic commentary on the idealist tone of Herbst's article.
15. *JCH*, p.154. This suggests, incidentally, some questions about the movement for scientific measurement of intelligence and ability in England centred at first round the LCC Education Department, and involving psychologists like Burt, and inspectors like Ballard – see e.g. Cyril Burt: *The Backward Child* (London, 1937), based largely on work done while he worked for the LCC, and P.B. Ballard: *The New Examiner* (London, 1923), especially chapter 1, and *Things I Cannot Forget* (London, 1937).
16. *JCH*, p.3, at the beginning of an article on 'The culture of a generation: students and others', pp.3–13.
17. I am grateful to John H. Goldthorpe for discussing with me some of the points which follow at an early stage in their formulation: he is not, of course, responsible for their final form.
18. *JCH*, pp.53–80.
19. *ibid.*, p.64.
20. *ibid.*, p.70.
21. *ibid.*, pp.78–80.
22. *ibid.*, p.70.
23. *Past and Present*, No. 36 (April, 1967), John E. Talbott: 'The Politics of Educational Reform in France during the Third Republic 1900–1940', p.130. Dr. Talbott was in fact commenting on an article with this title by D.R. Watson in a preceding number – No. 23 – of *Past and Present*; and the rapid-fire of his other questions provides a good guide to some of the other work needing to be done on French education.
24. *JCH*, pp.183–201.
25. *ibid.*, pp.123–38.
26. *ibid.*, p.138.
27. *ibid.*, pp.136–7.
28. *ibid.*, pp.136–7.
29. Throughout Ringer's article there runs the implication that scientists, industrialists and technicians were educationally very much the poor relations in nineteenth-century Germany. If this was really so, then why were English educational reformers obsessed with the German example? Why did Mundella, Samuelson and the rest perpetually insist that Germany was the example to the whole of Europe in providing adequate scientific and technical education for an industrial society? – see

83

e.g. George Haines IV: 'German Influences upon Scientific Instruction in England 1867–1887' in *Victorian Studies*, I (1958), pp.215–44.

30. Some clues can be found in Dr. J.G.C. Röhl's study 'Higher Civil Servants in Germany 1890–1900', *JCH*, pp.101–21, in which he shows a caste-like exclusiveness and arrogance in the higher levels of the government service. But this article deals with a briefer time-period, and touches only marginally on the educational qualifications and background of these bureaucrats, so detailed comparison of the data in the two articles is not possible.

31. London, 1968.

32. pp.37–52.

33. *ibid.*, p.52. One small point Ward neglects – and it contributed to the continuing pre-eminence of the classical curriculum – was the relative weakness of the case made for scientific and technical education, precisely because it was almost always presented in narrowly vocational terms, as appropriate for managers, entrepreneurs and technicians. Few of its advocates, T.H. Huxley apart, were skilled at arguing, in the manner of the defenders of the classics, that science also communicated immutable cultural, aesthetic and moral values. In addition, many of the reformers were unable to agree beyond a simple insistence on more science; they argued interminably about the proportions of pure and applied – T.H. Huxley, *Collected Essays*, vol. iii, *Science and Education*, London, 1902, and Cyril Bibby, *T.H. Huxley* (London, 1959), pp.133–5: also e.g. arguments about the nature of the Jubilee Institution in *Nature*, 1886–7.

34. Uppingham, nearly 20% of boys entering 1854–76; Marlborough, an increase from 2% of the entry 1843–4 to 8% of the entry 1892–3; Sedbergh, 30% of the entry 1885; Loretto 36% of the entry 1885. *JCH*, pp.45–6. Unfortunately, the work of Musgrove, although suggestive, does not throw any more light directly on this – F. Musgrove: 'Middle Class Education and Employment in the Nineteenth Century', in *Economic History Review*, 2nd series, vol. xii (1959), pp.99–111; H. Perkin: 'Middle Class Education ... A Critical Note', *ibid.*, vol. xiv (1961–2), pp.122–30; and F. Musgrove: 'Middle Class Education ... A Rejoinder', *ibid.*, pp.320–9.

35. *JCH*, pp.45–6.

36. *Past and Present*, No. 23, p.25.

37. *op. cit.* supra, note 3. By contrast, Mrs. Simon's meticulously detailed study of the expansion of facilities and curricula in her *Education and Society in Tudor England* is a little disappointing: clearly a great deal was going on, but the overall implications are a little obscure.

38. Musgrove's work, cited in note 34, constitutes an honourable exception.

39. Samuel Bamford: *Early Days*, first published 1848, 2 vol. edition also including *Passages in the Life of a Radical*, ed. H. Dunckerley (London, 1893), i, pp.87–8.

40. Charles Dickens: *Hard Times*, first published 1854, Everyman paperback edition, p.4.

41. Registrar-General: *Annual Report of Births Deaths and Marriages* II (1840), pp.8–9: Males and Females unable to sign their names in the marriage register, 1 July 1838 to 30 June 1839.

History and the Sociological Perspective in Educational Studies

R. SZRETER

I. A VIEW OF EDUCATION

The title of this paper has been decided upon with some care and deliberation. It is intended to consider in it certain aspects of the inter-relationship of the three 'subjects' of history, sociology, and education. This task demands some reflection upon their nature, and it may be contended that, in their epistemological nature, the three are very dissimilar.

Of the three, history alone – with no disparagement of the others – seems essentially a *discipline*. History alone among them, that is, is a relatively self-contained branch of knowledge in that the bulk of its subject-matter is not claimed by any other branch of knowledge, and its method has been evolved by its own practitioners and is largely peculiar to it. 'Relatively' self-contained, since it does not categorically say: 'keep out' to experts from other disciplines, or 'stay in' to its own avowed practitioners, and it is not implied that such intermediate studies – or 'sciences' – as, say, economic history, are inferior epistemo-logical species because they also form varieties of history. Otherwise, this is not the place to enlarge upon the nature of history, nor even to refer to the many treatises upon it. Perhaps *The Modern Researcher* by Barzun and Graff, and W.H. Burston's pamphlet on *Social Studies and the History Teacher*[1] may be mentioned here: the former because it is less well known than it deserves to be and ranges far more widely than its title implies, and the latter for a number of pertinent observations by one who is primarily an educationist.

Sociology, however, if rightfully a separate discipline in having its own university departments and specialist courses of study, as well as a significant body of findings and specialist literature, seems to be less of a separate discipline in virtue of what sociologists investigate and how they go about it. When sociologists agree that the origins and antecedents of their study are chiefly to be found in the philosophy of history[2] and in social surveys, they also agree that most, though not all, matters they have been investigating for the past hundred years or more, had been investigated for many centuries by students of other branches of knowledge, notably of history, and that, in the main, their method, where it is not essentially historical, is that of statistics. What sociology offers is a newer way of viewing human activities, circumstances, and relations, and of asking questions about them, and a new way of systematizing our knowledge. This new angle of vision, with its new conceptual categorization, amounts to a new *perspective*. The perspective would, moreover, appear to subsume what is nowadays referred to as 'the structure' of a science, i.e. a certain logical coherence and an explanatory mode of thinking of its own. In subtitling his *Invitation to Sociology* 'a humanistic perspective', Berger[3] seems to signify not just that sociology is capable of offering a humanistic perspective, but that it is yet another, new and important humanistic perspective, which 'makes us see in a new light the very world in which we have lived all our lives', without discovering any new things or experiences. C. Wright Mills' *Sociological Imagination*[4] similarly seems to argue the view of sociology as, basically, a perspective. It has thus been both legitimate and feasible to develop an endless proliferation of sociologies: of religion and industry, of nature and literature. True, there can also be history of anything and everything, from cabbages to kings, but one may submit that the element of time-sequence is a unique and distinctive thread, binding the many contents into a discipline in a way no specific category has yet been made to bind the many varieties of sociology.

Education, finally, is neither a discipline nor a perspective, but a *field of studies*. That is, of course, education as an academic 'subject', with special reference to the problems and practices that make up 'the educational system'; the term 'education' has, in the English language, several different meanings, confusing in their close interrelatedness. Some collegiate institutions whose designation includes the word 'education' may, baldly and blandly, name 'Education' in their official syllabuses, but, on closer inspection of time-tables, it turns out to be Educational Psychology or History of Education and so on, and the 'Education' of the syllabus might well claim to be the first inter-disciplinary study. Alternatively, it might be termed a 'secondary subject', as a large area of human behaviour and social organization, wherein interested students, trained in such 'primary subjects' as

86

psychology or history, fruitfully meet and research, applying the methods and perspectives proper to them. Thus 'Religion' or 'Management', rather than 'Geography' or 'Physics', offer parallels to 'education' in the academic curriculum. Among the 'primary subjects' venturing into the field of education, sociology has in – literally – the last few years become, in this country, justly important, if excessively fashionable partly because its prolonged neglect has resulted in a 'rush'. How far this entry and its swiftness have been in the nature of a reaction to, and supplementation of, the domination of the study of education by psychology, can only be speculated upon. Somewhat less speculative and more relevant to the present topic is the need for mutual aid and collaboration in educational studies by historians and sociologists; and judging by the respective contributions to an important recent programmatic volume on *The Study of Education*,[5] the former are more aware of this than the latter. For the history of education has not the most propitious of legacies: originating in pietistic accounts of schools and educational thinkers, it has suffered much from both anachronistic attentions by educationists and neglect by social historians.[6]

Before proceeding to consider, first in general and then in educational studies, why and how history and sociology need each other, it seems needful briefly to dwell upon the functional relationship of education to society. Education, be it noted, refers in this context not to some overall process whereby all the natural and social influences we experience shape our entire personalities, but primarily to the business of formal educational institutions: of schools, colleges, and their teachers. If the emphasis on formal education seems restrictive, especially in relation to early societies, it is not intended to be exclusive, and at least one eminent historian and one eminent sociologist of education may be cited in support of it. B. Simon writes: 'The history of education can hardly be confined to schools and colleges, but it is here that social and intellectual developments are, as it were, crystallised or reflected; there is some reason, then, for concentrating on ... the field of institutionalised education';[7] similarly, J. Floud holds it proper for the sociologist of education, particularly of education in advanced, industrial societies, to 'concentrate on formal provision for instruction and training through specialised agencies and personnel; formative influences brought to bear on the individual informally ... from other social sources are not ignored, insofar as these may promote or frustrate the implementation of educational policies or pedagogical aims, but they are not the primary focus of attention'.[8] And it may be added that educating the young is not the fundamental or exclusive *raison d'être* of such other social institutions – notably the family[9] – as are also concerned with it.

There appear to be four social functions of education. Since they merge into one another, it may, indeed, be better to speak of the four-fold social role of education, or of four aspects of the reciprocal nexus between society and education. Three of them are universal. First, the cultural function, taking the term 'culture' in the broad anthropological sense of 'the way of life', concerned with the transmission of values and attitudes essential to social cohesion and historical continuity. The over-inclusive and consequently vague term 'socialization', or the repulsive one of 'acculturation', have occasionally been applied to this process. Secondly, we may distinguish the instructional function of transmitting knowledge, from the elements of literacy and 'numeracy' and basic appreciation of arts and crafts upward – a function made increasingly complicated and difficult today by the rapid growth of the body of knowledge, and by the associated insistence on the inculcation of critical and creative attitudes towards the existing learning. Very closely related to it, if logically distinguishable, is the economic function of equipping the young – and often the not-so-young – for earning their livelihood. For the educationist, this is where the argument about general or liberal v. technical or vocational education, although long since exposed as specious by the Bryce Commission and by A.N. Whitehead,[10] comes in. The fourth function, which the educationist may see as different in kind, since its links with pedagogy are tenuous, has not been very important in earlier historical societies or in primitive ones, but is prominent in modern democratic-industrial ones. It has certainly attracted many researchers and controversialists in post-war England. This is the function of social selection through education. As the bond between education, occupation and general social status tightens, and that between birth and social rank loosens, educational attainment becomes – admittedly, slowly – more of a determinant than a by-product of one's position in society. In sociological parlance, 'achieved status' gains in importance, as a determinant of life-chances, at the expense of 'ascribed status'. Viewed thus, the selection function forms, moreover, one facet of the large and fundamentally unanswerable question of whether education goes in the vanguard of, or must necessarily lag behind, general social change.

The fourfold division is, basically, sociological, but any combination of the four aspects can, and often should, be studied historically. This applies whether the studies be – to borrow two terms from economics – predominantly micro-sociological, e.g., concerned with a particular college or a certain sub-group of the teaching occupation, or macro-sociological, i.e. investigating the relationship between the national educational system (or some large sector of it, say, higher education) and the social structure or the economy supportive of it. It seems arguable that if history and sociology join forces in such studies, difficult though this may often prove, then we would consistently avoid, on the one hand, the narrowness of some writing on educational history (a term best consistently dropped in favour of 'history of education'), and, on the other hand, the misplaced scientism and indigestibility of much sociological writing. Since education, in its processes and organization, is essentially social in character, and since sociology is the science of society ('science' meaning here no more and no less than 'systematic study'),[11] historical studies in this field may frequently be in need of the sociological perspective, an analysis of which term will be attempted anon.

II. THE SCALE OF THINKING IN HISTORY AND IN SOCIOLOGY

The thesis that in practice the sociologist needs the historian largely for facts, and the historian may need the sociologist for help in conceptualising and systematizing his facts, may be grossly oversimplified, but does not appear to be basically erroneous. And, if the foregoing epistemological differentiation is even only partially accepted, then it is not surprising that, on borderline themes, historians should, in practice, be the better able to produce good work without the aid of sociology than sociologists can without history. C. W. Mills' well-known phrase that: 'history is the shank of social study' is important here (even if its implications may be interpreted as derogatory to either side); again, P. L. Berger avers that 'disregard of the historical dimension is an offence ... against sociological reasoning itself, namely that part of it that deals with pre-definition'; and R. K. Merton warns that although 'one need not be Caesar in order to understand Caesar ... there is a temptation for us sociological theorists to act sometimes as though ... it is not even necessary to study Caesar'.[12] Nevertheless, S. W. F. Holloway seems too caustic when he contends, in a perceptive essay, that 'it is as fashionable for the historian to pretend an interest in sociology as it is for the sociologist to proclaim the relevance of history; the trouble is that the historian wants to use sociology without doing sociology and the sociologist wants to use history without doing history', and too sweeping in saying that 'the sociologist and the historian must become one'.[13] Collaboration and occasional integration are wanted – not a merger; the two branches of knowledge are complementary rather than identical, and for some purposes their differences rather than similarities need to be insisted upon.

There is ample evidence[14] that historians have in recent years been increasingly asking sociological questions, using the social scientists' methods, and some even including history *among* the social sciences. The trend has been with us for some half century, and it seems relevant to consider some factors behind its emergence and recent acceleration.

Central among these factors is the shift of interest in historical studies from political and constitutional to social and economic matters. This shift, unsurprising in our 'age of the common man', has yet correspondingly to affect historical work on education. In the 1920s, appropriate occupational sub-groups were scarcely, as yet, in existence, but there already were active historians, whose researches and, presumably, teaching, even if university syllabuses did not much reveal this, were concerned chiefly with social and economic phenomena. The latter were, perhaps, especially important here. For, while traditional historians had seldom entirely neglected social circumstances, and while social history can still generally dispense with what I shall later call 'the specific component' of the sociological perspective, economic historians had, already in the 1920s, to know their economic theory, and had attempted quantification. And if today it is still virtually always possible to tell a social historian from a sociologist,[15] the economic historian is indistinguishable from the economist in such areas as studies of economic growth or econometric history. Furthermore, it has been pointed out by the President of the International Economic History Association[16] that the conception of economic history was reformed in the 1920s by historical sociologists (M. Weber) or 'sociologizing' historians (Sombart, Lefebvre, etc.); conversely, the sociologist D.G. McRae[17] speaks of 'a fruitful parasitism of sociology on economic history, which endured until at least the time of Tawney'. Social and economic affairs apart, it seems, finally, relevant to mention Namier's work here, for, although he was a political historian par excellence, it is difficult to gainsay the latest appraisal of him as 'the single most important influence in the introduction of modern social science methodology into British political history ... [He] made the political historian ... ask questions about status, interest, and behaviour, [demanding] minute observation and precise quantification'.[18]

Secondly, the social sciences, including sociology, have, in the postwar period, been growing in stature and academic respectability (let alone in popularity and policy importance). A count of the chairs of sociology in British universities today and 20 years ago, even excluding the universities of recent birth, would readily provide a rough but serviceable index. This, despite the fact that this country offers no propitious soil for them if Asa Briggs[19] is right that 'sociology has often had highest status ... in those countries where the status of history is low – where the past is thought to be not particularly relevant to action in the present' (whether Soviet Russia forms an exception here depends, presumably, on the recognition or otherwise of Marxism as sociological). And K. Thomas,[20] in an article clamouring for social scientific history, remarks, perhaps debatably, that 'sociological thinking has usually been pioneered by rootless intellectuals, foreign observers and immigrants ... not ... the English academic who has always been more closely involved with the established social order'. One should, however, obviously beware of reading into appraisals like these any necessary association between the study of history as such (through its links with nationalism[21] rather than a cosmopolitan *Weltanschauung* and its fundamental concern with the past rather than the present or future) and social conservatism.

Insofar as world-wide interests have, in the 1960s, come to affect the Western historian's outlook, this seems to have been part and parcel of the third strand of the convergence of history and sociology, namely the growing cultivation of 'contemporary history', or, if any still see this as a contradiction in terms, of very recent history. The sociologist has always been future-oriented and, fundamentally, interested in the present, the contemporaneous, if only because social reformism has been one of his spiritual parents. But 'the present' is ever on the point of becoming 'the past', and 'as soon as the sociologist turns from the present to the past, his preoccupations are very hard to distinguish from those of the historian'.[22] Since the sociologist's 'present' is virtually always, in fact, the very recent past, and since historians now consider this as a part of their demesne, the rapprochement of the two studies has been advanced.

The development, however, is not to be confused with what Croce meant in his famous dictum that 'all history is contemporary history', in the sense, primarily, that past events and the historian's thinking about them are inseparable, and the latter is inevitably conditioned by the present environment.

G.R. Elton[23] holds that 'there has possibly never been an age which imposed its own, rather narrow, preoccupations, so devotedly upon the past'. Even if 'rather narrow' is debatable, it might be felt that the increasing rate of social change in recent times has meant that our world is so different from the mid-nineteenth-century world (as against, say, the mid-thirteenth-century world from the mid-twelfth-century one), that it is the *very* recent past alone that truly helps us to understand our own times, and hence the vogue for 'contemporary' history. But the logic, completeness, and conception of the history of this explanation would leave many dissatisfied. It is pertinent also to mention the appeal of the views of E.E.Y. Hales.[24] Looking especially at history school syllabuses, he cogently argued that teachers emphasised the recent to arrest a retreat of history in the face of demand for 'evident relevance to today's needs', but 'the most recent is not always the most relevant, and is often duller'. Contemporary history is, at any rate, here to stay: there has, indeed, since 1966, appeared a *Journal of Contemporary History*, and it is of doubly marked relevance to the present theme that its entire issue of Summer 1967 was devoted to 'Social Structure and Education'.

If history and sociology have, however, been drawing nearer, there are still some differences of outlook, and some conflict, between their practitioners. The disagreement seems to turn chiefly on the largeness of vision appropriate to each subject, on the level of generalisation, on the old debate, itself debatable, of 'theory v. facts'. It is not likely or desirable that the two subjects shall become one, but it does seem likely that the practitioners of either may increasingly move towards middle-of-the-road positions, and that this will facilitate growing collaboration between them.

From its parentage of philosophy of history and social survey, sociology has inherited, respectively, what C.W. Mills fiercely attacked in his *Sociological Imagination* as the 'grand theory' and 'abstracted empiricism' i.e. extremes of macroscopic and microscopic approaches, the latter sometimes resulting in work of the type (not unknown in educational research) that B. Wilson brands as 'impeccable at a technical level and puerile in terms of philosophical assumptions'.[25] Mills, whose thesis has not failed to attract some cogent critics, charged the 'abstracted empiricist' with being 'a-historical, non-comparative, and inclined to psychologism', while implying that the 'grand theorist' was supra-historical and divorced from reality. He felt that, between them, the two approaches were making for neglect of significant, substantive problems, which demand a fusion of macroscopic conception and detailed exposition in the Weberian tradition. He concluded that 'all sociology worthy of the name is historical sociology'.[26]

By the time *The Sociological Imagination* appeared in 1959, R.K. Merton had already, however, put forward his celebrated views on theories 'of the middle range'.[27] Merton, foreshadowed in the 1940s by T.H. Marshall of the London School of Economics,[28] was exercised, on the one hand, by the fact that comprehensive theories, such as Marxism,

Sorokin's 'integralism', or Parsons' theory of action, were, in logical truth, no more than 'broad theoretical orientations', and, on the other hand, by the extremes of exclusively statistical *or* wholly historical sociological standpoints. He now championed 'theories that lie between the minor but necessary working hypotheses [of] day-to-day research, and the all-inclusive systematic efforts to develop a unified theory that will explain all the observed uniformities of social behaviour ... organisation and change', and would be 'principally used in sociology to guide empirical enquiry ... involving abstractions, of course, but ... close enough to observed data to be incorporated in propositions that permit empirical testing'. Theories of the middle range, he held, moreover, such as those of reference group or role conflict, did not necessarily clash with any of the aforesaid 'broad theoretical orientations'.

In history, the problem has been stated differently – in terms of feasibility and legitimacy, or at least degrees, of generalizing – but it seems essentially to be the same problem.

The strength of the legacy of Ranke's decree that history be written 'wie es eigentlich gewesen' – as it actually occurred, is not to be gainsaid. M.M. Postan asserted, in a pre-war paper, that 'this famous formula was not, at the time of its conception, meant to be anything more than an appeal for suspension of generalization until more was known about facts',[29] but did not substantiate this interpretation. Even if it was in keeping with the general, if later, nineteenth-century positivist view, the *effect* of Ranke's decree accorded more with a literal interpretation, and, in practice, there was no way of setting a term to the 'suspension'. In the same volume, M.J. Oakeshott reduced Ranke's rule to ascertaining, at the very most, 'what the evidence obliges us to believe' – the word 'available', being conspicuously absent before 'evidence'. Ranke's legacy was upheld in the famous prefatory passage in H.A.L. Fisher's *History of Europe* (1938), 'confessing' a failure to 'discover in history a plot, a rhythm, a predetermined pattern ... only one emergency following upon another ... the one safe rule for the historian [being] that he should recognise ... the play of the contingent and the unforeseen'. A disrespectful critic has referred to this view of history as 'one damn thing after another', but life does not, indeed, appear to be a tidy business – especially, perhaps, over the short period.

In emphasizing the uniqueness – or, at any rate, the particularity – unrepeatability, and 'wholeness' of events with which they are concerned, many historians have, in truth, denied any scope for abstracting, comparing, and, indeed, generalizing in their discipline.

Some have been prepared to accept (not without persuasion) no more than that many labels or categories which they use but 'do not like to analyse',[30] such as 'barbarians', or 'voluntaryism', or 'the middle class', in fact *are* generalized abstractions, i.e. that 'generalisations in the form of taxonomic concepts are built into historical language'.[31] In practice, just as it is impossible to eliminate all bias and abstraction in selecting, so it also is to refrain from generalizing and pattern-making when explaining, and the underlying purpose of establishing facts as fully and accurately as possible is to produce a generalized picture that best approximates the truth.[32] If O. MacDonagh,[33] for instance, prefers to talk of 'general notions', and 'explanatory models' rather than broad regularities and theoretical generalizations, the difference is partly semantic and partly one of degree. Yet if the right question is not whether generalizing is admissible in history but the proper degree of it, it still is a vital one.

H.S. Hughes in an important paper of 1960[34] goes so far as to say: 'Throughout the past century ... the historian ... has generalised in a sweeping fashion, and he has given an almost compulsive heed to the minute details of his account ... thus oscillating wildly between extremes ... [with] little in the way of tentative hypotheses or middle ground.' He then proceeds to list four types of historical generalizations of different levels: the semantic; the grouping of statements; the schematizing; and the metahistorical – and he argues that the third of these (schematization) has been successfully employed by numerous fine historians, and should obtain even more widely. And if Hughes's views on the relation between the traditional historian and 'laws' are less convincing, it yet seems relevant to note R.G. Collingwood's[35] observation that historiographical inheritance of dual interest in events and in the laws governing them goes right back to Herodotus and Thucydides respectively.

In a less philosophical manner, F.C. Lane,[36] the economic historian, has discussed types of historical statements of different levels of generality, exemplifying them as follows:

1. In March 1440 the Senate of the Venetian Republic voted to charter four great galleys to carry specified cargoes to London and Bruges;
2. Nearly every year in the fifteenth century the Venetian government sent three to five galleys for the transport of high-priced cargoes on voyages to the English Channel;
3. In the later Middle Ages the Venetian government sent merchant galleys to all the main seaboard trade centres of the Mediterranean and western Europe to assure the safety of precious cargoes;

4. Medieval city-states made most elaborate provision for those branches of trade affecting most the income of the government, the supply of precious metals, and the food supply;
5. Governmental action in regard to commerce is always most intense on those exchanges which are believed to affect the income of the government, and the supply of food and of military stores, and the condition of the currency.

Lane inclined to the view that all these had, for different purposes, value and validity, and did not particularly advocate an 'intermediate' degree of generality. Insofar as a degree of advocacy is present in this article, it is not intended to be exclusive. In history, and more particularly in sociology, certain insights and understandings may be better secured by the 'grand theorists' or the pursuers of minutiae, but what seems, in fact, to be happening is that more students are coming to favour what may be termed 'medium-scale' interpretation, as generally more fruitful and meaningful.

Lane, who looked at the problem in terms of 'a contrast between a theoretical interest and a historical interest', pointing out that, e.g.: 'M. Bloch is interested in the particular instances examined not merely as examples, but as interesting and worthy of study in themselves ... as basically a historian', saw no conflict in the contrast, saying: 'each type of thought makes use of the other; the theoretical draws on the knowledge of particular cases in order to discover general principles, and the historical draws on theory in order to understand particular cases'.[37] Similarly, Barzun and Graff maintain that history is interested in life as such, and social science in charting its regularities, so that: 'there can be no question, then, of social science displacing history as a mode of understanding reality, any more than of history producing theory in the scientific sense. There should, accordingly, be no conflict between the two.'[38]

The real or pseudo-conflict has, however, existed, and has here been so far discussed on a theoretical plane. The major methodological issue which it seems operationally to entail is that of quantification.

Even if it is accepted that the historian cannot but generalize, and if we agree, with W.O. Aydelotte,[39] that his seemingly impressionistic 'generalisations are implicitly quantitative in character' (i.e. imply certain numerical regularities, discoverable in the mass of evidence), the historian's concern is with the past, making it hard for him, psychologically, to take to a method which social scientists have always hopefully claimed as essentially predictive. And to the argument that quantifying may equally well be used to increase the exactitude of the truth about the past, the historian may reply that it is not his kind of truth. For, if sociology wants pattern-revealing generalizations, and for that quantification is necessary even if it simplifies and distorts, many historians would emphasize the latter attributes as unacceptable.

Furthermore, the historian more often than not lacks the necessary figures. A.J.P. Taylor[40] in a provocative aside on historical work today suggests that 'facts, once sacred, are increasingly discredited and figures have become sacred in their place ... and the more inadequate the statistics, the more ingenious are the deductions drawn from them'.

The dilemma between what is proper in history and what is correct in statistics seems exaggerated here, because of a misunderstanding of the statistical method and the idea of sampling. Certainly, generalizing from few instances is a risky procedure, but the statistician, within certain limits and duly adjusting and emphasizing the margin of error and degree of uncertainty, holds that the 'thinner' the data the more likely he is to 'squeeze' something out of them by using the most sophisticated methods. What is indefensible, and not uncommon, is when, having told the reader how far his procedure is based on evidence and how far on conjecture, etc., the writer 'proceeds to treat the explicitly doubtful conclusions as safe ground for further confident inference'.[41] And what is sad and unnecessary is that historians appear today to be developing an inferiority complex vis-à-vis their colleagues from the social sciences, as if the latter's quantified findings had really and universally more validity than the most rigorous qualitative analysis, as if mere words could not hope, in this science-based age, to compete with figures in elucidating human experience, as if, indeed, there were a question of competing alternatives rather than alliance. Finally, not all is lost, even in socio-economic history, if the paucity of figures is extreme. A.H.M. Jones resigned himself, for this reason, to the proposition that 'ancient economic history can never be a science, comparable to modern economic history', but can 'analyse from the economic angle evidence which is available ... on political, administrative, legal and social institutions', and he has since, of course, produced one of a handful of great post-war works in this area of scholarship.[42]

Ultimately, the value of quantification is the same for the historian and the social scientist: never the only way, it sometimes is the best way, and most frequently – especially in socio-economic history to which the development of education belongs – a very useful way of complementing and verifying qualitative statements. Again, the pitfalls of quantification are similar for both: the abuse of 'our vulnerability to the belief that any alleged knowledge which can be expressed in figures is, in fact, as final and exact as the figures in which it is expressed';[43] and the spreading attitude that all social phenomena that can be measured are worth measuring (conversely, the danger of neglecting important problems which are – or appear – incapable of being measured).

To sum up: in both historical and sociological circles some concern has been evident about the polarities of fact-gathering – often of trivial facts, too, and of vast theoretical systems – from the mysticism of Toynbee to the inelegancies of Parsons and, beyond, to the rigidity of the tenets of Marx.[44] Both historians and sociologists may increasingly come to favour, in practice, 'medium-scale thinking', whereby their recent rapprochement is likely to become more pronounced.

III. EXAMPLES AND SUGGESTIONS

If sociology and history have been, albeit uneasily, drawing closer for some decades, sociology and education have, in this country, taken interest in each other only in the last few years. Until the 1960s, courses in the sociology of education in departments and colleges of education were extremely rare, and so were contributions to the subject in the sociological literature. A date worth mentioning here is 1965, when the new Professor of Education at Sheffield University, very much a historian, gave a largely sociological inaugural lecture on *The Teaching Profession*, while the new holder of the Chair of Sociology at Nottingham discussed *Sociology and Education* (in the same year, the new Professor of Economic History at Leicester duly chose for his topic *History and the Social Sciences*).[45]

There have, perhaps, been more satisfactory attempts by socio-logists to tackle historical themes in education than attempts by historians to explore such themes in a sociological manner. If so, the explanation may be, apart from the historians being the better able to do without sociology than vice versa, and indeed having generally no sociological training at all, that the history of education is a better established study than the sociology of education. The present dis-cussion is not, of course, concerned with the nascent institutional rivalry, but with the potential intellectual and cognitive interpenetra-tion, of the two. The problem at this stage, however, is not so much whether or how to 'sociologize' historical work on education, as to clarify just what the sociological perspective might involve.

In the first place, such studies call for a general awareness of the social, economic, and political context of education, involving a readiness to ask sociological types of questions. One may call this the 'general component' of the sociological perspective. It seems close to what Sir Fred Clarke was postulating nearly thirty years ago in his seminal (or at least would-be-seminal) brief study of *Education and Social Change* (1940). It is also close to H.S. Hughes' view that the historian should absorb social science into his thinking and let it inform his work and 'illuminate' his reasoning, if only implicitly, but should think of 'applying' social science theories to his materials in the sense of some mechanical superimposition.[46] The 'general component' should, next, incorporate some acquaintance with the analysis and application by sociologists of such conceptual terms as social structure, ideology, élite, etc. Lastly, it would, of course, involve being conversant with significant writings on historico-educational themes by students whose prime allegiance is to sociology. The 'general component' would seem to be quite indispensable in any historical work on education; if this postulate seems obvious to the point of being axiomatic, it has not been so to many authors in this province, and one could also mention here the strangely narrow view propagated very recently in an influential journal that 'the history of education is ... primarily ... the history of teaching'.[47]

Secondly, one may postulate a 'specific component' of the socio-logical perspective, subsisting in the ability to *use* sociological theories, concepts and methods in an expert way. Admittedly, history of education can, in general, be well and meaningfully written without the mastery of this component. Thus B. Simon says of Halévy's relevant sections that 'he closely related educational change to social and political change [and gave] perhaps the most illuminating analysis of the historical development of education that we possess'[48] – and Halévy was no sociologist, nor were the authors of many fine monographs listed by Simon. Nonetheless, in many areas the interpretation may gain in depth and accuracy if the sociological expertise is in evidence and a strictly sociological, rather than social-historical, framework is adopted. The presence of the 'specific' as well as of the 'general' component of the sociological perspective may enhance our ability, if not to solve problems in educational history, then to state them more clearly and precisely, or, at the very least, to 'raise the level of our thinking about them'.[49] Thus, if we want to ascertain whether and how far education has been an avenue of social mobility in various societies and periods, historical materials need to be treated within a sociological theoretical and conceptual framework. Again, if curricular changes, or their absence, in boarding schools are investigated, the sociology of élites and the concept of the 'total institution' are highly relevant. But

98

these are no easy lines to follow: few have yet attempted them and fewer still with marked success.

It may be useful to illustrate the possibilities and limitations of the historico-sociological study of education by reference to some publications of different types and from different areas. A monograph by O. Banks on *Parity and Prestige in English Secondary Education* (1955) has provided a successful example of historical sociology of education, explaining how, in the context of our social and economic and, particularly, occupational, structure, the secondary modern school could not attain parity of esteem. Another sociologist, M.K. Hopkins, also employed the sociological perspective in its full sense in his paper on the 'Social Mobility in the Later Roman Empire: the Evidence of Ausonius'[50] (a fourth-century scholar-schoolmaster who attained to high office). In the author's words, this is 'a pilot study in which we may see how the conflicting elements of social status were in practice reconciled and applied'. Again, P.W. Musgrave, in his *Society and Education in England since 1800* (1968) broke virtually new ground in producing a general textbook of the history of education written from the sociological standpoint. Some jarring errors apart, there is much sound history here. Moreover, Musgrave's sociological training enables him to pose some novel and pertinent questions, and some events of the history of education, that have been worn threadbare by traditional textbooks, have again been made significant and stimulating. The manual, nevertheless, illustrates also the difficulty of applying the sociological perspective, as understood here, in that the 'specific component', namely W.I. Thomas' concept of the 'definition of the situation', on balance cramps and over-schematizes the exposition, and it is, rather, the 'general component' that invests the book with a fresh and sharp focus. Last but not least, several major official Reports of recent years on various aspects of our educational system, notably, perhaps, the Crowther Report *15 to 18* (1959), with its marked economic orientation, have assembled materials, and have couched much of the exposition in terms that could be classed as either historical or sociological. And, for a more negative illustration, A.M. Kazamias' *Politics, Society and Secondary Education in England* (1966) may be noted. The author of this study, of the period 1895–1944, is clearly knowledgeable on education and his history is sound, if tending to be of what R.G. Collingwood termed 'scissors and paste' variety, but he offers very little sociological perspective which the theme patently requires. The outcome seems, to the present writer, that an opportunity has been missed of filling an important gap left by both the social historian and the educationist.

In suggesting themes for historico-sociological educational studies, it seems, similarly, desirable to look at a number of different areas. 'Macroscopic' studies could, for instance, take for their subject the rise of universities – either in the Europe of the twelfth–thirteenth centuries, or of the 'Redbrick' variety in this country a hundred years ago. The recent monography by G. Leff on the former theme (*The Universities of Paris and Oxford in the Thirteenth and Fourteenth Centuries*, 1968) is certainly a valuable contribution to educational and to intellectual history – but its emphasis on the curricula and mental life of the institutions makes it less than satisfying; and while S. Rothblatt has successfully employed the sociological approach (esp. in Pt. I, 'A Problem of Social Change' of his *The Revolution of the Dons*, 1968) in studying higher education in Victorian England, he was concerned solely with the University of Cambridge. Secondly, there is room for more than one study of the growth and socio-economic implications of school examinations[51] in this country, and, in a related field, of the growth of education by correspondence as an avenue of social mobility. Lastly, educational history and political sociology could fruitfully combine in studying the conflict and accommodation between centralization and localism in the evolution of various national educational systems – not least that of this country, now approaching its first centenary. On a 'microscopic' scale, one could suggest studies, say, of women in the teaching profession, of trends in the composition of staff and student bodies in technical colleges, or of links and their absence between schools and industry in selected areas.

Finally, it seems needful to suggest, however tentatively, some specific conceptual schemes from sociology that might be employed and, simultaneously, tested in this field. R.H. Turner's theory[52] – seemingly a theory of the middle-range, of 'sponsored' as against 'contest' modes of social mobility through education (the former akin to the more familiar metaphor of a steep and narrow 'ladder' of scholarships and the latter to the 'broad highway' with those wanting in ability or motivation gradually falling out by the wayside) seems to have extensive possibilities. Again, the 'cultural lag' theory (and in his 1957 discussion the author insisted that it was not 'merely a concept') of W.F. Ogburn's,[53] 'occurring when one of two parts of a culture, which are correlated, changes before, or in a greater degree, than the other part does, thereby causing less adjustment between them', might well prove valuable in the context of the dynamics of the relations between education and the social institutions of the family, church, state and the economic system.

Insofar as history and sociology are 'meant for each other', the course of their love has certainly not run smoothly, and even this article has voiced some reservations and pointed to some difficulties. Nearly half a century ago some historians (e.g., Pirenne)[54] saw the potential relationship of sociology to history as analogous to that of economic theory to economic history. R. Davis is right, however, in his recent pronouncement that 'it would be misleading to suggest that in this country any social science except economics has as yet contributed very much to history, [and even] economic development is not wholly, not even mainly, an economic matter'.[55] Yet if there are many reasons why the double harness of history and sociology may in practice prove difficult to wear frequently and comfortably in the field of education,[56] and why even its advocates may find that 'the methodological positions [they] explicitly adopt are not ones they are always able to uphold as they grapple with substantive ... problems',[57] over much of their respective plots in this field the sociologist cannot go far without historical materials and the historian will be well-advised to consider sociological concepts and understandings. For one thing, their 'primary subjects' may well gain from this. Moreover, in the study of education, the psychologists have of late appreciated the need to broaden their emphasis on the individual apart from society, which Durkheim criticized and protested against,[58] and philosophers have in recent years increasingly adopted the analytical approach, and thereby shed much of the normative outlook of the traditional 'Principles' courses. It seems no less important, for the fullness and balance of educational studies, that their third dimension should compound the strengths and attractions of both history and sociology.

NOTES

1. J. Barzun and H.F. Graff, *The Modern Researcher* (New York, 1957); W.H. Burston, *Social Studies and the History Teacher* (London (Hist.Assoc.), 1954).
2. Philosophy of history in its traditional meaning, as, say, in R.G. Collingwood's *Idea of History* (London, 1946), and not as the study of the nature of historical explanation, as, say, in W.H. Dray's *Laws and Explanation in History* (London, 1957).
3. P.L. Berger, *Invitation to Sociology* (New York, 1963).
4. C. Wright Mills, *The Sociological Imagination* (New York, 1959).
5. J.W. Tibble, ed., *The Study of Education* (London, 1966): the chapter on 'The History of Education' is by B. Simon, that on 'The Sociology of Education' by W. Taylor. See No.5 in this volume.

6. On this see B. Bailyn, *Education in the Forming of American Society* (New York, 1960), esp. pp.5–9; G. Sutherland, 'The Study of the History of Education', *History*, LIV, no.180 (1969), see No.6 in this volume; and B. Harrison, 'History at the Universities, 1968' in *History*, LIII, no.179 (1968).
7. B. Simon, op. cit., p.113. See no.5 in this volume.
8. J. Floud, 'Educational Sociology' in J. Gould and W.L. Kolb eds., *A Dictionary of the Social Sciences* (London, 1963), p.229.
9. See, however, F. Musgrove, 'Decline of the Educative Family', *Universities Quarterly*, XIV, no.4, 1960.
10. Royal Commission on Secondary Education (Bryce Commission) reported in 1895; A.N. Whitehead deals with the point in ch.IV, 'Technical Education and its Relation to Science and Literature' of his *The Aims of Education* (London, 1949).
11. The endless and often pointless controversy arising from J.B. Bury's well-known declaration that: 'history is a science, no less and no more', is a warning here.
12. Mills, op. cit., p.143; Berger, op. cit., p.191; R.K. Merton, *On Theoretical Sociology* (New York, 1967), p.vi.
13. S.W.F. Holloway, 'History and Sociology: What History is and What It Ought to Be' in W.H. Burston and D. Thompson eds., *Studies in the Nature and Teaching of History* (London, 1967), p.18 and p.21.
14. E.g., in the success of the sociology-minded journal *Past and Present*; in the three issues of *The Times Educational Supplement*, nos.3345, 3361 and 3367, of 1966, devoted to 'New Ways in History'; or in P. Laslett's 'History and the Social Sciences' in *International Encyclopaedia of Social Sciences*, 1968, vol.VI p.434 ff.
15. W.J.H. Sprott usefully distinguishes between the social historian and the historical sociologist, in *Sociology at the Seven Dials*, Hobhouse Memorial Lecture, 1962.
16. W. Kula, *Problemy i Metody Historii Gospodarczej* (Warsaw, 1963) chs.I and IX, esp. at p.35 (English translation, *Problems and Methods of Economic History*, forthcoming).
17. D.G. MacRae, *New Society*, no.318, 1968, p.649.
18. J.M. Price and G.L. Weinberg, article on Namier in *Internat. Encycl. of Social Sciences*, 1968, vol.XI p.3.
19. A. Briggs, 'Sociology and History' in A.T. Welford ed., *Society – Problems and Methods of Study* (London, 1962), p.95.
20. K. Thomas, 'Tools for the Job' in *Times Literary Supplement*, no.3345, 1966.
21. On this see F. Znaniecki, *Modern Nationalities* (Urbana, Ill., 1952) and, on a different plane, E.H. Dance, *History the Betrayer* (London, 1960).
22. Berger, op. cit. p.31.
23. G.R. Elton, 'Second Thoughts on History at the Universities' in *History*, LIV, no.180 (1969).
24. E.E.Y. Hales, 'School History in the Melting Pot' in History Today, XVI no.3 (1966). Cf. R.M. Franklin, 'The Challenge of Social Science', *Times Educational Supplement*, no.2814, 1969, p.1350.
25. B. Wilson, 'Analytical Studies of Social Institutions' in Welford, op. cit., p.110.
26. Mills, op. cit., p.146; Mills singled out T. Parsons' grand theories (and language) for particularly severe treatment. The castigations of fellow-sociologists by another 'grand theorist', P.A. Sorokin, in *Fads and Foibles of Modern Sociology* (London, 1956), covered a different area.
27. R.K. Merton discussed this concept in his *Social Theory and Social Structure* in 1957; for an expanded version see 'On Sociological Theories of the Middle Range' in his *On Theoretical Sociology*, 1967.
28. T.H. Marshall, considering the problem in terms of synthesis v. analysis as well as of abstraction v. reality in his Inaugural Lecture on *Sociology at the Crossroads*, 1947, suggests that 'wide generalisation and the interpretation of social phenomena lie far apart ... they need ... stepping-stones in the middle distance'.
29. See contributions by M.M. Postan and by M.J. Oakeshott to *The Social Sciences*, Le Play House, London, 1936, p.62 and p.73 respectively.

30. Kula, op. cit., p.36.
31. Holloway, op. cit., p.8.
32. Cf. G. Kitson Clark's regretful: 'the effect of such detailed work may well be disheartening: its result may be to break up an existing picture and replace it with nothing that can be seen as a whole', when he advocates more research in depth for the sake of fuller historical truth – eventually, *The Making of Victorian England*, 1962, p.17.
33. O. MacDonagh, 'The 19th-Century Revolution in Government: a Reappraisal' in *Historical Journal*, I, no.I, 1958.
34. H.S. Hughes, 'The Historian and the Social Scientist' in *American Historical Review*, LXVI, no.I, 1960 (reprinted in A.V. Riasanovsky and B. Riznik, eds., *Generalisations in Historical Writing*, 1962).
35. R.G. Collingwood, *The Idea of History* (Oxford, 1946) p.30.
36. F.C. Lane, 'Conclusion' in F.C. Lane and J. Riemersma, *Enterprise and Secular Change* (Homewood, Ill.) 1953, esp. p.533.
37. Ibid., p.523–4.
38. Barzun and Graff, op. cit., p.219.
39. W.O. Aydelotte, 'Quantification and History' in *American Historical Review*, LXXI, no.3, 1966.
40. In a review of J.R. Hale, *The Evolution of British Historiography*, in *The Observer*, 16 March 1967.
41. G.R. Elton, *The Practice of History* (Sydney, 1967) p.29.
42. A.H.M. Jones, *Ancient Economic History* (London, 1948) (Inaugural Lecture). The great work is his *The Later Roman Empire, 284–602 A.D.: A Social, Economic and Administrative Survey* (Oxford, 1964).
43. R. Hofstadter, *Anti-Intellectualism in American Life* (New York, 1964).
44. J.H. Hexter's view, *Reappraisals in History* (London, 1961), p.14 ff., of Marxist influence on social history as 'stultifying' seems wide of the mark, though he is right in judging that many social historians use the Marxist approach unconsciously and therefore incompetently, as in accepting (correctly) his stress on the importance of the economic factor, they fail to discriminate against his unsatisfactory general theory of social change.
45. Professors J.P.C. Roach, J. Gould and R. Davis respectively.
46. H.S. Hughes, op. cit.; cf. H.R. Trevor-Roper: 'Today, I cannot conceive of good history without a sociological dimension', 'The Past and the Present. History and Sociology' in *Past and Present*, no.42, 1969, p.12.
47. D. Hopkinson, 'Teachers and the History of Education' in *Trends in Education*, no.II, 1968.
48. B. Simon, op. cit., p.122.
49. I have borrowed this phrase from H.L. Elvin, *Education and Contemporary Society* (London, 1965).
50. *Classical Quarterly*, N.S., XI, no.2, 1961. Numerous articles that might have been used here as examples are listed in R. Szreter, 'The History of Education in Non-Education Periodicals, 1939–1967: a Bibliography', *British Journal of Educational Studies*, XVI, no.3, 1968.
51. Useful discussions by N. Morris (a historian here having to 'sociologise'), 'A Historian's View of Examinations' in S. Wiseman ed., *Examinations and English Education*, 1961, and by W. Taylor (a sociologist having to be historical) in *The Secondary Modern School*, 1963, passim, are too brief and too sectional respectively.
52. R.H. Turner, 'Modes of Social Ascent through Education: Sponsored and Contest Mobility', *American Sociological Review*, XXV, 1960; E.I. Hopper, 'A Typology for the Classification of Educational Systems' in *Sociology*, II, no.I, 1968, uses it non-historically for comparative education, and L. Stone, 'Literacy and Education in England 1640–1900' in *Past and Present*, no.42, 1969, only touches upon it in passing.

53. W.F. Ogburn, *Social Change* (New York, 1922); cf. his 'Cultural Lag as Theory' in *Sociology and Social Research*, XLXI, 1957.
54. A point noted by M. Ginsberg, 'History and Sociology' in his *Studies in Sociology*, 1932, p.29.
55. R. Davis, op. cit. Cf. B.F. Hoselitz, *Sociological Aspects of Economic Growth* (Glencoe, 1960) and 'Investment in Education and its Political Impact' in J.S. Coleman, ed., *Education and Political Development* (Princeton, 1965); also F. Harbison and C.A. Myers, *Education, Manpower and Economic Growth* (New York, 1964).
56. W.J. Cahnman and A. Boskoff, eds., *Sociology and History* (New York, 1964) in a selection of over thirty readings include none that touches on education.
57. J.H. Goldthorpe, 'Introduction' to T. Raison, ed., *The Founding Fathers of Social Science*, 1969, p.12.
58. See esp. ch.IV, 'Pedagogy and Sociology' of Durkheim's *Education and Sociology* (Glencoe, 1956).

8

The Historiography of Education

H.C. BARNARD

The study of educational history is today very generally included in the professional training of the teacher. The development of the subject, however, is a comparatively modern phenomenon, especially as far as Great Britain is concerned, yet it has surely justified itself as an academic discipline in its own right. Its aims and its content have been defined by such writers as J.W. Adamson in his collection of essays entitled *The Illiterate Anglo-Saxon* (1946) or Brian Simon in 'The History of Education'.[1] The scope of history is indeed so wide that some degree of sectionalization is necessary if it is to be satisfactorily dealt with. Thus we have the history of a limited period or of a limited area – for example, Ancient Greece or England under the Tudors or Revolutionary Europe. We can have histories of institutions such as schools or colleges; and local studies are a fruitful field of research. Biographies of individuals often shed light on the social conditions under which they lived. But the tendency to departmentalize is perhaps especially marked in treating some particular aspect of general history. Thus we have economic, political, ecclesiastical and military history; we have histories of science, medicine, law, art, agriculture, and so on. It was natural therefore that similar developments should have been made in the case of education. Foster Watson points out that 'the slightest attempt to analyse the present state of an organism leads us to the past'; and Brian Simon, commenting on this statement, adds, 'The idea that education could also become more scientific, and that one of the essential means to this end was a rigorous study of its history, was a particular stimulus to historical inquiry.'[2]

At the same time it is true, as Adamson has reminded us, that education is essentially concerned with ends and therefore has a philosophic outlook. In the study of philosophy we consider the principles which the chief thinkers of the past have laid down, and from these we can synthesize a system for ourselves which will affect the means by which we seek to attain those ends. Thus in education a study of the theories and the resultant practice of the great educationists may well have important bearings on our own practice and planning. If so, even though the study of educational history is in origin an academic matter, it can not only be a source of inspiration to the practising teacher, but may even be brought down into the everyday life of the classroom or into the details of school administration. The influence of such reformers as Rousseau and Froebel and the 'educational innovators' dealt with in W. A. C. Stewart's two volumes bearing that title (published in 1967 and 1968) can be fully appreciated only by those who have studied the contemporary educational background; and quite apart from all this the present educational arrangements in a country like England or France or the United States can be properly understood only in relation to its historical development.

The study of education as an academic discipline has therefore involved an investigation of its history, though it began on the continent of Europe long before it was taken up in England. Gabriel Compayré points out in a valuable contribution to Paul Monroe's *A Cyclopedia of Education*,[3] that a considerable, if rather sporadic, amount of investigation into the subject had already been made in Germany in the latter years of the eighteenth century and the early part of the nineteenth. But the most significant and comprehensive survey is that of Karl von Raumer whose *Geschichte der Pädagogik* (three volumes, 1857) carried the history of education from the end of the medieval period down to the middle of the nineteenth century. Von Raumer's original interest was in geology and mineralogy, but he was impressed by Pestalozzi's work and writings and by Fichte who, in his *Addresses to the German Nation* (1807–8), urged a reorganization of the German school system on Pestalozzian lines. At the University of Erlangen, in addition to his duties as professor of mineralogy, von Raumer delivered lectures on the history of education, and these are the origin of his treatise on the subject. It consists of five volumes: the first deals with the Middle Ages down to Montaigne, and was published in 1842; in the next year appeared volume 2 which carried on the account from the death of Bacon to that of Pestalozzi; volume 3 (1852) deals with the development of the curriculum, with technical education and with the education of girls; while volume 4 (1854) describes the growth of the German universities and institutions of higher education. A fifth volume was added by G. Lothholz in 1897, thirty-two years after von Raumer's death and according to the preface it 'continued and supplemented' the original work, and contained studies of individual German educationists from the eighteenth century onwards.

Von Raumer's work was followed up by several other German scholars. Particular mention should be made of Carl Schmidt's *Die Geschichte der Pädagogik* in four volumes, published in 1860–2; its full title claims that the subject is treated in its world-wide development and in its essential relation to national cultures. Schmidt was also the author of *Die Geschichte der Erziehung und des Unterrichts*, published in 1863. He should be distinguished from Carl Adolph Schmid, whose *Encyklopädie des gesammten Erziehungs- und Unterrichtswesens* in eleven volumes was published between 1859 and 1875. In his *Geschichte der Erziehung* (1884–1902), which covers the whole period from the earliest times to his own days, Schmid had the co-operation of several other educationists. The influence of these German writers on the subsequent evolution of educational history was – as we shall see – considerable, especially in England and the United States.

The outstanding contribution to the subject made by Germany is, however, the *Monumenta Germaniae Paedagogica*. It was inaugurated by Karl Kehrbach, with the co-operation of a number of specialists, and published by the *Gesellschaft für deutsche Erziehungs- und Schulgeschichte*. The first volume appeared in 1886 and up to 1938 sixty-two volumes were published; unfortunately the series has since been discontinued. The general scope of the work covers the regulations for school-systems in various German states, together with information as to their development, some account of school books, and miscellaneous details about education in countries where German is the native language. But the volumes also contain a large amount of sheer historical information as well as reprints of such important documents as the Jesuit *Ratio Studiorum*, Melanchthon's *Enchiridion* and other sixteenth-century Protestant catechisms, the *Doctrinale* of Alexander Villa Dei, and some of the writings of such educational reformers as Comenius and Pestalozzi. The emphasis throughout is naturally on the development of education in Germany, but the work as a whole is a most valuable mine of information. It covers a wide range and is an indispensable source for research on German educational history.

The German contribution to both national and general educational history has been supplemented by a number of other works. Among them may be mentioned Carl Gottlob Hergang's *Pädagogische Real-Encyklopädie* which was published in 1843–7. In 1871 appeared Friedrich Dittes's *Geschichte der Erziehung und des Unterrichts*; and

107

to August Vogel we owe a *Geschichte der Pädagogik als Wissenschaft* (1877) which stresses the academic aspect of the subject. Vogel was also responsible for a *Systematische Encyklopädie der Pädagogik* (1881). A more recent contribution to the history of education is Theobald Ziegler's *Geschichte der Pädagogik mit besonderer Rücksicht auf das höhere Unterrichtswesen* (1895) which, as the title suggests, lays particular stress on the development of higher education. Friedrich Paulsen's *Geschichte des gelehrten Unterrichts auf den deutschen Schulen und Universitäten* was published in 1885 and appeared in a revised edition (two volumes) in 1896. The same author's *Das deutsche Bildungswesen in seiner geschichtlichen Entwicklung* dates from 1906 and was translated into English with the title *German Education, Past and Present* (1908). It is perhaps the most convenient and accessible work on educational history in Germany and has a very useful short bibliography. Wilhelm Rein, in addition to his writings on educational psychology, edited a ten-volume *Encyclopädisches Handbuch der Pädagogik* (1902–11) which contains some historical material and is described by the German *Lexicon der Pädagogik* (1952)[4] as the most important educational work of reference.

France is notably rich in monographs dealing with the history of individual educational institutions and of educational developments in particular regions. The University of Paris and its colleges have not unnaturally attracted a good deal of interest. The earliest study, published between 1665 and 1673, was that of César Égasse du Boulay, who had been rector of the University and obviously had ready access to the relevant source material. His account was continued through the seventeenth and eighteenth centuries by Charles-Marie-Gabriel Bréchillet-Jourdain whose work was published in 1862–6. He also edited a most useful *Index chronologicus chartarum pertinentium ad historiam Universitatis Parisiensis*. The Abbé Fleury, who was one of the most distinguished educational writers of the seventeenth century, devoted the earlier part of his *Traité du Choix et de la Méthode des Études* (1686) to a history of the subject. He describes, and where necessary criticizes, education among the Greeks and Romans, the early Christians, the Arabs, and during the Middle Ages, the Renaissance and in his own day. The treatise is interesting because it deals with current problems of method, curriculum and other educational matters, but adopts a definitely historical approach to them.

But for the first specific general history of education from a French source we turn to Auguste Vallet de Viriville's *Histoire de l'Instruction publique en Europe* which appeared in 1849 – seven years after the publication of von Raumer's first volume. It is a most attractive work, but it seems to have incurred some ill-deserved neglect even in its own country. In his preface de Viriville calls attention to the lack of 'une histoire générale des établissements consacrés à l'instruction publique'; he endeavours to fill this gap. His experience as a professor at the École des Chartes had given him an interest in the archives of the University of Paris, and this had led him on to a more general study of the whole field of educational history. There is throughout some emphasis on France and the account is carried from Celtic and Gallo-Roman times to the restoration of Louis-Philippe. The book is rather like a series of monographs, but is full of interest and a valuable source of information. A feature of the work is the 'pièces justificatives', especially those concerning the University of Paris; and there is a large number of delightful illustrations – some of them steel-plate engravings – and a selection of coats of arms, in full colour, relating to the various French universities and colleges.

After Vallet de Viriville's engaging book, the *Histoire de l'Éducation en France depuis le cinquième siècle jusqu'à nos jours* of A.F. Théry is something of an anticlimax. It appeared in two volumes in 1858. If it lacks the liveliness and attractive appearance of its predecessor, it covers the ground more fully and claims to have been based on a thorough study of original sources. Another general history starting from 'peuples sauvages' and working through the educational arrangements of the ancient Chinese, Phoenicians and Jews, education in classical times, in the Middle Ages, the Renaissance, and modern times, was the work of Jules Paroz. The first edition was published in 1867. An interesting addition to thè purely historical work is a comparative treatment of contemporary education in England, Germany, France and Switzerland. There is a tendency to improve on the bare narrative, and, as Paroz says in the preface, 'Above all theories and practice I have not ceased to place the holy truths of Christianity without which education – as also civilization which is derived from it – will lose itself in the desert of doubt and materialism.' The author acknowledges his great debt to German sources, and especially to von Raumer and to C. Schmid.

An outstanding nineteenth-century French contribution to educational history was made by Gabriel Compayré who was both an academic and a politician. He became rector of the University of Lyons and was a writer not only on this subject, but also on the theory and practice of education. His *Histoire critique des Doctrines de l'Éducation en France depuis le seizième siècle* in two volumes was published in 1879 and went through a number of subsequent editions. As the title suggests, the book is concerned mainly with the history of educational

109

theories and with France, but it is not restricted in either direction and, taken altogether, it is a reliable and informative guide. Compayré afterwards developed his *Histoire critique* into a more general history of education under the title of *Histoire de la Pédagogie* (1883) which was translated into English (1886) by Professor W.H. Payne of the University of Michigan; it contains a handy bibliography. In his preface Payne calls attention to the small number of works in English dealing with educational history:

If we allow that a teacher should first of all be a man of culture, and that an invaluable factor in his professional education is a knowledge of what has hitherto been done within his field of activity, there are the best of reasons why the claims of this study should be urged upon the teaching profession.

Compayré's own introduction setting forth the value and scope of educational history is an expansion of this theme.

In addition to his major contributions to this subject, Compayré wrote on the philosophy of Hume and on Darwinism, translated Locke's *Thoughts on Education*, and wrote a series of monographs dealing with such educationists as Rousseau, Spencer, Pestalozzi, Herbart and Montaigne – men 'who deserve to have their names on the honour list in the history of education'. These books are also available in English translations. Nor must we overlook Compayré's historical contributions to F. Buisson's *Dictionnaire de Pédagogie et d'Instruction publique*. This four-volume work, a mine of information upon almost any subject connected with educational history in France, was first issued between 1878 and 1887, and a revised and modernized edition appeared in 1911. It may be supplemented by A. Silvy's *Essai d'une Bibliographie historique* which was reprinted from the *Bulletin* of the Société générale d'Éducation et d'Enseignement. This is pretty complete so far as it goes, but it includes only books and articles dealing with the educational history of France up to the Revolution and published in that country before 1892.

When one comes to more recent French works it is difficult, and perhaps invidious, to make a selection. However, mention may be made of the following: for a general history from the Renaissance onwards, the sociologist Émile Durkheim's *L'Évolution pédagogique en France*, two volumes (1938), and Louis-Grimaud's *Histoire de la Liberté d'Enseignement en France*, four volumes (1944–6). Michel Glatigny's paperback *Histoire de l'Enseignement en France* (1949) is a handy short account. For special periods one can consult G. Weill, *Histoire de l'Enseignement secondaire en France, 1802–1920* (1921) and F. Vial, *Trois Siècles d'Histoire de l'Enseignement Secondaire* (1936). The education of women and girls is studied by P. Rousselot, *Histoire de l'Éducation des Femmes en France*, two volumes (1883), and O. Gréard, *L'Éducation des Femmes par les Femmes* (1907). The development of higher education since the Revolution is discussed in L. Liard, *L'Enseignement supérieur en France, 1789–1889* (1889); and that of technical education in F.B. Artz, *The Development of Technical Education in France, 1500–1850* (1966). This book is based on three monographs which were written in French and appeared in issues of the *Revue d'Histoire moderne*.

As far as English contributions to this subject are concerned Matthew Arnold's *Schools and Universities in France* (1868) contains a good deal of historical material, and Geraldine Hodgson, *Studies in French Education* (1908) is also a valuable source of information. Another English work is F.S. Farrington, *French Secondary Schools* (1910), and perhaps the present writer may be allowed to refer to his *The Little Schools of Port Royal* (1913), *The French Tradition in Education* (1922), *Mme de Maintenon and Saint-Cyr* (1934), *Education and the French Revolution* (1968) and other writings dealing with the history of education in France. To these we should add the educational articles contributed by A.G. Little to *Medieval France* and by J.W. Adamson to *Modern France* – both volumes edited by Arthur Tilley and published in 1922. Some interesting material will also be found in W.D. Halls, *Society, Schools and Progress in France* (1965) and in W.H.G. Armytage, *The French Influence on English Education* (1968).

In the United States Henry Barnard,[5] who lived from 1811 to 1900, may be regarded as the earliest and perhaps the most eminent exponent of the study of educational history. He was not a teacher, but after graduating at Yale he entered the legal profession, served in various administrative posts and in 1851 became 'superintendent of common schools' in Connecticut and principal of the State Normal School. He was afterwards chancellor of the University of Wisconsin and from 1867 to 1870 the first United States commissioner for education. Alongside this official work he was a voluminous writer of books and articles dealing with educational topics, and he had a special interest in the history of education. He made several visits to Europe and was impressed by the work of de Fellenberg and the disciples of Pestalozzi; he also made known in America the kindergarten movement. His greatest contribution to educational literature was the *American Journal of Education* which began publication in 1855 and which he continued to edit for twenty-six years. It is far more than a mere 'journal', but is better described in the words of W.S. Monroe as 'a vast encyclopaedia of educational literature'. R.K. Morris, in his *Henry*

Barnard Sesquicentennial Address at Trinity College, Hartford, Connecticut, says of it that 'it stands today as a classic repository of educational history, catholic in scope, scholarly in treatment'.[6] The contributors included many of the most distinguished American educationists of the day, and their work was supplemented by reprints of famous educational writings from Plato to Pestalozzi. Some of these were republished as separate volumes under such titles as *National Education in Europe* (1854), *German Educational Reformers* (1861) and *English Pedagogy* (1862). The thoroughness and detail of the work is amazing. It certainly owes something to von Raumer – some of the articles in the German volume are directly translated from the earlier author's *Geschichte der Pädagogik*; but Henry Barnard has an importance all his own. To quote the article in Monroe's *Cyclopedia of Education*, 'He gave America her earliest literature of education'[7] – and much of that literature was directly concerned with the history of the subject.

The study of educational history so notably inaugurated in America by Henry Barnard set a tradition which has been worthily followed there, especially within recent times; but at first it was of rather slow growth. Mention, however, should be made of the work of Thomas Davidson, a graduate of Aberdeen who, after experience as a schoolmaster in England, emigrated to America in 1866. His primary interest was in philosophy and he translated and edited the *Philosophical System of Rosmini* (1882); but he also wrote on Greek education (1894) and on Rousseau (1898), and his *History of Education* was published in 1900 – the year of his death. Meanwhile a movement in America to make teacher-training a more definite responsibility of universities and colleges was contemporary with somewhat similar recommendations of the Cross Commission in England and with the consequent formation of day training colleges.[8] An advocate of this type of training was Charles Kendall Adams who had been professor of history at the University of Michigan. He afterwards became president first of Cornell University and then of the University of Wisconsin. He was the author of several historical works and of *Higher Education in Germany* (1882). In a speech delivered in 1888 to the New England Association of Colleges and Preparatory Schools he stresses the duty of universities to provide professional training for teachers, and at the head of his syllabus he puts 'The History of Education, ancient, medieval and modern'; and for a textbook he prescribes Compayré's *History of Pedagogy*.

But it is in the present century that we have seen the real florescence of the study of educational history in the United States. Conspicuous among the contributors to this is Paul Monroe who held a chair specifically devoted to the subject in Teachers College, Columbia. *The Cyclopedia of Education* (1911) in five volumes which he edited, although naturally oriented towards American interests and institutions, is of the utmost value to the student of educational history and is in the same class as Buisson's *Dictionnaire*. Monroe was also the author of a useful *Text Book in the History of Education* (1905), as well as of a *Source Book in the History of Education for the Greek and Roman Period* (1901) and other contributions to the literature of his subject.

Paul Monroe has been followed within more recent years by a host of American educational historians. F.P. Graves, *History of Education* (1909–13) is a handy compendium for students. E.F. Cubberley, who is the author of *History of Education* (1920) and *Readings in the History of Education* (1943) as well as of other works, has come in for a certain amount of criticism lately from some of his American colleagues; but as this concerns mainly his treatment of certain aspects of his own country's educational history the present writer does not presume to pass any judgment. E.H. Reisner, *Nationalism and Education since 1789* (1922), is a stimulating analysis of a topic the relevance of which has greatly increased since the appearance of his book. Another interesting approach is R. Freeman Butts, *A Cultural History of Education* (1947); and a less known, but hardly less attractive treatment of the subject is J. Franklin Messenger, *An Interpretative History of Education* (1931). Mention also must certainly be made of H.G. Good, *A History of Western Education* (1947), J.S. Brubacher, *A History of the Problems of Education* (1947), and R. Ulich, *History of Educational Thought* (1950) and *The Education of Nations* (1961) – all scholarly contributions to the literature of their subject. Brubacher's *History*, in particular, has a most complete and interesting 'biographical commentary' addressed to the student of educational history. I.L. Kandel, who was born in Romania, educated at Manchester University, and became professor of education at Teachers College, Columbia, may perhaps be classified as an American writer. He has done his chief work in the field of comparative education and educational sociology, but his *History of Secondary Education* (1931) is a valuable book. W.W. Brickman, professor of the history of education and comparative education in the University of Pennsylvania, has done important work in both fields and has contributed many articles to specialist journals. He has written a very comprehensive historical introduction to *A History of International and Comparative Education* (1968) of which he is joint author with S.E.

Fraser. His *Guide to Research in Educational History* (1949) will prove invaluable to the candidate for a higher degree in this subject.

Particular reference should be made to the work of Lawrence A. Cremin who is professor of education at Teachers College, Columbia; his most important book, *The Transformation of the School* (1961), discusses the development of 'progressivism' in American education between 1876 and 1957. But we owe to him in particular a most valuable series of paperback 'Classics in Education'. They include not only a number of volumes illustrating the educational history of America, but also reprints of such sources as *Émile* and Rousseau's minor educational writings, Locke *On Education*, as well as modern classics such as W.H. Woodward on Vittorino da Feltre and Erasmus.

In England the study of educational history was, in its early stages, closely bound up with the development of the professional training of secondary teachers. The Head Masters' Conference inaugurated a movement which led to the formation in 1878 of the Teachers' Training Syndicate at the University of Cambridge. The courses of lectures which were provided included one on the history of education given by R.H. Quick. Quick had been educated at Harrow and Trinity College, Cambridge, and after a short spell as a curate turned to schoolteaching. His interest in educational history seems to have dated from his visits to Germany and resulted in a volume of essays which were published in 1868 under the title *Essays on Educational Reformers*. The book owes much to von Raumer's *Geschichte der Pädagogik*. As Quick himself says, he is 'the authority I have had recourse to most frequently'. Quick also made use of C.A. Schmid's *Encyklopädie des gesammten Erziehungs- und Unterrichtswesens*, which he describes as 'a vast mine of information on everything connected with education', as well as C.G. Hergang's *Pädagogische Real-Encyklopädie*. In short, quoting his friend Professor J.R. Seeley, he says, 'I have found that on the history of education, not only all good books, but *all* books are in German or some other foreign language.'[9]

There is no doubt also that Quick owed something to Henry Barnard, even if his main inspiration was from von Raumer. A revised edition of *Educational Reformers*, published in 1890, was indeed dedicated to 'Dr. Henry Barnard who in a long life of sacrificing labour has given the English language an educational literature.' At the same time the claim in Monroe's *Cyclopedia of Education* that Quick originally got the inspiration for his *Educational Reformers* from the 'American Journal of Education by Henry Barnard' is obviously unjustified. In Quick's own memoirs he says quite definitely 'When I wrote Educational Reformers I had never heard of Barnard's *American Journal of*

Education'; and he adds with regret how greatly it would have helped him had he known of it.[10]

In view of what has been said it was natural that when the Cambridge Teachers' Training Syndicate was formed Quick should have been asked to take the course in educational history. He held this post until 1883 when indifferent health compelled him to abandon it. He was presented by his old college to the living of Sedbergh in Yorkshire which he held until 1887 and he then retired to Redhill where he died in 1891. The success of his *Educational Reformers* was initially due in no small measure to its popularity in America where it was extensively pirated; but it has since been accepted as the first and one of the greatest classics of educational history from an English source.

Quick's work at Cambridge was carried on by his friend and colleague Oscar Browning. He had been a master of Eton and was a fellow of King's College and university lecturer in history. He acted as secretary of the Teachers' Training Syndicate and in 1891 was appointed principal of the Cambridge University Day Training College. The provision of such institutions was due largely to the recommendations of the Cross Commission and during the 1890s training departments of this kind were set up at several universities and university colleges. The Cambridge college, however, in its early days received lukewarm support but, continuing Quick's work, Browning published in 1914 an *Introduction to the History of Educational Theories*. Whereas *Educational Reformers* had started at the Renaissance, Oscar Browning goes back to the Greeks and deals with the teachings of Plato and Aristotle. He discusses Roman and humanist education and then overlaps somewhat with the topics treated by Quick. Like his predecessor, he makes use of von Raumer's *Geschichte* and C.A. Schmid's *Encyklopädie*, as well as of Compayré's *History* and the work of Henry Barnard. For his early period he refers to A.S. Wilkins's essay on *National Education in Greece* (1873) and R.L. Nettleship's work, *Education in the Republic of Plato* (1880). Thus, although the book owes a good deal to earlier writers, it forms a compendium to Quick, and it links up with the contemporary movement for the extension and deepening of teacher-training, especially that of secondary teachers.

The development of university day training colleges led to the growth of university education departments and the institution of specialist diplomas in education. The University of London had in fact inaugurated such a diploma as far back as 1883; but in the early 1890s, as has already been indicated, training colleges for secondary teachers were set up not only at Cambridge, but also at King's College London, at Durham, at Manchester, and at the university colleges of

Birmingham, Nottingham and Cardiff. Oxford also dates from 1892, and soon all the universities and university colleges had established such departments. In practically every case a study of educational history was required.[11] A particularly interesting diploma course was that developed by Sir Michael Sadler when he was professor of education in the University of Manchester. Various types of teacher were provided for, but those who proposed to work in secondary or elementary schools or in schools for handicapped children were required to study 'the history of modern education, with special reference to English education in the nineteenth century'.This was a fairly typical syllabus, but some universities prescribed in addition a study of special educationists – for example, at Cambridge, Locke or Thomas Arnold. At Oxford a wider general conspectus was prescribed together with a special period – the sixteenth and seventeenth centuries, or the eighteenth or the nineteenth and up to date. Lance Jones, writing in 1924, says:

The History of Education is perhaps the least valiantly defended part of the Diploma syllabus. A purely biographical treatment is now almost a thing of the past. So far as classical and medieval times are concerned, emphasis is laid on the development of educational ideas by the few outstanding thinkers of the period, while in more modern times attention is also directed to the sociological and institutional aspects of the subject.[12]

This attitude to the academic study of educational history in the graduate diploma course has remained, but there has also been a considerable development of research in this field.

Even before the development of professional training in the universities an attempt to provide it had been made by the College of Preceptors. This institution, founded in 1846 and granted a Royal Charter three years later, aimed to promote 'sound learning and advancing the interests of Education'. It instituted diplomas to give some indication of professional competence, and it also hoped to found and endow normal (or training) schools, and to establish 'lectureships on any subject concerned with the Theory and Practice of Education'. Lack of funds and support seriously hampered the work of the College but in 1871 it succeeded in instituting a lectureship in education to which Joseph Payne was appointed. He had been a schoolmaster for many years, had already interested himself in the work of Jacotot, and had established a successful private school. He then retired from this work in 1863 and devoted himself to the study of educational theory and methods. Payne's lectures at the College of Preceptors proved popular and in 1872 he was promoted to be professor of education – the first Chair in this subject to be set up in England. The course of lectures

116

which he provided included not only educational theory and practice, but also the history of education. This covered the whole ground from early Chinese, Egyptian, Jewish and Persian education, to the writings of Aristotle, Plato and Quintilian, and the theories of Froebel and Herbert Spencer. Unfortunately, for financial reasons it was found impossible to continue the professorship at the College and it was closed down after the 1874 course; but in 1883 Payne's chief lectures and essays were published in two volumes, entitled *Works of Joseph Payne*, which were edited by his son Dr J.F. Payne. Like his friend Quick, Payne had obviously made good use of German sources and in preparing his lectures on educational history he was, as he acknowledges, indebted to the *Educational Reformers*. Included in the *Works* is 'A Visit to German Schools' which is really a separate book and deals with kindergarten and elementary schools seen by Payne in Germany. He was also the author of an article, 'The Higher Education of the United States', which appeared in the British *Quarterly Review*, Summer 1870. Altogether he has claims to be considered one of the English pioneers both of educational history and of comparative education.

About the time that the College of Preceptors was endeavouring to establish a Chair of Education the Universities of St Andrews and Edinburgh succeeded in providing something more settled and permanent. They were enabled to do this by funds from a bequest by Dr Andrew Bell, of monitorial schools fame. The Chairs were to be in the 'Theory, History and Practice of Education'. At St Andrews the professor was J.M.D. Meiklejohn who had been a schoolmaster in the Lake District and in London, had interested himself in German philosophy, acted as an assistant commissioner for the Endowed Schools (Scotland) Commission in 1872–5, and was also the author of a number of school books. In his inaugural address in 1876 he emphasized the value of the historical approach to the study of education because of its humanizing influence.

At Edinburgh an even more important contributor to the history of education was appointed in the person of S.S. Laurie who held the Chair until 1903. He took a prominent part in Scottish educational activities, was secretary to the Endowed Schools Commission, and was largely responsible for the three reports on secondary education in Scotland which were presented to Parliament. His published work on educational history included an account of the life and writings of Comenius (1881), a treatise on the medieval universities (1886), an historical survey of pre-Christian education (1895) and *Studies in the History of Educational Opinion since the Renaissance* (1903). In the

117

preface to the work on pre-Christian education he acknowledges his debt to Schmidt's *Die Geschichte der Pädagogik* and C.A. Schmid's *Geschichte der Erziehung* – yet one more example of the influence of German writers on educational historians in other countries. It will be seen that Laurie's works covered a wide field of educational history. His *Pre-Christian Education* carries us back to Egypt, the Semitic races, China and India, as well as to Greek and Roman times. His description of the rise of the universities continues the account into the Middle Ages, and his work on the period after the Renaissance and on Comenius takes it from the fourteenth century to the educational writings of Bacon, Milton, Locke and finally Herbert Spencer. In addition, Laurie wrote several philosophical works and was particularly interested in the teachings of Kant. In his *Institutes of Education* (1892) he shows the influence not only of Kant himself, but also to a lesser degree of Fichte and Hegel. When Laurie retired, the University Senate put on record that 'his grasp of philosophical principles and his intimate practical knowledge combined with the influence of a strong and many-sided personality to make his tenure of office a memorable one and to set a high standard for all future occupants of the Chair.'

One of the first university day training colleges to be established was at King's College, London. It dated from October 1890. The College appointed one of its old students, John William Adamson, to be its head and 'normal master'. His duties were 'to give lectures in the history and theory of Education, to superintend the students' work in the practising school, to give a course of model lessons, and to preside at the criticism lesson' – a model on which the modern university departments of education have been formed. Adamson had started his career as a pupil teacher and then trained at St Paul's College, Cheltenham; he had taken a London degree by part-time evening work, and at the time of his translation to King's was head of a London board school. His students soon constituted a major part of the College's arts faculty, and his part in this was recognized by his appointment as lecturer in education in 1901, and professor in 1903. Together with the initial training of students Adamson encouraged the academic study of education, and he was largely responsible for the introduction in 1915 of an M.A. degree in this subject. The number of candidates working for this qualification increased year by year.

Besides developing the Department of Education at King's, Adamson soon established himself as a writer on his subject. He edited a handbook of method, entitled *The Practice of Instruction*, which appeared in 1907, but his special interest in educational history had been manifested in his *Pioneers of Modern Education, 1600–1700*, which Cambridge University Press published in 1905. This dealt not only with the educational theories of such thinkers as Bacon and Comenius, Hartlib and Petty, but also with the schoolroom practice of the period, as mirrored in the writings of John Dury, Hoole and Brinsley. J.-B. de la Salle and A.H. Franke were also introduced to English readers. This book was followed, in 1912, by an annotated selection from the educational writings of Locke which formed one of a series of 'Educational Classics' edited by Adamson himself, and including volumes on Froebel by S.S.F. Fletcher, on Rousseau by R.L. Archer, on Pestalozzi by J.A. Green, and on Vives by Foster Watson – a massive contribution to educational history. In 1919 the whole subject was pulled together in Adamson's own *Short History of Education*. In spite of its title, the book – as the preface makes clear – 'treats primarily of English education and its agencies', but due attention is given to those foreign tendencies, ideas and activities which affected it. A number of treatises of this general type have been published as the academic study of education has developed, but Adamson's book remains a classic.

Although Adamson was based at King's College, London, his eminence as an educational historian was soon recognized outside his own university. He was associated particularly with the University of Cambridge where as we have seen, the study of educational history had already been developed by Quick and Oscar Browning. For many years he acted as examiner for the Education Syndicate and he used to visit Cambridge regularly in order to lecture on the history of education. He also acted as an adviser to Cambridge University Press. He was the author of the chapters dealing with education in the Cambridge *History of English Literature* (1907). The valuable bibliographies which these volumes contain are supplemented in the Cambridge *Bibliography of English Literature* (1940) to which Adamson contributed comprehensive booklists. He thus furnished an invaluable conspectus of educational works from the Middle Ages to the eve of the 1902 Act. The result is a piece of technical apparatus of great value to those who are working in the field which Adamson made so conspicuously his own and which first acquired for the Education Department at King's College, London, that reputation for research in educational history which has been so worthily carried on by his successors.

There is no space to list all of Adamson's minor contributions, but after his retirement from his Chair in 1924 he was free to devote himself solely to scholarship and the result was his *magnum opus* – *English Education, 1789–1902* – which was published in 1930 and reissued in

1965. It is a standard work and will remain a landmark in the literature of educational history. Charles Birchenough had published in 1914 his *History of Elementary Education in England and Wales from 1800*, Frank Smith's *English Elementary Education, 1760–1902* dates from 1931, and R.L. Archer's *Secondary Education in the Nineteenth Century* appeared in 1921. But Adamson draws all these threads together and his work is based on a wide and thorough knowledge of the original authorities.

It is noticeable that during the period when Adamson was adviser to the Cambridge University Press (that is, during approximately the first two decades of this century) there issued from it a number of important books dealing with various aspects of educational history in this and other European countries. To this period and to this publishing house we owe not only editions of Comenius, Milton and Locke, but also W.H. Woodward, *Vittorino da Feltre* (1897), *Erasmus* (1904) and *Education during the Age of the Renaissance* (1906), J.E.G. de Montmorency, *State of Intervention in English Education* (1902), S.S. Laurie, *Educational Opinion from the Renaissance* (1905), J.W. Adamson, *Pioneers of Modern Education 1600–1700* (1905) and *A Short History of Education* (1919), Foster Watson, *English Grammar Schools to 1660* (1908), *Vives on Education* (1913) and *The Old Grammar Schools* (1916), Geraldine Hodgson, *Studies in French Education* (1908), A.F. Leach, *Educational Charters* (1911), R.S. Rait, *Life in the Medieval University* (1912), H.C. Barnard, *The Little Schools of Port-Royal* (1913), *The Port-Royalists on Education* (1918) and *The French Tradition in Education* (1922), Irene Parker, *Dissenting Academies* (1914), and R.L. Archer, *Secondary Education in the Nineteenth Century* (1921) – all in a little over twenty years. This important accession to the literature of educational history was in large measure due to the inspiration, advice and encouragement of Adamson himself.

In the list just given there are two names which have a particular significance in the historiography of education – those of A.F. Leach and Foster Watson. Leach was a historian of the antiquarian type whose particular interest was the early history of the older English schools. He was above all things a researcher concerned with documents and records. After a distinguished career at Oxford he became a Charity Commissioner and this gave him exceptional opportunities of access to the material with which he was concerned. He contributed articles on the history of individual schools to many volumes of the *Victoria County History of England* and was a sub-editor of Monroe's American *Cyclopedia of Education*. Apart from histories

120

of such institutions as Winchester College (1899) and Warwick School (1906), he wrote a large number of articles published in various antiquarian and educational journals; but more comprehensive studies are his *English Schools at the Reformation* (1894) and *The Schools of Medieval England* (1915). The latter contains a complete bibliography of Leach's books and articles, and this illustrates the wide range of his researches into the history of English education. One of his chief contributions to the subject was his collection of *Educational Charters and Documents, 598 to 1909*, published in 1911, which is a source-book of the first importance to the student. A useful supplement to this is J.S. Maclure's *Educational Documents, England and Wales, 1816–1963*, which appeared in 1965.

There is no doubt about the importance of Leach's work. Its meticulous research into the history of education is on a level with the similar research which is carried out in other branches of history. At the same time some of Leach's conclusions and his interpretations of his researches have been called in question, and he is said to have been hasty in forming his opinions. The matter has been fully and competently discussed by Joan Simon in articles contributed to the *British Journal of Educational Studies*.[13] *The Centenary History of King's College, London* says that Adamson followed in the steps of A.F. Leach, but that is far from being the case. Leach was a historian of the antiquarian type who was interested in educational institutions. Adamson doubtless made good use of his work but, though a scholarly historian if ever there was one, he was primarily an educationist. He was much more in the Cambridge tradition, and that, as we have seen, was influenced by German pioneers. However, it remains true that the monographs on the history of individual schools which form the subject of so many theses and articles nowadays owe a good deal to the example of Leach and they are doing much to co-ordinate and extend our knowledge of English educational history.

Foster Watson, like Adamson and unlike Leach, was fundamentally an educationist, and his contributions to educational history over a wide range are outstanding. He graduated in English at Owens College, Manchester, and afterwards took an M.A. degree at London. After some experience in a preparatory school he was appointed vice-master of the Central Foundation School in London, but he also became associated with the neighbouring Finsbury Training College. This had been opened in 1883 as an institution for the professional training of secondary teachers, but the experiment proved unsuccessful and the college had to be closed in 1886. Foster Watson, however, ceased not in the Convocation of London University and elsewhere to advocate the equality of education with other academic disciplines and to urge the establishment of higher degrees in this subject. In 1894 he was appointed head of the training department at University College, Aberystwyth, a constituent college of the University of Wales; and this gave him an opportunity to put some of his ideas into practice. The department rapidly developed under his guidance and not only turned out yearly 'a large body of well-equipped teachers who cannot fail to benefit popular education',[14] but also afforded him scope to develop and encourage the study of educational history which henceforth became one of his main interests. In 1909 he published *The Beginnings of the Teaching of Modern Subjects in England*, a book remarkable – like all of Foster Watson's writings – for the wide range of background knowledge which it displays, and the innumerable suggestive side-issues which the student may be encouraged to follow up. But the main issue is never lost sight of and the book remains a standard work. It is very much to be regretted that it is now out of print and that attempts to get it reissued have so far proved abortive.

Foster Watson had a particular interest in the work of the Spanish Renaissance educationist Vives. This is shown in his *Tudor School-Boy Life: The dialogues of Juan Luis Vives*, which were translated into English for the first time in 1908. It was followed in 1912 by *Vives and the Renaissance Education of Women*, and in 1913 by a translation of *De Tradendis Disciplinis*, published by Cambridge University Press under the title *Vives on Education*. But Foster Watson's interest in educational history was by no means confined to this subject. He was the author of innumerable articles dealing with English and other European educationists, and his *The English Grammar Schools to 1660*, published in 1908, forms a valuable and balanced supplement to the work of A.F. Leach in the same field. W.A. Vincent, *The Grammar Schools, 1660–1714* (London, 1969), carries on this work. Foster Watson also contributed a large number of historical articles to Monroe's *Cyclopedia*, and he edited an *Encyclopaedia and Dictionary of Education* (1921–2) in four volumes. This may be regarded as the English equivalent of Buisson's *Dictionnaire de Pédagogie* or Monroe's American work. It forms a comprehensive guide not only on topics connected with educational history, but also with principles, practice and administration, and with comparative education. This valuable compendium has quite recently been reprinted by the Sale Research Company of Detroit.

The foundations of the study of educational history in England were laid by such scholars as Quick, Joseph Payne, Leach, Adamson and Foster Watson. Perhaps to their names we can add that of Sir John

122

Adams whose *Evolution of Educational Theory* was published in 1909. As a history of educational ideas and as a contribution to the development of educational philosophy the book is unsurpassed. The work of these pioneers has been carried forward in more recent years by a large number of specialists. In practically every case they are, or have been, connected with a university Department of Education where, in addition to their literary work, they have been able to apply the study of educational history in the postgraduate training course for intending teachers, and also to encourage and supervise research in the subject for higher degrees.

An attempt, no easy one, must now be made to list some of the works on educational history which we owe to these authors. For a general history we may turn to Helen Wodehouse's *A Survey of the History of Education* (1924), which, although rather slight, is full of interest. A more compendious treatment is that of William Boyd whose *The History of Western Education* was first published in 1921. It has been most competently revised by E.J. King (1965) who has added two chapters in order to bring it up to date. It covers the whole story from Greek education down to the twentieth century and it may be regarded as the modern standard work. Another useful general treatise is S.J. Curtis and M.E.A. Boultwood, *A Short History of Educational Ideas* (1953) which describes the development of educational theory from the earliest times.

Apart from these histories which cover the whole field there is a large number of works dealing with special subjects or special periods or special areas. For example, Greek and Roman education is treated in H.I. Marrou, *History of Education in Antiquity* (1956) and in Werner Jaeger's *Paideia*, three volumes (1933) – the former translated from the French and the latter from the German. A shorter but very stimulating account is given in the paperback *Ancient Education and Today* (1961) by E.B. Castle. To these we should add K.J. Freeman, *Schools of Hellas* (1922), a charming piece of work, and also T. Haarhoff, *Schools of Gaul* (1920) which carries the education of classical times over into the Christian era.

An outstanding contribution to educational history during the Middle Ages is Mother F.R. Drane, *Christian Schools and Scholars* (1867 and 1924), and for the earlier part of this period we have Geraldine Hodgson, *Early Christian Education* (1906). A.W. Parry, *Education in the Middle Ages* (1920) is confined to England and owes a good deal to Foster Watson. The educational work of the Roman Church and of its teaching Orders in many parts of the world is a subject which has hardly received the attention which it deserves, and we still await a comprehensive treatise on this subject. However, the Ursulines are dealt with in Gaëtan Bernoville, *Sainte Angèle Merici: Les Ursulines de France et de l'Union Romaine* (1947), and there are many published biographies of the founders or foundresses of individual teaching orders. The Jesuits, not unnaturally, have received some particular attention. The standard history is J. Crétineau-Joly, *Histoire de la Compagnie de Jésus*, six volumes (1845–6), which contains a good deal of information about the educational work of the Society in many countries. A more specialized account is R. Schwickerath, *Jesuit Education: Its history and principles* (1903). The work of J.-B. de la Salle and his Institute of the Christian Schools is fully treated in the numerous works on this subject which we owe to W.J. Battersby. Perhaps the best account of the subject as a whole is to be found in M. O'Leary, *Education with a Tradition* (1936). It deals primarily with the work of the Order of the Sacred Heart, but the introductory chapters treat of the general history of conventual education. As far as England is concerned there is some historical material in H.O. Evennett, *The Catholic Schools of England and Wales* (1944), and reference may also be made to A.C.F. Beales, *Education under Penalty* (1963), and to the contributions by Beales, Battersby and Evennett to *The English Catholics, 1850–1950* (1950).

The educational work of other religious bodies and societies has been investigated and recorded in such works as W.A.C. Stewart, *Quakers and Education* (1953), F.C. Pritchard, *Methodist Secondary Education* (1949), and M.G. Jones, *The Charity School Movement* (1938). The development of the National Society is described in H.J. Burgess, *Enterprise in Education* (1958), and that of the British and Foreign School Society in H.B. Binns, *A Century of Education* (1908). M. Cruickshank, *Church and State in English Education* deals with the working of the dual system since 1870; while E.G. West's *Education and the State* is a very critical survey of this compromise in educational administration.

For a general history of British education from the earliest times to the present one naturally turns to S.J. Curtis, *History of Education in Great Britain*, which was published in 1948 and has since been revised and enlarged. It covers a wide range, dealing with education not only in England and Wales but also in Scotland and gives special attention to the development of adult and technical education and education in the Armed Forces. For a special study of the educational history of Scotland we can refer to M. Mackintosh, *Education in Scotland, Yesterday and Today* (1962). Another interesting treatment of the development of education in England more especially is T.L. Jarman,

Landmarks in the History of Education (1951). It discusses the subject from its origins in Greece and Rome and treats English education as part of the European tradition.

There exists a large number of works which deal with special periods of English education and to which reference has not already been made. The following should certainly be included: J. Lawson, *Medieval Education and the Reformation* (1967); K. Charlton, *Education in Renaissance England* (1965); N. Wood, *The Reformation and English Schools* (1931); G.H. Turnbull, *Hartlib, Dury and Comenius* (1947); W.H.G. Armytage, *Four Hundred Years of English Education* (1964); Nicholas Hans, *New Trends in Education in the Eighteenth Century* (1951); A.E. Dobbs, *Education and Social Movements, 1700–1850* (1919); Brian Simon, *History of Education 1780–1870* (1960) which deals with England only and is particularly concerned with efforts to extend popular education; A.D.C. Peterson, *A Hundred Years of Education* (1952); J. Graves, *Policy and Progress in Secondary Education, 1902–1942* (1943); H.C. Dent, *Change in English Education* (1952); H.C. Barnard, *A History of English Education from 1760* (1947, 1961); G.A.N. Lowndes, *The Silent Social Revolution* (1937).

Innumerable biographies of individual educationists have also been written and once again it is not easy to discriminate among them. Rousseau, Pestalozzi and Froebel have been fully exploited by writers in European countries and in America. Special reference may perhaps be made to W. Boyd's book on Rousseau (1911) and J. Russell's translation of De Guimp's *Life of Pestalozzi* (1890). As far as England is concerned we may note chapter 8 in G.D.H. Cole, *Robert Owen* (1925); Frank Smith, *The Life and Work of Sir James Kay-Shuttleworth* (1923) and B.M. Allen, *Sir Robert Morant* (1914). Collective volumes of this type are A.V. Judges (ed.), *Pioneers of English Education* (1952), and H.M. Pollard, *Pioneers of Popular Education* (1956). The former deals with English educationists from Robert Owen to modern times and contains noteworthy contributions on J.H. Newman (by A.C.F. Beales) and on Herbert Spencer (by J.A. Lauwerys); the latter is concerned with the second part of the eighteenth century and the early part of the nineteenth, not only in Great Britain but also on the Continent. A special study of Newman is that by F. McGrath, S.J., entitled *Newman's University* (1950). The many editions of Spencer, *Education, Intellectual, Moral and Physical* are usually provided with an introduction containing some historical material. As a corrective to this writer we may consult C. Bibby, *T.H. Huxley* (1959).

J. Fitch, *Thomas and Matthew Arnold* (1897) deals with the

125

life and work of two outstanding English educationists of modern times. The achievement of the former as a headmaster is the theme more particularly of J.J. Findlay's *Arnold of Rugby* (1897). Other studies of individual headmasters include G.R. Parkin, *Life and Letters of Edward Thring* (1898) and F.D. How, *Six Great Schoolmasters* (1904) – Hawtrey of Eton, Moberly of Winchester, Kennedy of Shrewsbury, Vaughan of Harrow, Temple of Rugby and Bradley of Marlborough – all in the public school tradition. H.G. Wells wrote *The Story of a Great Schoolmaster* (1924), which is an account of the work of Sanderson of Oundle. The reforms of some other heads who experimented in 'progressive' schools are dealt with in W.A.C. Stewart, *The Educational Innovators*, two volumes (1967–8). Nor must we overlook the great headmistresses – for example, E. Raikes, *Dorothea Beale of Cheltenham* (1908) and A.R. Ridley, *Frances Mary Buss* (1895).

Educational history deals not only with the work of famous teachers or theorists but also with the development and achievements of institutions. As far as universities are concerned the fundamental and monumental work is Hastings Rashdall, *The Medieval Universities*, three volumes. This book, originally published in 1895, was edited by F.M. Powicke and A.B. Emden and reissued in 1936. N. Schachner, *The Medieval Universities* (1938) in one volume suffers by comparison with Rashdall's work. To these we may add Anthony à Wood, *History and Antiquities of the Colleges and Halls of the University of Oxford*, edited by J. Gutch and published in 1786, and also C. Wordsworth, *Social Life at the English Universities in the Eighteenth Century* (1874). C.E. Mallett, *History of the University of Oxford*, three volumes (1924–7) is a classic, and J. Bass Mullinger, *A History of the University of Cambridge*, three volumes (1873–84), with a shorter version in one volume published in 1888, performs a similar service in the sister university. W.H.G. Armytage, *Civic Universities* (1955), covers a wider field than its title would suggest. It goes back to the earliest times and refers to Oxford and Cambridge as well as to more modern foundations. Like all of Armytage's works it draws on a wide background knowledge which illuminates the subject matter and delights the reader. In this respect this author resembles Foster Watson. Histories of individual colleges at Oxford and Cambridge and of other universities and also of many schools are numerous, but a fairly complete list of the volumes available will be found in Adamson's Cambridge *Bibliography of English Literature* lists – see vol. 2, pp. 368–74, vol. 3, pp. 115–18, and vol. 4, pp. 121–34. The ancestor of all school histories is of course N. Carlisle, *A Concise Description of the Endowed*

Grammar Schools in England and Wales, two volumes (1818) – a fascinating work.

The history of teacher-training is dealt with in the first chapter of Lance Jones, *The Training of Teachers* (1924) and in R.W. Rich, *The Training of Teachers in England and Wales during the Nineteenth Century* (1933). G. Ögren, *Trends in English Teachers' Training from 1800* (1953), written by a Swedish author and published in Stockholm, is largely a compilation from English sources. A. Tropp, *The School Teachers* (1957), gives some attention to the growth of the National Union of Teachers.

M.E. Sadler, *Continuation Schools in England and Elsewhere* (1908), includes 'a historical review of certain agencies for further education in England'. Adult education is more specifically dealt with in J.F.C. Harrison, *Living and Learning, 1790–1960* (1961), which gives an account of the development of this activity in England. A fuller treatment is that of T. Kelly, *A History of Adult Education in Great Britain* (1962). M. Stocks, *The Workers' Educational Association: The first fifty years* (1953) and I. Jenkins, *History of the Women's Institute Movement* (1953) are also contributions to this subject. S.F. Cotgrove, *Technical Education and Social Change* (1958), gives a fair amount of attention to history and one can also consult the introductory chapter of P.F.R. Venables, *Technical Education* (1955).

The history of the education of women and girls has given rise to a considerable literature. The following may perhaps be listed: D. Gardiner, *English Girlhood at School* (1929), which carries the story through from Saxon times, A.C. Percival, *The English Miss*, which was published in 1939 and covers the previous hundred years, A. Zimmern, *Renaissance of Girls' Education in England* (1938), J. Kamm, *Hope Deferred* (1965). A.M.A.H. Rogers, *Degrees by Degrees* (1938) and Vera Brittain, *The Women at Oxford* (1960) describe the progress of the attempts made to admit women to university degrees.

In addition to the ever-increasing number of books dealing with educational history there are of course other sources. Journals and publications of societies are often of great assistance, *Paedagogica Historica*, published twice annually in Ghent, with an international editorial board at the Centre for the Study of the History of Education, is devoted – as the name indicates – solely to historical articles. *The History of Education Quarterly*, which is issued in co-operation with the School of Education of New York University, is the official organ of the American History of Education Society. *The Review of Educational Research*, published by the American Educational

Research Association, although by no means confined to historical topics, often contains valuable studies in this field. The same may be said of *Paedagogica Europaea*, 'published with the support of the Council of Europe', and also of *I Problemi della Pedagogia* from Rome. In England there are the *British Journal of Educational Studies* which specializes to some extent on educational history and also from time to time includes useful bibliographical articles, and the *Journal of Educational Administration and History* twice a year from the University of Leeds; the recently formed History of Education Society issues a bulletin (the editor of which is M. Seaborne of Leicester University).

The Library Association's *Sources for the History of Education* (1967) and its supplements, compiled by C.W.J. Higson, list books relating to this subject which have been published between the fifteenth century and 1870. Most of the volumes also mentioned in this monograph are of course provided with bibliographies. In passing, too, it should be noted that a good many treatises concerned primarily with comparative education contain historical material. Good examples are I.L. Kandel, *Comparative Education* (1933), N. Hans, *Comparative Education* (1949), and special studies like N. Hans, *The Russian Tradition in Education* (1963) or V. Mallinson, *Power and Politics in Belgian Education, 1815–1961* (1963).

Another source of information is that afforded by the year-books issued by London University Institute of Education and by Teachers College, Columbia. The former, entitled *The Year Book of Education*, is edited by G. Bereday and J.A. Lauwerys and its volumes cover a wide range of topics among which the history of education holds an important place. The latter is the *Educational Yearbook of the International Institute of Teachers Colleges*, Columbia; it has appeared annually since 1924 and is edited by I.L. Kandel. It also contains historical articles. Official reports, again, sometimes are provided with a historical introduction. For example, the *Schools Inquiry Commission Report* of 1868 contains some historical details concerning endowed schools in all parts of the country. Matthew Arnold's *Reports on Elementary Schools* (edited by F.S. Marvin, 1908) gives a vivid picture of primary education between the years 1852 and 1882. Some of the Board of Education's *Special Reports on Educational Subjects*, issued under the aegis of M.E. Sadler between 1896 and 1903, contain historical material. The reports of the Consultative Committee and special commissions in more modern times are particularly useful. The Hadow report, *The Education of the Adolescent* (1926) has an account of the development of full-time post-primary education in England and

Wales from 1800 to 1918; while the Spens Report, *Secondary Education (Grammar Schools and Technical High Schools)* (1938), contains a 'sketch of the development of the traditional curriculum in secondary schools of different types in England and Wales'. We owe these two valuable articles to the secretary of the Consultative Committee, R. Fitzgibbon Young who also, incidentally, was the author of a very interesting *Comenius in England* (1932). The Fleming *Report on the Public Schools* (1942) has two preliminary chapters which give an historical account of these institutions from the earliest times to the present day, and there is a valuable appendix on the meaning of the term 'public school'. The report of the Robbins Committee, *Higher Education* (1963), devotes some attention to the historical aspects of its terms of reference.

An important contribution towards the extension and deepening of our knowledge of educational history is being made by candidates for higher degrees. The value of some of their theses may perhaps be questioned, but they do involve real research and something more than the broadcasting of a questionnaire and adding up the results. Information as to these theses may be found in the lists compiled by Mrs A.M. Blackwell and published by the National Foundation for Educational Research, London. The five volumes available cover the years 1918–48, 1949–51, 1952–3, 1954–5 and 1956–7. Unfortunately, since Mrs Blackwell's death in 1963, this most valuable service has not been carried on, but it is very much to be desired that the work should be brought up to date. *Sources for the History of Education*, edited by C.W.J. Higson and published by the Library Association of London (1967), gives a useful, though rather limited bibliography relating not only to works dealing with educational history but also to children's books and government publications. There seems to be no lack of suitable topics for further research in educational history, and even yet there remain some subjects which would give ample scope for further investigation and record – for example, the educational work of the London city companies.

During the present century there has been a great development of the academic study of education, and one evidence of this has been an outpouring of works devoted to various aspects of the subject – psychology, sociology, administration, method, even economics. But in no respect has the interest been greater than in the field of educational history; and this has been particularly marked in the case of Britain and the United States. What has been said in this article may perhaps serve to show in some measure the extent and variety of the contribution which has already been made.

NOTES

1. For Adamson, see No. 3 in this volume. For Simon, see J.W. Tibble (ed.), *The Study of Education* (London, 1966), pp.91–132, and No.5 in this volume.
2. Ibid., p.104. See No.5 in this volume.
3. New York, 1912, vol.3, pp.293–7.
4. Vol.3.
5. It should be mentioned that the present writer is in no way related to him.
6. 'The Barnard Legacy', *School and Society*, vol.89, no.2199 (1961), p.394. W.S. Monroe's comment is from P. Monroe, op. cit., vol.3, p.564.
7. Vol.1, p.324.
8. See p.245.
9. *Essays on Educational Reformers* (1890 ed.), pp.x-xi.
10. F. Storr (ed.), *Life and Remains of the Rev. R.H. Quick* (London, 1899).
11. G.E. Lance Jones, *The Training of Teachers* (London, 1924), pp.140–1.
12. Ibid.
13. Vol.3, no.2 (1955), pp.128–43; vol.4, no.1 (1955), pp.32–48; vol.12, no.1 (1963), pp.41–50.
14. Quoted in W.H.E. Armytage, 'Foster Watson: 1880–1929', *British Journal of Educational Studies*, vol.10, no.1 (1981), p.9.

9

The Place of the History of Education in the Training of Teachers

A.C.F. BEALES

I

When the era of teacher-training colleges began in this country in 1840, the history of education was no part of the curriculum. For some time to come the stress was on the craftsmanship of class management and the pedagogy of basic school subjects. Despite the genius of Kay at Battersea, and despite the example of David Stow in his Glasgow Normal Seminary, the English training college had for long to be academically a secondary school for carrying its students beyond the elementary scholastic equipment with which they came to it. Even when Education had begun to be discussed among contemporary scholars as a discipline in its own right, alongside the venerable subjects of study classified originally by Aristotle, Alexander Bain could write as late as 1879, of history itself, that it was but 'an interesting form of literature', and that, in a crowded curriculum, 'when there is any doubt, we may settle the matter by leaving it out'.[1]

Only when the Victorian public ceased to regard its elementary school teachers as primarily craftsmen, as artisans with a veneer of culture, could the training of these teachers take on a new dimension, and their vocation be appreciated as that not only of teacher but of educator.

There is indeed a significant distinction between the two conceptions. Ever since the time of Socrates and Plato the business of education had been appreciated by philosophers and great pedagogues as a double process of instruction and of discovery. The development of a child, both physically and intellectually, was essentially *self*-development. It could be accelerated by treating him as an active, ever-curious little person. It could be retarded by handling him as a passive receptacle

131

for impressions coming to him didactically from outside. Ironically the actual tradition of the earlier grammar schools and the later charity and elementary schools reflects this latter view, with Locke as its seventeenth-century formulator and Owen and Herbart as its leading nineteenth-century impresarios. The pedagogical theory of the other view, the 'active' view of self-development, has long been available for study in the writings of Aquinas, Vives, Comenius, Rousseau, and Pestalozzi. But it was not to come into its own till the activity method of the late John Dewey (and then for not by any means the same philosophical reasons).

What produced the additional dimension in late Victorian educational practice, i.e. that the schoolmaster was (ought to be) an educator in the full sense as well as an instructor, was a flux of many influences but primarily the need to clarify the distinction between the two prevailing notions of elementary and further education, based at the time on differences more social than anything else. The raw material for studying this debate is embalmed in the volumes of the Cross Commission of 1888 and the Bryce Commission of 1895. The theorizing on it is a major reason today, still, why we study Spencer's *Essays on Education* (1861) and Matthew Arnold's *Culture and Anarchy* (1869). In the end, the present century dawned with a new kind of teacher-training, already by then a decade old: that of the graduate teacher. And this, perhaps more than any other single development, was *the* breakthrough in helping Education to become a subject of study mature enough for universities, and (therefore) on its mettle to prove that in both theory and practice it could be academically respectable.

II

Once enshrined in university chairs, and with modern scholarship in the 'pure' subjects to draw upon and adapt to professional ends, Education began to establish itself on a triple basis of theory: educational philosophy and principles, educational psychology, and the history of education from Plato onwards. It emerged as a subject in its own right, as centuries ago Canon Law had hived off from Theology and Civil Law from Rhetoric, in the medieval university.

There had of course already been pioneers asserting that the educational aspect of history at large was as worthy of study in depth as the political, ecclesiastical, constitutional, colonial and (latterly) economic aspects. In England perhaps the first scholarly works to demonstrate this were R. H. Quick's *Essays on Educational Reformers*

(1868) and Theodora Drane's *Christian Schools and Scholars* (1876). The subject was to find its first major historian in the United States in 1900, with Thomas Davidson's *History of Education*. The greatest (even today) of the English pioneers, John William Adamson of King's College London, published his first substantial work in 1902, though his *magnum opus* had to wait till after his retirement, in 1931.[2] The magnificent series of Cambridge monographs in the history of education – by W.H. Woodward, Foster Watson, J.W. Adamson and others – began almost with the century.

For a whole generation, from about 1910 till 1932, Education was a subject in the B.A. general degree course of London University. Its structure was the one already established – principles, psychology, history; and surviving examination papers reveal that the history syllabus, prescribed in sections to accommodate the preferences of students, covered the whole of Western educational history. But, insofar as there was no concomitant teaching practice, undergraduate Education remained academic, and as the four-year course developed (degree plus postgraduate professional training) its days became more clearly numbered.

Within the postgraduate one-year course the history of education has all along held an integral place, though latterly as essential background in syllabuses on the current English Educational System (with the general history of education, as such, taught as one of a number of options). To some extent, in America as well as in England and Scotland, it is today losing ground. For this there are several reasons.

One is the advent of a new 'discipline', formerly subsumed in the study of the history of education itself and of comparative education – the sociology of education. Its pedigree is from Herbert Spencer and Durkheim and Max Weber, by way of Mannheim. It is carving out a place for itself in college curricula at the expense of time formerly spent on other aspects of education, including the historical.

A second factor is the extent to which by no means all those lecturers in our colleges of education who are charged with the task of teaching the history of education are themselves graduates in history, whereof the implications are obvious and serious.

There are thirdly the experiments going on – already prior to the inquiries of the former Secretary for Education and Science (Mr. Short) and the forthcoming James Committee report – in curriculum reform within the colleges and the university departments of education. Many of these experiments will involve an overhaul not only of options available but of fundamental approach to the main foundation courses in the training. The traditional subject basis – philosophy, pyschology, history – may partly disappear, to be superseded by topic-centred study, topic-centred examinations, set in terms of interdisciplinary answers and essays. It will be for the coming generations of tutors and students to clarify by experience how (if at all) some of these very beguiling polysyllabic phantasies may be made to mean something tangible, at the far from advanced level and depth of study that is the most an initial course in teacher-training can ever hope in fact to be. Meanwhile, history will be among the time-honoured segments of global study that may find its frontiers increasingly overgrown and its relevance challenged.

One way and another, then, the subject is in some quarters on the defensive, and engaged in a rearguard action, just as in some parts of the Western world (notably Canada) it has on the contrary yet even to establish itself firmly and produce a rich historiography.

But above all, finally, is the notion that it is the business of the history of education to be relevant to the student in his daily and professional life; wherefore, if it is not so (for reasons of syllabus or lecture course or indifferent teaching) it should indeed be dropped from the curriculum of the colleges. This cult of relevance – a criterion now increasingly applied to all the subjects of study, and one reason why student participation is being demanded in the realms of even syllabus and examinations – is perhaps the most dangerous snare in higher education today.

We speak of 'the uses of the past'. Certainly the past is useful; and since the history of education is a part of history itself, the history of education can be useful. In the field of history at large, no monarch since Canute has been prompted to take a beach-chair and sit in it below high-water mark. No general, in the light of 1812 and 1941, is henceforth likely to march an infantry army towards Moscow. On the corresponding positive side, mankind has benefited richly from such humble occasions as when James Watt first looked at a boiling kettle, J.H. Fabre at bees and wasps, Alexander Fleming at cobwebs and pondweed. *Everything* has its uses.

And that is where the current relevance criterion becomes idle and jejune. For love and affection have their uses – but is that their proper essence and business? Convalescence after illness has its uses, in terms of grapes and books and *dolce far niente*: but these are merely by-products of what convalescence is properly about, as the dictionary at least well knows.

Contemporary relevance, as *the* criterion and motivation for study, is today's version of the utilitarian criterion that was already under attack and in retreat a century ago. Utilitarianism, as a philosophy in

134

Jeremy Bentham, and as a pedagogy in James and John Stuart Mill, was the result of the unprecedented industrial conditions of the early nineteenth century, just as our current relevance is the result of new and unprecedented technological and sociological conditions. Most certainly there was need for deliberate attention to the usefulness of subjects and studies, if the Victorians were not to be outstripped in fields of material prosperity by lesser, foreign breeds without the law. Most certainly the classical and traditional view, that learning (whether as joy or as drudgery) was for its own sake, needed to be challenged and re-appraised. But the battle that raged, with John Henry Newman and Matthew Arnold asserting the liberal conception of education, and the Mills and Spencer and Huxley asserting over against it the utilitarian conception, was fought lest in the end the baby be thrown out with the bath-water.

The past has its uses. Demonstrably. But that is not its primary business. Its primary business is to have been fully itself. Its responsibility to posterity has always been that of not leaving to them a *worse* world than it had itself inherited. And the result would accrue as a by-product of its efforts to make its own world as good as possible for its own time. All this is the eternal truth (formulated best by Newman) that the utilitarian (or today the relevance-to-life protagonist) may surely secure his useful ends but without any guarantee of ensuring anything else; the liberal, stressing learning as a good without strings attached, will also secure (as a by-product) the utilitarian's desires. The liberal approach to study, by going beyond the relevant approach, includes it.

Nevertheless the criterion of relevance to daily and professional life is in the ascendant today, and is perhaps the major challenge to college disciplines to justify their claim for study. How far this is the result of defects in the teaching, or of syllabuses too narrow and merely traditional (Acts of Parliament and Royal Commissions as against social changes and cultural trends), may defy generalization.

III

But fortunately the prevailing self-consciousness, about the history of education in particular, need be no more than a phase. For the urge to ask 'why' of the past is as old as man himself, and indeed is one of the characteristics that make him man; and the enchantment of a 'story' lies already at the heart of the earliest of man's heroic legends, in Homer to Hesiod. It is something ineradicable, a part of human nature, a dimension of awareness and understanding. The need for history does not have to be pleaded, but only to be demonstrated. Even *with* a historical grasp of today one may seem no more than merely antiquarian. But without a historical grasp there is academically no full grasp, for very little that is new is really new, and we need always to know why not.

No doubt there have been occasions when something radically new has come into the teaching of history: for example when Lord Acton said teach problems rather than periods; or when Leopold von Ranke, following John Lingard, set a standard of impartiality (not detached, but certainly non-partisan and objective) in writing of the great disputes in which men had both died and killed; or when J.R. Green argued that in history the national is but the local writ large; or when M.V.C. Jeffreys introduced the techniques of teaching by Lines of Development. But all these salutary innovations can also be found somewhere earlier. What historical discussion does is to rearrange emphases, and (later on) to reflect upon the rearrangement.

It is not the purpose of historical events and trends to be useful, but events and trends, having happened, may have their uses. Herbert Butterfield,[3] long ago conceiving history as 'the spirit of man brooding on man's past', and impressed no less by the unlikeness than by the likeness of present to past, was insistent that it is profoundly unhistorical to ask such a question as 'To whom should we be grateful for the emergence of modern religious tolerance?' For it is not the function of the historian to envisage the past as a preparation for the present, nor to pity sixteenth-century persecutors as having been (so to speak) born too early to appreciate the benefits of ecumenism. The proper question for this historian is 'Why did men persecute in the sixteenth century?' But, at the same time, we can learn from what they did, and should be wanton not to. The past and tradition have not only their (by-product) uses, but indeed a fundamental survival-value. This has been most cogently stressed by T.S. Eliot:

Tradition ... cannot be inherited, and if you want it you must obtain it by great effort. It involves, in the first place, the historical sense ... and the historical sense involves a perception, not only of the pastness of the past, but of its presence. ... a sense of the timeless as well as of the temporal, and of the timeless and of the temporal together. ... The mind of Europe is a mind which changes, and this change is *a development which abandons nothing* en route, *which does not superannuate.*[4]

That is why, as we said above, the educated person whose sense of history has been underdeveloped or allowed to atrophy is deficient in his understanding of anything in human affairs at all. This can be illustrated at will; from short-term problems on a local scale and from long-term problems on a world scale.

IV

There are discussions going on in England today, for example, to reorganize the local government of education. One current plan is to administer our national education under some sixty or so local authorities of one kind. The object? To secure greater efficiency, and evenness of administration, and consequent equality of opportunity for children, by reducing the present much larger number of LEAs. So far so good: and all very relevant.

But what of this multitude (150) of authorities existing today? Whence did they come, and (if they are to go) why did they come? The answer to this lies in the events of 1944 a generation ago, enshrined in the Education Act of that year and the White Paper that preceded it. There was to be a simple pattern of *two* sorts of LEA, the counties and the county boroughs, each responsible for *all* the public education within its boundary.

Had this been the beginning? No. The 1944 arrangements reformed those made a generation earlier still; and the answer to what these were lies in the Balfour Education Act of 1902. The object on that occasion had been to establish a simple pattern of *four* kinds of authority (totalling 318): counties, county boroughs, municipal boroughs, and urban districts, according (broadly) to population and historic importance. Of these, only *some* had responsibility for *all* the public education inside their boundaries; the others were enclaves of autonomy within them.

Nor had this been the beginning. For that, we have to go back still one more generation, to the Gladstone Education Act of 1870, the first to visualize English schooling as a national matter of universal importance. The arrangements here made took notice that the private and voluntary (religious) bodies alone in the field as yet were unable (from their limited financial resources) to provide a school place for every child entitled to one; and proceeded to 'fill the gaps' by allowing (but not ordering) locally-elected School Boards to come into existence (aided by local education rates specially levied). In due time there were over 3000 of these boards.

The trend from 1870 to 1970 is thus spectacular. With education as a national service locally administered, the map of local authorities has been successively reduced: from 3000 to 318, then to 150, and now maybe to 60. By stages the decentralization has become more and more streamlined, and the element of control from a centre more patent.

Why? The argument today is that, in deference to social mobility and educational egalitarianism, school administration needs more even material and financial arrangements and therefore larger areas. But these considerations have been operative throughout the whole century since the Gladstone Act. Why then did the original pattern, or that of 1902 or that of 1944, not have them in mind? The historical answer is that at each of those turning-points such considerations *were* prominently in mind: but they were not the dominant ones. Perhaps the best single source in which to find this current issue about LEAs thoroughly thought through is the debates of 1902.

There was a tension between *two* essential needs. One was for efficiency and equality of opportunity by an even distribution of resources. For this, to administer education through large local authorities was the obvious answer. The other need was to preserve (and foster) strong local interest in education – without which there would be no life in the business. For this, small authorities as in the past seemed the precedent best worth adapting.

The final decisions of 1902 were a compromise between the two allegiances: hence the complicated fourfold framework that resulted, full of anomalies as it proved by 1944 to have been. Hence too 1944 in turn was a compromise of a different kind, directed still to accommodating the same two paradoxical needs for national efficiency and live local interest. The 1944 Act reduced the number of independent LEAs but allowed each (should it see fit) to delegate certain powers to local divisional executives. But the 1970 suggestions cannot so readily be assessed as a means directed to that same dual end. They smack far more of increasing centralization as such.

Our point here, however, is not to argue that issue, but rather to use it as an illustration of how a full grasp of an educational problem needs the historical as well as all the other insights. Details change. Population structure and occupational structure change, and drive Acts of Parliament out of date. But the realities behind the details remain constant. They were thought of as such – efficiency versus local vitality – in 1870 and still more in 1902. The point is how far they are being kept in mind today. Anyone may assess that for himself: from the bent of the arguments about LEAs canvassed in the public press at the moment, and the degree to which the ruminations of our fathers and grandfathers upon it all are held sufficiently relevant to be recalled.

A like example comes in the present inquiries, all over the country, about overhauling the training of teachers. These inquiries result from an initiative by the late Secretary and the present Secretary, for Education and Science. Their focus is the James Committee, which is already in process of being inundated by evidence from all over the country, earnestly assembled in every college of education and university department of education in England and Wales.

There is no need to go into the details of these self-examinations and heart searchings. They centre on crucial issues such as the balance of the initial training course for teachers graduate and (not much longer) non-graduate; the relation of this training to higher degrees in Education; the in-service additional training of qualified teachers already in the schools; the pattern of school-teaching-practice during training (full-time or part-time? one block-practice or several? teacher-tutors in the practising schools?); and so on. What is germane here is not the details, but the extent to which the discussion – even on so permanent a question as the function of teaching, or the role of the teacher – is being done 'from scratch'. The large-scale ramifications of the past decade, following especially the revelations of the Robbins Report of 1963 on the 'pool of untapped ability', have changed the sheer size of the training problem out of all recognition. But nothing has happened that modifies the basic issues, on which the literature of the past is rich, and at hand to be drawn upon. No doubt the coming report will feature a historical chapter, as did the Fleming Report on the Public Schools in 1944. The classic example of such a historical chapter, bringing down to date all the threads of the past and drawing inferences for the future from within the *existing* social set-up, which was still taken for granted, is that in the Spens Report of 1938. Within less than a decade that social structure was to be challenged and altered *ex professo* by His Majesty's Government. The Spens Report was written for an England supposed to be still socially permanent. This was a shortcoming. Neglect of the historical aspect of a problem is the obverse of it: as if nothing was sure in the light of experience, and as if overhaul meant re-creation. 'It is impossible to gauge accurately the relevance of a previous idea or practice to our own day unless we understand both the present context and the original context in which the idea of practice arose.'[5]

These have been British and local examples of what can happen for *lack* of due attention to the past and its experience. One that affects the wellbeing of the entire globe is the difference between the United Nations Organization of today and the League of Nations that preceded it. Here there has been loss.

The League of Nations Covenant of 1918 was fully a twentieth-century document, the climax of two millenia of experiments in trying to get rid of war and to order the world. By virtue of the experiments, bits of international machinery had been forged and had long proved their worth: arbitrations, arbitration treaties, international law, an international tribunal. Under the Covenant these were all integrated into an organic machine of international order, in which each member-State was a legal person, and all were equal before the law and the World Court. The United Nations Charter of 1944 is by contrast an eighteenth-century document. It enshrines no such principle of equality – whereof the sign is the veto arrogated to the Great Power members of its Security Council. One may argue, and validly, that in a real world the peace will depend upon how man, however obligated, will in fact act if he has the power. But, in superseding the Covenant by the Charter, principle has given way to expediency; and this is a *loss*. Likewise in the contrast between the medieval guild, which had amongst its characteristics a built-in responsibility to the consumer and customer, and the modern trade union, which has not. Though the past has no duty to warn us, we do well to look to it for warnings and 'lessons'.

V

The place of the history of education becomes clearest, indeed, when one essays to grasp a great problem without it.

One may go on a tour of English-speaking countries, having in mind (say) the problem of State versus Church in education, focused on the matter of denominational (confessional) schools.[6]

In Scotland, for all its historic religiosity, there are today *no* confessional schools in the public sector. All are owned by, and their teachers paid by, the local authorities. But no parent is dismayed at this on religious grounds, because the Concordat of 1918 safeguarded every conscience through the procedure laid down for the actual appointment of teachers. In Ireland nearly *all* the schools are confessional, and the Protestant minority is content because, under the Constitution of 1936, the (Catholic) local authorities are obliged to treat all schools equally. In England and Wales the confessional schools of the Anglicans, Roman Catholics and Free Churchmen do not enjoy full financial equality with the schools of the LEAs; they receive grants up to 80%. In the United States there are no grants to confessional schools as such at all: the First Amendment to the Constitution of 1789 forbade any establishment of any religion. 'Not one red cent.' In Australia and New Zealand, likewise, there is no support from public funds at all for denominational schools; the twin schools systems, confessional and public, are parallel and separate.

Such a descriptive comparison gives data, and by its apparent chaos and inconsequence demands explanation. For with respect to one and the same matter in each country, namely the role of State and Church(es) in education, current practice ranges from no support for confessional schools whatever (U.S.A., Australia, N.Z.) to full support for the confessional principle (Scotland), with England and Ireland at seemingly arbitrary points between the two extremes.

Shrewd students will be prone at this point to look behind the contrary details laid bare by the comparative educationist, and seek from the philosopher and the theologian the general principles that govern *all* such problems. These principles are profound and timeless. They include such considerations as the ultimate responsibility (under God) of the parent for what happens to the child; the right of the citizen not to be discriminated against by being obliged to contribute financially to religious teaching that offends his conscience or by having to furnish at his own expense one that does; the rights in general of minorities, religious and racial, and so on.

But does a grasp of these principles explain how and why the absence of confessional schools in Scotland leaves nobody feeling aggrieved? Or why England, with an Established religion, does not support the schools of even that Establishment fully? Or why Australia and New Zealand, fashioned from British stock, have in fact adopted (in 'Not one red cent') a situation not British but American? Above all, how can Catholic principles explain how and why, though the situation of the few Protestant schools in Ireland is of a kind to evoke gratitude, that of the few Protestant schools in Spain amounts to discrimination up to the frontier of persecution?

The principles have a place in study, but they are not the only key, nor the decisive key. Descriptive comparison itself defies them. The full answer is multiple, and its solvent is the historical approach. Despite the principles, despite object-lessons from elsewhere, what obtains today in Spain is so because it is done by Spaniards, not Irishmen; and vice versa. The reason for the difference lies 'far back in the past, in the recesses of the mentality that the past has fashioned; the long centuries, since the Renaissance, of Irish Catholicism on the defensive, and introverted, Spanish Catholicism extraverted and crusading'. By the same token, the Anglo-Saxon stock in Australia and New Zealand opted in the 1870s for an 'American' separation of Church and State in education not because it was American but because, given the local difficulty they had to face, with no possibility of a form of religious instruction that would satisfy the rival denominations, they felt constrained to legislate for a secular public school system. By the same token again, the Scottish Concordat of 1918 (unique in the world) was achieved not so much by fidelity to solemn principles all round as because its three chief negotiators knew and trusted one another absolutely.

The answers to human problems, once past, are historical problems, each uniquely local, and each (despite all the abstract principles of the traditional disciplines) decidedly personal. Every event is unique; and history is expressly the study of that uniqeness. No student of human affairs can do without it: the education student most of all.

Moreover the basic problems are timeless, the best minds have been devoted to grasping them since man first began to think, and the resultant literature is unlikely, surely, to have left *nothing* yet fixed and firm, on which to climb and build. Certainly the first great writer on education as such, St. Augustine, saw it that way. To him the teacher was a *disciple*, a willing follower – of what was best in the past to date. Contrariwise, he who does not study the past is altogether at its mercy.

How the history of education is to fill its place in the training of teachers, is a very important but derivative matter. It has been suggested above that the auguries are best if (to start with) he who has to teach the subject in colleges is himself a trained historian.

What has been argued here is as to the place itself: that the historical approach is complementary to the philosophical and the psychological and the others; that together they form a whole; that history, like every other branch of learning, has no *use* as part of its essential *raison d'être*; but that it has uses, since all experience can be learned from; that we are therefore wayward and perverse to the extent we neglect to use and learn from it; and that in the final analysis there is no full understanding without it.

NOTES

1. *Education as a Science* (London, 1879), p.287.
2. *English Education 1789–1902* (reprinted (C.U.P.) 1965; and see 'The Historiography of Education', by H.C. Barnard, *Melbourne Studies in Education* 1970 (1971) printed as No. 5 in this volume. For the history of the subject see also Bernard Bailyn, *Education in the Forming of American Society* (North Carolina, U.P., 1961). A standard current exposition of the place of the history of education in academic study is that by Brian Simon in J.W. Tibble (ed.), *The Study of Education* (London, 1966), pp.92–131. See No.5 in this volume.
3. *The Whig Interpretation of History* (London, 1931).
4. Quoted in G.H. Bantock, *T.S. Eliot and Education* (London, 1970), p.46.
5. Paul Nash (ed.), *History and Education* (N.Y.: Random House, 1970), p.19.
6. I have examined this in detail in the book edited by Paul Nash (above), pp.256–82.

10

The History of Education

JOHN E. TALBOTT

Historians have begun to stake new claims in the history of education. Over the past decade a number of pioneering books and articles have appeared on subjects whose long neglect now seems quite remarkable – from the Spanish universities under the Habsburgs to childrearing practices in colonial America. Despite the great diversity of themes and problems with which these studies are concerned, they share a similarity of approach. Nearly all seek, to use Bernard Bailyn's phrase, 'to see education in its elaborate, intricate involvements with the rest of society'.[1] This approach has opened new perspectives in a field historians had long ignored.

Not that the history of education has been neglected. The bibliography in the field is enormous. But it is lopsided, mainly concerned with 'house history' and the ideas of pedagogical reformers. Countless histories of individual schools and universities have been published, describing aims, organization, faculty, curricula, finances, student life, and so forth; histories of pedagogical ideas have surveyed the views of leading theorists from Plato through Dewey. To be sure, great monuments of historical scholarship stand forth in the field; such studies as Hastings Rashdall's *The Universities of Europe in the Middle Ages* and Werner W. Jaeger's *Paideia* are not likely soon to be surpassed.

But to the contemporary historian much of the older literature seems inadequate – impressive in bulk but insubstantial, seldom addressed to the sorts of questions with which historical scholarship is now concerned. A good share of the institutional history has been the work of antiquaries and devoted alumni, who uncovered much valuable information but rarely sought to interpret it. With the professionalization of schoolteaching and the establishment of teachers' colleges educational history became nearly a separate

143

discipline, isolated from the mainstream of historical study. The educationists who founded and sustained these institutions sought to give prospective schoolteachers a historical sense of mission, certainly a not unworthy aim. But in the hands of some of them educational history became a weapon against adversaries living and dead, a vindication of their own ideas and efforts in the struggle for public schooling; in the hands of others it became a whiggish chronicle, a quick guided tour of the past in search of the antecedents of contemporary educational institutions.

If historians were frequently heard to lament the inadequacies of traditional approaches to the history of education, they were slow to do anything about them. Only after the Second World War, when educational issues began to loom larger in the public consciousness, did they turn in any numbers to the subject. The deepening crisis in education, charted in issues of the journal *Daedalus*, from the neutral-sounding 'The Contemporary University: U.S.A.' of 1964, to 'The Embattled University' of 1970, is likely to accelerate this trend.

Trends in the professional study of history also encouraged the new interest. Chief among these, perhaps, was what might be called an increasing concern for the interrelatedness of past experience, brought on by the pervasive influence of social history, the emphasis on interdisciplinary approaches to the past, and the collapse of the internal boundaries that once delineated 'areas' of historical study. Historians began to recognize that education touches upon nearly all aspects of a particular society. The historical study of education came to be seen not only as an end in itself but as a promising and hitherto neglected avenue of approach to an extremely broad range of problems.

New approaches to the history of education differ from the old primarily in the attention now being given to the interplay between education and society. But this is a very great difference indeed. What was once a narrow specialty is now seen to have such broad ramifications that it has become hopelessly ill-defined. For if the role of education in the historical process is to be understood, attention must be paid to the external influences that shape the educational arrangements a society has made; to the ways in which these external influences impinge upon each other at the same time they are acting upon education; and to the ways in which education itself influences the society. The social composition of an elite educational institution, for example, is the consequence of the interaction of economic factors, of patterns of social stratification, of the conscious political decisions of the estab-lished authorities, and so forth.

It is one thing, however, to recognize all the influences that need to be taken into account in the study of a particular problem in the history of education. It is quite another thing to determine the relative weight that is to be assigned each of them, especially over long periods of time. Research is at an early stage, and has not moved far beyond an enumeration of influences. In some important areas, such as the study of literacy in pre- and early industrial societies, the collection of raw data has scarcely begun; only recently have statistics long available in manuscript form been published and useful manuscript sources rescued from neglect.[2] In advanced industrial societies, where statistics on literacy abound, nearly the entire adult population is formally literate. But these figures conceal the functional illiteracy that is one of the consequences of technological change, and about which very little is now known. The questions that need to be asked in the new educational history are only beginning to be clarified. Conceptual models for dealing with these questions have yet to be devised; the methodological controversies that have enlivened more developed areas of study have yet to take place.

Thus the history of education is an area of study whose potentialities are only beginning to be exploited and the inchoate state in which it now exists is precisely what makes it attractive. So varied are the purposes now brought to the history of education, so patchy is the present state of knowledge, that the field does not lend itself to systematic treatment. Nevertheless, an idea of present concerns and problems can be conveyed by tugging at a few strands in the network of relationships that bind education to society.

I

Conventional histories of education are filled with generalizations about relationships between education and social structure. It has been a common practice, for example, to attach a class label to an educational institution, which is then held to respond to the 'needs' or 'demands' of a particular social class. Who determines these needs, or whether, if such needs exist, the institution in fact responds to them, is left unclear. Moreover, such static descriptive statements, based on implicit assumptions about how the class system works, explain very little about the dynamics of the interaction between education and the structure of society. Nor do they allow for the possibility that cultural values and styles of education once presumably moored to a particular social class may drift loose from that class and become the common property of an entire society – in which case they are not particularly amenable to class analysis except in its crudest forms. It is hard to see how describing an

145

American university education as 'middle class' explains very much about either the American university or American society. To be sure, education and social class have been, and continue to be, intimately connected. But the complexity of the historical connections between them has only begun to receive the carefully nuanced analysis it requires.[3] One would expect to find a large number of aristocrats' sons in an institution labeled 'aristocratic'. But one would also find some people who were not the sons of aristocrats. Who were they? Furthermore, one might also find aristocrats' sons in fairly large numbers in institutions not traditionally associated with the aristocracy. What were they doing there? Detailed research has only recently begun on who actually received the education a particular society has offered, how this has changed, and what the causes and consequences of change have been.[4]

With more attention being paid to who actually got educated, historians are now beginning to see that relationships between education and social structure have often been different from what the providers of education intended. It is roughly true that, until very recently, the structure of education in most European countries had the effect of reinforcing class distinctions and reducing the flow of social mobility – and was often intentionally designed to do so. Different social classes received different kinds of education in different schools; the upper levels of education were the preserve of the upper classes, a means of maintaining their children in established social positions and of bolstering their own political and social authority. But attempts to make patterns of education conform to the pattern of society have often been frustrated, both by forces the established authorities have been unable to control and by changes in other sectors of society which they have promoted themselves. One example of the latter is an expansion of job opportunities. Lawrence Stone has shown that in early modern England, economic growth and the proliferation of the bureaucracy of the state triggered an educational expansion: 'So great was the boom ... that all classes above a certain level took their part,'...[5] – a consequence not entirely welcome to the ruling class of a highly stratified society. Other forces, of which demographic change is one, need to be identified and assessed.[6]

Patterns of social stratification affect the structure of education. But educational arrangements also turn back upon the structure of society and exert their own influences upon it: the relationship between education and social stratification is a two-way street. This process can be seen at work in the history of European secondary education. Elitist patterns that took shape during the sixteenth and seventeenth

146

centuries, when the hereditary ruling classes sent their sons to secondary schools in increasing numbers, persisted well into modern times. Recent studies of the English public school have addressed themselves to some of the consequences of this persistence. Among the most important and far-reaching of these consequences was the preservation of the values and attitudes – and therefore the social ascendancy – of the aristocracy, in a fully industrialized and formally democratic society.[7]

Research into who actually got educated will lend a good deal more precision to statements about the historical role of education in the promotion of social mobility and in the maintenance of established social positions. Until recently, these have possessed all the rigor of the notorious generalizations about the rising middle classes. Such research should shed light on changes and continuities in the recruitment of elites, matters of particular concern to social and political historians. What has been the role of education in this process, in the long movement away from a society in which status was based on birth to a society in which status is increasingly based on achievement? What have been the social and political consequences of the paradoxical principle of the career open to talent, which holds that everyone should have an equal chance to become unequal? To what extent were traditional elites able to adjust themselves to the pressures for merito-cratic standards of recruitment which emerged from the economic and political revolutions of the eighteenth century? To what extent did the implementation of such standards truly open the way for new men? For the upper levels of education, which prepared their clientele for elite positions, abundant evidence is available on the social origins of students over long periods of time. University matriculation registers, for example, are waiting to be tapped.

But it is not enough simply to describe with greater precision the role of education in the promotion of social mobility (or in the maintenance of established social positions). It also needs to be asked what the consequences of this form of mobility have been, what it has meant to the individuals who experienced it and the societies in which they lived. Such qualitative questions may be exceedingly difficult to answer.

The education of the lower classes presents the historian with equally difficult problems. What influences have primary schools exerted on the values and attitudes of their clientele? Recent studies of elite institutions offer persuasive evidence of the ways in which education acts upon social structure through the medium of values and attitudes. But for lower levels of education, the kinds of literary evidence that permit one to generalize about the gentlemanly life-style of the public school, or the bourgeois ethos of the lycée, rarely exist. So far,

147

historical studies of the impact of popular education on values and attitudes have been mainly concerned with such public issues as the promotion of nationalism and nation building – as in the case of the Third French Republic, whose founders quite consciously undertook a sweeping reform and extension of a state-supported system of primary education in order to provide a new regime with republicans. Comparatively little is known about the role of the school in shaping attitudes toward more ostensibly private matters, such as sex, or toward such divisive questions as social class. Analysis of the content of textbooks would at least suggest what attitudes the authorities sought to inculcate, though the degree to which they succeeded is quite another question.[8]

Attention to the social consequences that educational arrangements have produced, apart from what their designers intended, should help put to rest the largely speculative leaps of the kind which assume an exact correspondence between the structure of a society and the structure of its education. Indeed, given the extraordinarily high incidence of anachronistic features that educational arrangements exhibit (such as the persistence of classical studies in the West), it is hard to see how such a direct correspondence could ever have been drawn. Instead, historical relationships between education and social structure, as one sociologist has perceptively remarked, 'are various, involve structural discontinuities and are singularly lacking in symmetry'.[9]

Nevertheless, the sons of the rich are usually better educated (or spend more time in school) than the sons of the poor. As soon as education began to confer social, economic, or political benefits, the question of who should be educated became a source of bitter controversy. Some of the involvements of education in politics have received considerable attention: the intervention of the state in the provision of popular education has been one traditional area of concern. State intervention followed on centuries of debate about the wisdom of providing widespread education; seldom has a question been agonized over so long and settled so swiftly. The arguments for and against popular education, the activities of certain reform groups, the legislative aspects of reform, the church–state struggle, have all been treated in a number of studies. These questions fall within the traditional preoccupations of political history. But a vast amount of territory remains to be explored, and older interpretations need to be reexamined.

Older studies, for example, regarded the extension of popular education as an aspect of the process of democratization, a necessary consequence of the implications of liberal political philosophy. More recent work has held that the decisive motive in the drive for public schooling was social control of the lower classes in an industrializing and urbanizing society.[10]

But both interpretations are mainly concerned with the attitudes of the upper-class proponents of widespread schooling; they stress the intentions of the reformers, not the consequences of the reforms. Very little is known about the attitudes toward education of the people whom the upper classes quarreled over. Popular education needs to be studied 'from below', and several works have opened the way. E.P. Thompson, for example, has shown how an eagerness for learning and an enthusiasm for the printed word were important elements in the radical culture of the English working class.[11] Inquiry is now moving beyond the confines of the politically-conscious elements of that class. What were the attitudes toward education of the unskilled and illiterate laborers who poured into the factories with their wives and children in the early stages of industrialization? Literary evidence is likely to yield very few answers; such evidence as does exist is likely to be testimony from men who were not themselves workers. An investigation of this kind must rely on indirect evidence: census records, school attendance records, the reports of factory inspectors, and so forth; new methods must be added to those already devised for dealing with the inarticulate.

Traditional governing elites, from their point of view, at least, had reason to fear the possible consequences of widespread literacy. To be sure, there existed conservative arguments in support of popular instruction. In Protestant countries, Christian duty seemed to require that the people be enabled to read the Bible, the idea that popular literacy was one more means of teaching the lowly respect for their betters and resignation to their lot bolstered the moral and religious arguments in its favor. But once people had been taught to read, it was nearly impossible to control what they read, without resort to the extraordinary measures which only twentieth-century dictatorships have been willing, or able, to undertake. Events of our own times provide abundant evidence that education can influence political behavior and the structure of politics in ways that the established authorities by no means intend. This aspect of the relationship between politics and education offers many promising lines of historical inquiry.

In recent studies of revolution, for example, attention has been given to the conditions which produce that ubiquitous revolutionary figure, the alienated intellectual. An oversupply of overeducated and under-employed men seems to be a common plight of countries in the early stages of development.[12] These conditions existed in both seventeenth-century England and eighteenth-century France. In both countries an

149

expansion of enrollments at the upper levels of education produced too many educated men seeking too few places, frustrated in their ambitions and ready to turn against a society that had no use for their talents. All that was needed to create an extremely dangerous situation for the established authorities was an ideology which enabled personal grievances to be elevated into opposition to the regime: Puritanism in the case of England; a radical version of the Enlightenment in the case of France.[13]

If historians have begun to hammer out answers to important questions concerning the relationship between education and politics, in the equally significant area of education's links with the economy they are just beginning their work. Economists since Adam Smith have been interested in the relationship of education to the economy, and particularly to economic development, in the last decade the economics of education has become a vigorous subdiscipline. But historians have their own contribution to make, especially since the vexing question of the ways in which education has influenced economic growth demands historical treatment. As David McClelland has put it, 'Did increases in educational investment precede rapid rates of economic growth, or were rapid increases in wealth followed by increased spending on education? Or did both occur together? These are the critical questions of social dynamics that cry out for an answer.'[14] Historians are just starting to attempt to break the vicious circle in which such questions have been enclosed.

Take, for example, the problem of literacy – a topic which itself is only beginning to be investigated systematically. R.S. Schofield has remarked, 'Today literacy is considered to be a necessary precondition for economic development; but the historian might well ask himself whether this was so in England at the end of the eighteenth century.'[15] It would be plausible to argue that the relatively high rate of literacy that had long prevailed in England had much to do with that country's becoming the first industrial power. But on closer examination it is far from clear how literacy and schooling have contributed to rapid growth, especially in the early stages. In the first decades of industrialization, the factory system put no premium on even low-level intellectual skills. Whatever relationships existed between widespread literacy and early industrial development must have been quite roundabout. In one of the best treatments of this problem, Ronald Dore has shown that what was actually learned in school mattered less than the discipline involved in learning anything at all:

But what does widespread literacy do for a developing country? At the very least it constitutes a training in being trained. The man who has in childhood submitted to some process of disciplined and conscious learning is more likely to respond to further training, be it in a conscript army, in a factory, or at lectures arranged by his village agricultural association. And such training can be more precise and efficient, and more nationally standardized, if the written word can be used to supplement the spoken.[16]

Directing his attention to a higher level of training, David Landes has recently argued that the links between technical and scientific education on the one hand and economic development on the other are much more direct than the links between literacy and development.[17] Certainly, the prima facie evidence in the classic comparison between the sluggishness of the British and the explosiveness of the German economies in the late nineteenth century, when industrial processes came increasingly to depend upon scientific innovation, would appear to support Landes's case: German scientific education was undoubtedly superior to British, and German entrepreneurs were more willing to hire and to heed the advice of graduates of scientific and technical institutes than were their British counterparts. But too little is now known about scientific education in the industrial age; historians of science have so far given more attention to the early modern period. When work in progress on scientific education in later times appears, it may well complicate, even if it does not substantially modify, the picture Landes presents.[18]

Such studies, which define education as a process that takes place in specialized institutions, are likely to remain at the center of attention in historical writing. Nevertheless, any definition of education must be broad enough to include learning experiences which take place outside the framework of formal institutions, particularly within the family, whose role in the educational process remains of primary importance. But historical research on the family is now at a rudimentary stage. Very little is known, for example, about the ways in which responsibility for education after the earliest years of childhood shifted over a period of centuries, from the family to specialized institutions, such as the apprenticeship system and schools. Nor have we discovered much about the interaction between changes in the structure of the family and changes in the structure of education, or about how these changes have differed from class to class and among various levels of education. Did changes in family structure make formal educational institutions increasingly important agencies of socialization, or did pressures outside the family, from government or from social and religious institutions, provide the impetus for this shift in educational responsibilities? What have been the social and psychological consequences of these changes? How has submission to the discipline of the school altered the experience of childhood and affected patterns of adult behavior? Only in the last decade have such questions begun to receive the attention they deserve.[19]

II

If the exploration of 'the involvements of education with the rest of society' is the new credo, it is a credo not without its own ambiguities and difficulties. The phrase can be interpreted in a variety of ways. It has been employed in a specific critical sense, to suggest the inadequacies of the history of education, old style, without meaning to lay down a program for the new. It has been used superficially, to dress up straightforward descriptions of educational institutions hardly different from older institutional histories.

More significantly, the phrase also lends itself to a quasi-functionalist interpretation which may distort the role of education in the historical process. This interpretation assumes that everything which may be identified with education responds to or fulfills the needs of society; that the structure of an educational system is merely a reflection of the class structure; that the pace of change in education is roughly equal to, indeed responds to, the pace of other changes in the larger society. First of all, it is never easy to decide what constitutes 'society', the abstract entity to which education responds. Moreover, the functionalist view runs afoul of empirical evidence which suggests that the pace of change in education has often been widely at variance with the pace of social change. And this view is hard-pressed to allow for the anomalies and anachronisms so frequently found in educational systems. The relationship between change in an educational system and changes in the society of which it is a part is certainly one of the most important and least understood problems confronting the historian of education. An explanatory model which could be applied to this relationship would be an extremely useful tool, but for all its compelling simplicity – indeed, because of it – the functionalist approach is inadequate.[20]

The new credo may also be interpreted too broadly. An undiscriminating concern with relationships between education and society can lead to an emphasis on certain aspects of the role of education in the historical process at the expense of others. If the historical study of education is too preoccupied with relationships and interconnections, it may slight certain problems internal to the process of education itself,

152

problems which may not be very satisfactorily explained in terms of external influences. Along with our attempts to understand how the larger society influences education, perhaps we need to understand the ways it does not.

For this very reason the study of educational institutions remains important – but what is needed is institutional history in a new key. The new studies should indeed take into account the larger social context in which educational institutions are located, but their viewpoints should be from the inside looking out. Only in this way are we likely to understand such matters as the consequences of educational reform as opposed to the intentions of reformers, or such significant topics in intellectual history as the influence which institutional settings exercise on patterns of thought and intellectual creativity.

Sheldon Rothblatt has attacked some of the foregoing problems in his recent book on nineteenth-century Cambridge, an important example of the new institutional history.[21] He argues that two historiographical traditions can be traced in the writing of English university history. The Whig interpretation assumed that university history could be written as an extension of political history: the ancient universities were seen as plain tools of the Georgian Establishment. Unable and unwilling to respond to the challenge of industrialism, Oxbridge was forced into the modern world only by pressure administered from the outside, in the form of investigations by royal commissions. Of course the Whig version applauded these nineteenth-century changes. A second historiographical tradition, the class-conflict interpretation, holds that 'the function of the university is to serve whichever social class is in power'. This view reverses the Whig judgment: it does not regard the nineteenth-century reforms as progressive but as merely the transfer of control of the universities from one class to another. Whatever their respective merits, Rothblatt argues, both the Whig and the class-conflict versions have assumed much too close a fit between society's wishes and the response of educational institutions to them. Especially in a pluralistic society, 'it is entirely possible that the university and society will be in subtle and complex states of disagreement as well as agreement with one another, that the direction of university change may not be completely obvious, that surprises will occur'.[22] Rothblatt elaborates this thesis by showing how the reform of Cambridge, though quickened by external pressures, sprang largely from within the university, from the reformulation of donnish traditions which had very little to do with either the presumed needs of an industrial society or the 'demands' of a rising middle class, and which in fact set itself against them.

The new institutional history is valuable not only as an illustration of the dangers in interpreting the new credo too broadly. There are other good reasons for maintaining institutional history amid the central concerns of the history of education. Despite the wealth of old-style studies of institutions, little is known about most of the problems with which contemporary historians are now engaged. Modeled on the constitutional history that dominated nineteenth-century scholarship, the older studies were preoccupied with formal structures; contemporary historical writing, on the other hand, might be characterized as mainly concerned with processes, with relationships of power and influence and social interaction that may have been widely at variance with the dictates of formal institutional structures. There are many histories of individual American universities, for example, but there is not even a handful of trans-institutional, comparative studies of the caliber of Laurence R. Veysey's *The Emergence of the American University*.[23] The standard history of the French universities, published at the end of the nineteenth century, is surely not the last word that can be written on the subject.[24] And the histories of many other important educational institutions remain to be written.

Moreover, the study of universities is an ideal theater for historians interested in problems of the *longue durée*. For universities are one of the oldest forms of corporate organization in the West. Few institutions have been at once so fragile and so durable; few have been altered so radically, both internally and in their relationship to the larger society, adding new purposes, allowing others to lapse, and managing to maintain some of those for which they were originally founded. And perhaps because their existence and purpose presuppose an acute sense of the past, universities are rich repositories of information about themselves.

No scholar working alone can expect to take full advantage of these vast sources, nor can he exploit on his own that unique opportunity for the investigation of long-term problems offered by the university as a subject of study. The new institutional history demands collaborative efforts which will press into service the methods of several disciplines as well as the computer.

One such project, under the direction of Allan Bullock and T.H. Aston, is concerned with the social history of Oxford University from earliest times to the present. Another collaborative study, a statistical survey of universities in the West, is under way at the Shelby Cullom Davis Center for Historical Studies of Princeton University. A major goal of the project is to explore the cyclical patterns of expanding and contracting enrollments in Western universities, a phenomenon whose

154

causes are not understood. Universities in England, Spain, and Germany exhibited similar patterns of rising enrollments in the sixteenth and early seventeenth centuries, of rapid decline beginning in the mid-seventeenth century, and of stagnation throughout the eighteenth. English and German enrollments again rose sharply in the nineteenth century. Was there a general decline in university matriculation throughout the West between about 1650 and 1800? If so, what were its causes, and what were its social, cultural, economic, and political consequences? Why did expansion resume in the nineteenth century? How did these cycles affect the pace and character of modernization in the West?

The Davis Center project is also concerned with two other problems: one, patterns in the relationship of university education to social mobility and to recruitment for professional, political, and administrative elites; two, the role of universities as transmitters of culture. The latter problem will consider education both as an intellectual and a socializing process and will ask how the structure, composition, and intellectual activities of the faculty changed over time – how and why the university was eventually able to become the critic of society as well as its servant.

Such collaborative enterprises can make significant contributions to our knowledge of the internal history of universities. But each study will eventually have to face the general problem with which much of this essay has been concerned: the establishment of cause-and-effect relationships between changes in education and changes in other sectors of society. This task, though the most difficult, may also prove the most rewarding.

III

Why has the history of education undergone such extreme change in recent years? The resurgence of interest is in part a consequence of the troubled state of contemporary education. New questions shaped by the dilemmas of our own times require new approaches to the past. The older historiography was found inadequate both because it was too narrow and inward-looking, and because it was ignorant of some essential facts concerning education itself. Long untouched by the great changes that have overtaken historical research in this century, the history of education became one of the last refuges of the Whig interpretation. So long as its practitioners were mainly concerned with searching the past for the antecedents of their own contemporary institutions, they could believe that education in the West had followed an upward linear progression. We now find this view hard to accept. We know, for example, that periods in which formal instruction was fairly widespread have been followed by periods in which it was restricted to small groups. The older historiography could neither accommodate such findings nor answer the questions they raise. Their exploration requires new modes of analysis. To pursue our example, it is clear that any satisfactory explanation of these expansions and contractions will have to take into account changes in demographic patterns and in the family, in the economy, the social structure, and the political system, in beliefs about the nature and purpose of human life. And it will also have to be recognized that education has turned back upon these influences in subtle and complex ways, working changes on its own.

Such a task is clearly beyond the old-style historian of education and the old-style historiography. But the demands of the task will not be satisfied by a new historiography of education as such. It may be doubted whether education, a process so deeply entangled in the life of an entire society, deserves to be called an 'area of study' at all. Surely there can be little justification for making education a particular genre of historical scholarship. The history of education touches upon all the varieties of history. It is a task for the generalist, who must bring to the study of education a thorough knowledge of the society of which it is a part.

NOTES

1. Bernard Bailyn, *Education in the Forming of American Society: Needs and Opportunities for Research* (Chapel Hill: University of North Carolina Press, 1960), p.14. I am grateful to my friends and colleagues in the Shelby Cullom Davis Center for Historical Studies of Princeton University, whose comments in a seminar on The University in Society provided suggestions for this essay. They are: Robert Church, Richard Kagan, Tom Laqueur, Sheldon Rothblatt, Henry Smith II, and Lawrence Stone.
2. See, for example, Michel Fleury and Pierre Valmary, 'Les progrès de l'instruction élémentaire de Louis XIV à Napoléon III, d'après l'enquête de Louis Maggiolo, 1877–1879', *Population*, 12 (1957), 71–92.
3. For a brilliant example of the analyses now going on see Pierre Bourdieu and Jean-Claude Passeron, *Les héritiers: les étudiants et la culture* (Paris: Editions de Minuit, 1964).
4. For a pioneer effort see J.H. Hexter, 'The Education of the Aristocracy in the Renaissance', *Reappraisals in History* (New York: Harper and Row, 1961), pp.45–70, an earlier version of which appeared in the *Journal of Modern History* (March 1950); also Hester Jenkins and D. Caradog Jones, 'Social Class of Cambridge University Alumni of the 18th and 19th Centuries', *British Journal of Sociology*, 1 (1950), 93–116.
5. Lawrence Stone, 'The Educational Revolution in England, 1560–1640', *Past and Present*, no.28 (July 1964), 68.

6. See, for example, François de Dainville, 'Effectifs des collèges et scolarité aux XVIIe et XVIIIe siècles dans le nord-est de la France', *Population*, 10 (1955), 455–88. 'Collèges et fréquentation scolaire au XVIIe siècle', *Population*, 12 (1957), 467–94; Frank Musgrove, 'Population Changes and the Status of the Young in England Since the 18th Century', *Sociological Review*, 11 (1963), 69–93.

7. See, for example, David Ward, 'The Public Schools and Industry in Britain after 1870', *Journal of Contemporary History*, 2, no.3 (1967), 37–52; two studies by Rupert Wilkinson, *Gentlemanly Power: British Leadership and the Public School Tradition* (New York: Oxford University Press, 1964), and with T.J.H. Bishop, *Winchester and the Public School Elite* (London: Faber, 1967). On the French lycée see John E. Talbott, *The Politics of Educational Reform in France, 1918–1940* (Princeton: Princeton University Press, 1969); Paul Gerbod, *La condition universitaire en France au XIXe siècle* (Paris: Presses universitaires de France, 1965).

8. For an early and still useful discussion of the role of primary education in the promotion of nationalism see Carleton J.H. Hayes, *France, A Nation of Patriots* (New York: Columbia University Press, 1930); also Charles E. Merriam, *The Making of Citizens: A Comparative Study of Methods of Civic Training* (Chicago: University of Chicago Press, 1931); for recent work see, for instance, Pierre Nora, 'Ernest Lavisse, son rôle dans la formation du sentiment national', *Revue historique*, 228 (July–Sept. 1962), 73–106; Jacques and Mona Ozouf, 'Le thème du patriotisme dans les manuels primaires', *Le Mouvement Social*, no.49 (Oct.–Nov. 1964), 5–32.

9. Donald G. MacCrae, 'The Culture of a Generation: Students and Others,' *Journal of Contemporary History*, 2, no.3 (1967), 3.

10. For an early suggestion that the American common school may not have been the spearhead of democracy, see the essay in intellectual history of Merle Curti, *The Social Ideas of American Educators* (New York: C. Scribner's Sons, 1935); more recently, Michael Katz has expressed a similar view from the perspective of social history in *The Irony of Early School Reform: Educational Innovation in Mid-Nineteenth Century Massachusetts* (Cambridge, Mass.: Harvard University Press, 1968).

11. E.P. Thompson, *The Making of the English Working Class* (New York: Vintage, 1963), especially pp.711–45; also Georges Duveau, *La pensée ouvrière sur l'éducation pendant la Second République et le Second Empire* (Paris: Domat-Montchrestien, 1948); R.K. Webb, *The British Working-Class Reader, 1790–1848* (London: Allen and Unwin, 1955); R.D. Altick, *The English Common Reader* (Chicago: University of Chicago Press, 1957); J.F.C. Harrison, *Learning and Living, 1790–1960: A Study in the History of the English Adult Education Movement* (London: Routledge and Kegan Paul, 1961).

12. Edward Shils, 'Intellectuals in the Political Development of the New States', *World Politics*, 12 (April 1960), 329–68.

13. See Lawrence Stone, 'The Educational Revolution in England, 1540–1640', *Past and Present*, no.28 (July 1964), 41–80. In a more recent essay Stone has concluded: 'More and more it looks as if this educational expansion was a necessary – but not sufficient – reason for the peculiar and ultimately radical course the revolution took.' 'The Causes of the English Revolution', in Robert Forster and Jack P. Greene, eds., *Preconditions of Revolution in Early Modern Europe* (Baltimore: Johns Hopkins University Press, 1970); Mark H. Curtis, 'The Alienated Intellectuals of Early Stuart England', *Past and Present*, no.23 (November 1962), 25–43; J.H. Elliot, 'Revolution and Continuity in Early Modern Europe', *Past and Present*, no.42 (Feb. 1969), 35–56; Robert Darnton, 'Social Tensions in the Intelligentsia of Pre-Revolutionary France', paper read at the annual meeting of the American Historical Association, Dec. 1969. On the importance of a similar phenomenon in 19th-century Spain see Raymond Carr, *Spain, 1806–1939* (Oxford: Oxford University Press, 1966), p.167; on 19th-century

157

Germany see Lenore O'Boyle, 'The Democratic Left in Germany, 1848', *Journal of Modern History*, 33 (1961), 374–83; John R. Gillis, 'Aristocracy and Bureaucracy in Nineteenth-Century Prussia', *Past and Present*, no.41 (Dec. 1968), 105–29.

14. David C. McClelland, 'Does Education Accelerate Economic Growth?', *Economic Development and Cultural Change*, 14, no.3 (April 1966), 259.

15. R.S. Schofield, 'The Measurement of Literacy in Pre-Industrial England', in Jack Goody, ed., *Literacy in Traditional Societies* (Cambridge, Eng.: Cambridge University Press, 1969), p.312 and n: 'The necessity of literacy as a pre-condition for economic growth is a persistent theme running through many Unesco publications ... These measures [established by Unesco] are very general and throw no light at all on the question of why literacy should be considered essential to economic growth.' See also Lawrence Stone, 'Literacy and Education in England, 1640–1900', *Past and Present*, no.42 (Feb. 1969), 69–139; Carlo M. Cipolla, *Literacy and Development in the West* (Baltimore: Penguin, 1969).

16. Ronald P. Dore, *Education in Tokugawa Japan* (Berkeley: University of California Press, 1965), p.292.

17. David Landes, *The Unbound Prometheus: Technological Change and Industrial Development in Western Europe from 1750 to the Present* (Cambridge, Eng.: Cambridge University Press, 1969), pp.343–8.

18. One of the few studies of nineteenth-century scientific education is D.S.L. Cardwell, *The Organisation of Science in England* (Melbourne: Heinemann, 1957). On literature on scientific education see Thomas G. Kuhn, 'The History of Science', *International Encyclopedia of the Social Sciences*, XIV, 78. John H. Weiss is writing a Harvard University doctoral dissertation on scientific education in 19th-century France; Steven Turner is preparing a Princeton University dissertation on scientific education in Germany.

19. For a brief discussion of some of these problems, see Stone, 'Literacy and Education in England, 1640–1900,' pp.93–95; Bailyn, *Education in the Forming of American Society*, pp.75–78. One of the boldest and most widely-heralded inquiries into these questions to have appeared in recent years is Philippe Ariès, *Centuries of Childhood: A Social History of Family Life* (New York: Knopf, 1962). The idea of childhood as a distinct phase of life, Ariès argues, is an invention of the late Middle Ages, when changes in the family and a new concern for education led to the removal of the child from the adult society in which he had formerly been free to roam. This practice, at first limited to the upper classes, gradually permeated the rest of society. Though Ariès has perhaps done more than anyone to stimulate interest in the historical study of the family, the argument of his book, despite – or because of – his ingenious use of iconographical evidence, is not entirely convincing. For a study that owes much to Ariès but has a great deal more to say about education see Georges Snyders, *La pédagogie en France aux XVIIe et XVIIIe siècles* (Paris: Presses Universitaires de France, 1965). Important historical work on the family is now beginning to appear in the United States, pursuing lines of inquiry established by Edmund S. Morgan and Bernard Bailyn. See, for example, John Demos, *A Little Commonwealth: Family Life in Plymouth Colony* (New York: Oxford University Press, 1970); Philip J. Greven, Jr., *Four Generations: Population, Land and Family in Colonial Andover, Massachusetts* (Ithaca: Cornell University Press, 1970). Demos has more to say about education. For England see, among the articles of Frank Musgrove, 'The Decline of the Educative Family', *Universities Quarterly*, 14 (Sept. 1960), pp.377–406.

20. For an interesting discussion of functionalism see Olive Banks, *The Sociology of Education* (London: Schocken, 1968). See also Gillian Sutherland, 'The Study of the History of Education', *History*, 54 (Feb. 1969), 53–4, and printed as No. 6 in this volume.

21. Sheldon Rothblatt, *The Revolution of the Dons: Cambridge and Society in Victorian England* (New York: Basic Books, 1968).

158

22. *Ibid.*, pp.17–26.
23. Laurence R. Veysey, *The Emergence of the American University* (Chicago: University of Chicago Press, 1965). Veysey follows ground broken by Richard Hofstadter and Walter P. Metzger in *The Development of Academic Freedom in the United States* (New York: Columbia University Press, 1955), which is about much else besides academic freedom. Veysey's study of the movement to redefine the purpose and structure of American higher education in the post-Civil War era also shows how much can be missed by assuming too close a fit between a society's needs and the response of educational institutions to these needs. 'During the early years of the American university movement, until about 1890,' he contends, 'academic efforts burgeoned largely in spite of the public, not as the result of popular acclaim ... Academic and popular aspirations seemed rarely to meet' (p.16).
24. Louis Liard, *L'enseignement supérieur en France, 1789–1889*, 2 vols. (Paris, 1888–94).

11

The Study of the History of Education

ASA BRIGGS

I

The study of the history of education is best considered as part of the wider study of the history of society, social history broadly interpreted with the politics, the economics and, it is necessary to add, the religion put in. Yet for long the study was either neglected or left to a small and scattered group of specialists, some of whom were unaware of the broad trends of historical scholarship. During recent years changes both in education and in the study of history have altered the picture. Education has once more become a major social, political and economic issue; it is natural in such circumstances that there should be a reinterpretation of old issues and the struggles surrounding them. We are already far removed, in consequence, from the attitudes eloquently expressed by J.L. Garvin in his biography of Joseph Chamberlain. 'No Ezekiel's wind,' Garvin exclaimed, 'can make dry bones live in some valleys. Nothing seems more dead and gone today than the educational battles of the early seventies in the Victorian age.'[1] A year after the centenary of the Education Act of 1870, which itself stimulated the production of large numbers of local studies based on the examination of source materials which had long been buried and forgotten, the mood of the times is a very different one. It is easy to understand why the 'battles' were so fiercely contested. As for changes in the study of history, they have been sufficiently comprehensive for slogans like 'the new history' to be bandied around in academic circles. Several of these are of special interest and importance to historians of education, and this paper is particularly concerned with six of them.

The first is a new approach to local history, a far more sophisticated version of local history than that common in the past. The study has cast off the shackles of antiquarianism, has moved from a rural to an urban ambiance, and has begun to take account not only of institutions or of

160

personalities but of structures and processes.[2] At its best, such study does not divide the past into convenient periods: it searches across the centuries for continuities and discontinuities. Moreover, as it broadens out, it ceases to involve an exercise in illustrating what is already known about national history from local examples and becomes a means of reconstructing national history afresh from local materials. We can already trace the breaking down of set interpretations of national history and the building up of new interpretations in their place.[3]

The second is a new approach to comparative history, a natural sequel to the rediscovery of the variety of experience embedded in local, regional and national sub-cultures. Comparative studies pivot on the discovery of what was common between and what was distinctive to different societies. 'When an analyst cannot experiment with his subject matter through replication, establishment of controls and the manipulation of variables', an American historian has observed recently, 'then he resorts to the comparative method in the hope of achieving the same explanatory results.'[4] Whatever the difficulties in establishing categories and definitions – and to establish them is essential if historians are to ask similar questions of similar materials – the approach implies both greater care for methodology in research and greater analytical power.

The third is the study of quantitative history, 'cliometrics', as some Americans have christened it. What began with 'new' economic history has subsequently been paralleled in the writing of social history, with historical demography playing a strategic part in the development of scholarship.[5] There are dangers in a commitment to quantitative approaches which excludes other approaches and in a multiplication of quantitative studies at a low level of argument, but given a critical frame of mind and the ability to ask relevant questions on the part of the historian, quantitative studies, assisted by statistical techniques and supported when necessary by computers, can point to fascinating and sometimes unexpected conclusions. In one respect they are particularly important. 'A quantitative discrepancy between theory and observation', Professor Kuhn has written, 'is obtrusive. No crisis is so hard to suppress as that which derives from a quantitative anomaly that has resisted all the usual efforts at reconciliation.'[6] Moreover, the analysis of bodies of data which were often collected for strictly limited immediate purposes, very different from the purposes of the historian, can in itself stimulate the asking of new questions. As Schumpeter put it, 'we need statistics not only for explaining things but in order to know precisely what there is to be explained'.[7]

Quantitative history has attracted many able, pioneering minds. So too has the 'new social history', 'history from below', which is still in the process of articulation and development. This, indeed, is the fourth approach which deserves to be identified. Such history makes use of concepts derived from sociology, anthropology and psychology without (when it is at its best) being imprisoned in borrowed social science categories. It also directs attention to people whose names never figured in the older history books, the people who were deprived or neglected in their own time and whose participation in government was minimal or non-existent, whose attitudes towards 'authority' could be deferential or resentful, passive or hostile. The study of 'history from below' often creates a greater sense of understanding along with a recovery of immediacy. It quickens the curiosity of the historian and leads him into the examination of related patterns of work and 'leisure', participation and 'apathy'.[8]

The fifth change in the study of history – at the opposite end of the spectrum – has been the development of a more analytical kind of political history, with attention moving from particular pieces of legislation, though these are still studied within a different frame, to cumulative administrative processes, to the making of critical decisions, to the changing scale and role of organization. A re-scrutiny of nineteenth-century administrative history is in process, carrying with it useful controversy. It involves less concentration on the 'landmarks' and more on the interplay of people and problems. It will eventually produce a new synthesis, particularly in relation, perhaps, to the forging of social policies.[9]

The sixth change relates to intellectual and cultural history. The history of ideas is beginning to come into its own, not merely the history of the ideas of 'great thinkers' but the history of chains of ideas and their mode of communication through different 'media', the shifting relationships between 'minority' and 'mass' communication, the significance of 'language' and the forms of 'control'. The new history of ideas has been associated with a re-examination of such crucial changes as the invention and development of printing and the subsequent history of literacy and the more recent 'communications revolution'.[10] Yet it has encouraged new tendencies within political and social history also. The kind of interpretation advanced by A.V. Dicey in his still influential *Law and Public Opinion in the Nineteenth Century*, first published in 1905, has been challenged without so far being fully replaced.[11] Although Dicey had very little specifically to say about education, his approach to the broad subject of the making of social policy has done much to influence writers of every kind, many of whom have sharply questioned his assumptions and conclusions.

It is the main argument of this paper that each of these new approaches – and they are related to each other – needs to be studied carefully by historians of education. To some extent they all reflect, as most historiographical change has always reflected, current preoccupations. To some extent they are made possible by the availability of new materials and techniques, although techniques (including oral interview) are, of course, instrumental and depend for their success on the quality of the questions asked. Most important of all, the new approaches represent a somewhat new balance between specialization and generalization. Historical study must involve specialization if it is to advance, but the old barriers between the different sub-branches of history are breaking down and new efforts at synthesis are being made.

The study of the history of education will not, in my view, be adequately furthered if there is to be new departmentalization with a new sub-branch of history, 'the history of education', being increasingly separated out from the rest. There may be something to learn in this connection from recent developments in the study of labour history and of urban history. In both of these cases groups of interested historians have been created in this country in recent years, each with its own meetings and its own system of scholarly communication.[12] Unfortunately there are always historians who are more aware of their separate identity as specialists, even of their status, than of the potential contribution which they can make to the study of history as a whole. Yet the wisest among the labour and urban historians have recognized that critical issues in the history of labour and of cities cannot be studied in isolation from other branches of history. Against this background the History of Education Society, founded in 1967, is poised at a particularly interesting moment in its short life.[13] There are so many questions to ask about educational history (curriculum as well as policy) that it is essential that they should be placed in their general context and that the answers should be related, when possible, to the kind of answers which social historians are seeking to provide.

Although the six developments outlined in this paper are 'new', less new perhaps than some of their practitioners realize, there are old guides in the history of education who point in the same direction. One of the most stimulating of them was R.H. Tawney, who was always looking for a synthesis. In an essay written as long ago as 1914 he argued that 'educational problems cannot be considered in isolation' and that in every period of history – he himself was mainly concerned with preindustrial periods – 'educational policy reflects its conceptions of human society'.[14] Much of the later Tawney is forecast in this early statement. In one of the key passages in *Equality* (1931) he emphasised

163

that in considering the place of education in English society it is always necessary to bear in mind that the English social system has been shaped by pre-industrial as well as industrial influences, that it is marked not by a single set of class relations but by two. 'It is at once as businesslike as Manchester and as gentlemanly as Eton; if its hands can be as rough as those of Esau, its voice is as mellifluous as that of Jacob.'[15] The remark has often been overlooked by those who have generalised too simply about English experience, and it reminds us that historians of education must concern themselves not only with 'crises' or 'struggles' of a dramatic kind but with long-term influences and trends. Tawney also reminds us perpetually that society in the last resort must be looked at not in terms of categories, however valuable they may be, but in terms of people. He was willing to look for evidence in every kind of place from 'high literature' to 'common experience'.

II

Each of the six approaches outlined above is relevant to the study of the history of education in this country. The first, indeed, is basic. The new approach to local history and its relationship to national history must be grasped because of the 'localism' of the English educational pattern. It was from the periphery not from the centre that English education developed. As Sir Joshua Fitch, for 26 years a leading HMI, put it in a magisterial article in the *Encyclopedia Britannica* which deserves to be reprinted, educational provision in England was

not the product of any theory or plan formulated beforehand by statesmen or philosophers. It has come into existence through a long course of experiments, compromises, traditions, successes, failures and religious controversies. What has been done in this department of public policy is the resultant of many diverse forces, and of slow evolution and growth rather than of clear purpose and well-defined national aims.[16]

If it is necessary to turn to foreign writers, like de Tocqueville, to grasp the significance of 'localism' and 'de-centralization' when viewed in international terms,[17] it is equally necessary to explore local economic, social (including religious) and political structures, to understand why initiatives and activities in education varied as much as they did before the passing of the Education Act of 1870; and it is necessary to examine in this way a body like the Lancashire Public School Association which, like the Anti-Corn Law League, to which it owed much, professed itself a 'national' body in 1850. The contrast between Manchester and Birmingham, about which so much has recently been written in relation to nineteenth-century history as a whole, has its significance in relation

164

to the history of education. The point was clear enough, indeed, to Francis Adams, the Birmingham-born and based secretary of the National Education League, founded in 1869. After directing attention to the Manchester Education Aid Society, established in 1864, he went on to quote the words of George Dixon, the chairman of the League:

Had my suggestions been favourably received by the gentlemen [in Manchester] to whom they were made, Birmingham would not have originated the League, but would have followed Manchester, which, in my opinion, ought to have headed and was entitled to lead a national movement.[18]

Given comments of this kind and what we already know of the contrasting profiles of England's two largest cities,[19] it is obviously not sufficient in discussing what happened in English education before 1870 to talk in simple terms of differences between 'rural' and 'urban' areas. A far more intensive survey and analysis of particular places is necessary.

After 1870, though the framework changed, the same kind of survey and analysis remains necessary, with the additional point to consider – the relationship between 'national' pressures and local provision. The fact that between 1870 and 1902 the first development of a deliberately organised pattern of national primary education was left to locally based 'school boards' is of major importance, as is, of course, the role of local education authorities since 1902. Several histories of individual boards have been written, often in the form of theses,[20] but few of them move into the kind of comparative local history which is most rewarding. There were more than 2,000 boards in 1902, and there are some interesting aspects of their distribution. Yorkshire, for example, had 280 boards; Lancashire with a population nearly a million larger had only around 50. The contrast here is worth studying, as is the contrast between Lancashire and Yorkshire in other matters of education, including technical education.[21] Within Yorkshire it would be interesting to compare Leeds and Bradford. Turning to comparative national histories, we still lack studies of the way in which primary education was developed 'on the ground', say in one British and one French or German city or in two agricultural areas.[22] The next stage in our understanding of nineteenth-century English history as a whole may well be to follow up the local breakdown of structures and processes within England by comparing across national boundaries.

In this connection it is useful to turn back again to Fitch's *Encyclopedia Britannica* article which was written at the time of the debate on the Education Act of 1902 and remains a good starting point for further exploration. Fitch went out of his way to outline developments in other countries, drawing out what seemed to him the relevant comparisons and contrasts. The same approach had been followed in a more limited way by Francis Adams in the last decades of the nineteenth century when he preceded his important book on *The Elementary School Contest* (1882) with an earlier study of *The Free School System of the United States* (1875). Such 'anatomization' had been pursued even earlier by Bulwer Lytton in his still valuable book (one of the first nineteenth-century examples of a *genre* which has led up to Anthony Sampson), *England and the English* (1834, reprinted in 1874 in the aftermath of the Education Act).[23] Books of this kind have been used far too little by historians of education, yet backed by contemporary evidence they help us to understand (i) the place of 'voluntarism' within the English context, (ii) the lateness of 'national development' (G.M. Young rightly called education 'the great Victorian omission'), and (iii) the lack of 'system'. It is important to note that none of these points can be explored adequately in terms of the history of education narrowly interpreted.

There is a further way in which comparative approaches are useful. It is interesting to compare the successive *Encyclopedia Britannica* articles on education with each other, going back to James Mill's famous essay for the fifth edition. Fitch, perceptive as always, showed how the approach had changed. In particular, he drew attention to the contrast between his own article and that of Oscar Browning, the famous Eton master, which had been printed in the main volumes of the ninth edition. Browning, writing very much in dilettante style, had been concerned with 'the ideals which have prevailed from time to time' in education (going back to the ancient world); Fitch concentrated on tracing 'the gradual growth of what may be called the English system, the forces which have controlled it, and the results it effected during the last quarter of the nineteenth century'.[24]

At this point, the third new approach to the writing of history becomes directly relevant – the use of quantitative techniques. It was always evident in the nineteenth century, at least from the time of the foundation of the local statistical societies in the 1830s, that the case for educational reform was buttressed by if not grounded in the exposition of statistics. The Act of 1870 was itself preceded by the major local statistical inquiries of the 1860s, some of which were deliberately comparative in character. The mass of nineteenth-century material is worth sifting as it stands, yet it is worth noting that far more can be done with it than was done in the nineteenth century itself. Increased statistical sophistication has already influenced the way in which educational issues are being presented in the twentieth century,[25] and more attention is being paid in current debate to the 'economics of education' (claims on national resources; shares of national income devoted to education; modes of financing numbers, buildings and equipment) than has ever been the case before.[26] The reason has doubtless been the growing volume of public educational expenditure and the need to formulate policies. At the same time, quantitative methods have been applied to educational sociology also, with reference both to class differentials and mobility.[27]

So far these increasingly fashionable approaches have had little impact on historical studies, although one interesting article by E.G. West, who has been actively involved in current debate, is of a pioneering kind, and on the basis of rigorous quantitative analysis questions a number of accepted assumptions about relative educational provision in England and Scotland in the early nineteenth century. The contrast between England and Scotland is one which must be explored by all students of British educational history, and this article is far more than a gloss.[28] There is as much scope for assessing quantitatively the economic limitations to the expansion of voluntary primary education in the nineteenth century (and its social limitations) as there is for examining comparable aspects of public provision in the 1970s. We know far too little about the economics of voluntary effort in every field of social policy and the financial and manpower 'crises' which were a feature of the 'system' both locally and nationally. It is perhaps important to bear in mind also that the Education Act of 1870 which shifted the locus of finance was passed in a year of exceptional business prosperity.

The fourth of the new approaches to the study of history – the emergence of a new kind of social history – has such obvious bearings on the study of educational history that it is not necessary to do more than identify a number of key issues. As far as the relationship between social history and sociology is concerned (terminology, methodologies, boundary questions), there has already been one paper in the *Bulletin* of the History of Education Society,[29] and one textbook, P.W. Musgrave's *Society and Education in England since 1800* (1968), draws fully on sociological analysis.[30] It is important to bear in mind that in any partnership between historian and sociologist (even the most manageable of partnerships, that where historian and sociologist are the same person), the role of the historian is not simply to supply facts and to correct errors.

History has always been a borrower from other disciplines, and in that sense social-scientific history is just another example of a time-honoured process; but history has always been a lender, and all the social sciences would be immeasurably poorer without knowledge of the historical record. The social sciences are not a self-contained system, one of whose boundaries lies in some fringe area of the historical sciences. Rather the study of man is a continuum, and social-scientific history is a bridge between the social sciences and the humanities.[31]

It would be unfortunate if there were to be boundary disputes in relation to the history and sociology of education, given the need of both for each other. Musgrave has rightly related the history of education to changes within the family, the economy and the social-class system, and the historian of education must be interested in such matters as 'education' through agencies outside the school and relative 'mobility' through education and other routes or agencies in society (a basic problem in nineteenth-century social history), even if these are not his primary focus of interest. It is absurdly restrictive to argue that the history of education is primarily the history of teaching.[32]

At every point in the history of education institutions and motivations, facts and values must be considered together. Take any key passage from the past relating to educational provision and it immediately provokes questions. In 1851, for example, Nathaniel Woodard, founder of the Woodard schools, had this to say:

It is the glory of a Christian State that it regards all its children with an eye of equal love and our institutions place no impassable barrier between the cottage and the front of the throne; but still parity of rights does not imply equality of power or capacities, of natural or accidental advantages. Common sense forbids that we should lavish our care on those least able to profit from it while we withhold it from those by whom it would be largely repaid. The class compelled to give the greater part of each day to the toilsome earning of its daily bread may be as richly endowed as that which is exempt from this necessity but it is manifest that those who are subject to such a pressure must, as a body, enjoy less opportunities of cultivating their natural endowments.[33]

Whenever the historian of education comes across terms like 'common sense' or 'it is manifest that' he must begin to probe deeply. Indeed, he must be sensitive at every stage to the language of the past (vocabulary, tone, rhetoric). It is important to bear in mind that in the middle years of the nineteenth century, to which this passage belongs, the relationship between education and social class was posed most frequently within the context of relations between the 'middle classes' and the aristocracy and gentry. The leading voices were Tawney's two voices of Eton and Manchester, not those to whom we have become accustomed in twentieth-century dialogue. The Taunton Commission, which does not figure in Eric Midwinter's useful booklet in Seminar Studies on History called *Nineteenth-Century Education*, is an essential source.[34] It needed an unorthodox thinker like Lytton to get away from mid-Victorian 'common sense' about education and society. 'One great advantage of diffusing knowledge among the lower classes', he wrote provocatively, 'is the necessity thus imposed on the higher of increasing knowledge among themselves. I suspect that the new modes and systems of education which succeed the most among the people will ultimately be adopted by the gentry.'[35] During the last two decades of the nineteenth century attitudes towards education and society changed as much as attitudes towards other aspects of organization and policy, with H.G. Wells playing a prominent part in shifting the terms of the debate about education and class to the middle-class working-class matrix. The Education Act of 1870 was for him 'an act to educate the lower classes for employment on lower class lines, and with specially trained inferior teachers'.[36]

At this point 'history from below' comes into its own. Since the Act of 1870 owed little to working-class pressure and aspects of its implementation were often bitterly resented in working-class areas – the 'school bobby' was never a popular figure[37] – it is essential to examine what happened after 1870 from the vantage point of those who were 'receiving' education as well as from the vantage point of those who were 'supplying' it or causing it to be supplied.[38] Recently it has been clearly realized also that the same kind of examination is necessary even in the period of voluntary provision before 1870 when education was thought of as an instrument of social control, not least by Kay-Shuttleworth.[39] It was difficult for those engaged in promoting education fully to understand the attitudes of those *for* whom they were promoting it, as was frankly recognized by Henry Moseley (a scientist as well as a clergyman), one of the first HMIs. 'The fact is', he wrote in a minute of 1845, 'that the inner life of the classes below us in society is never penetrated by us. We are profoundly ignorant of the springs of public opinion, the elements of thought and the principles of action among them – those things which we recognize at once as constituting our own social life, in all the moral features which give it thought and substance.'[40] The same kind of point has been made about social policy as a whole in the nineteenth and early twentieth centuries by R.M. Titmuss:

The poor law, with its quasi-disciplinary functions, rested on assumptions about how people ought to behave. ... Valuations about the nature of man were written into the social legislation of the day. They informed the means of policy. Derived, as they commonly were, from the norms of behaviour expected by one class from another, and founded on outer rather than inner observation ... their application to social questions led the new services to treat manifestations of disorder in the individual rather than the underlying causes in the family or social group.[41]

In examining the detailed history of schools it is essential, therefore, to look critically at 'behaviour' and 'discipline' as well as at curricula and methods of teaching. What can we make of such comments as that of the Rotherham School Board Inspector who wrote in a log book of 1890 'found boys and girls in the same playground. Witnessed much indecent behaviour'?[42] The relationship between discipline and 'drill' is well brought out in many late nineteenth-century logbooks, including that of the head teacher of another infant school in Rotherham who hired a drill sergeant to visit school every Tuesday afternoon after being criticised by an inspector.[43] Logbooks and diaries are particularly useful sources, but we have to penetrate beneath the surface to some of the fundamental problems of language and communication which were as crucial in the nineteenth century as they are today.[44] To understand what was 'going on' in a school it is necessary to take account of complex systems of personal and social interaction, involving complex relationships between the experience, language and values which children brought into the school from their own (sometimes contrasting) neighbourhoods and those imparted by their teachers. Questions of curriculum and methods of teaching are best examined when these complexities are properly understood. The sixth new approach to the study of history identified earlier in this paper depends, like the fourth, on insights as much as techniques, although there is much to be gained from the work of anthropologists and of social psychologists.

III

The fifth approach is worth very full consideration in relation to the whole field of educational policy-making, since too often the history of educational legislation is treated in functional terms of a general kind as a necessary adaptation to new sets of economic or political circumstances. The difficulty is that similar circumstances produced different kinds of results in a different order in other societies. To understand what happened in each case we have to look at the intricate interplay of individuals and groups, ideas and interests, and pressures and restraints. The point was well made by John Rex in his *Key Problems of Sociological Theory* when, after urging 'the reshaping of sociological theory so that it is built around the notions of conflict, imperative coordination and balance of power', he went on to take the Education Act of 1902 as his example:

Some sections of the ruling classes were opposed to the ideas of secondary education altogether. Those who were in favour of it vied with each other about controlling it because they had different ideas about the content of education. And the working classes demanded it either in the hope that their children would 'get on' in the existing order, or because they recognised that such education would help them in the establishment of a new social system. The resulting educational system was the outcome of a compromise between these competing pressures. It is not a system which can in any way be explained in terms of orthodox functionalist theory. But the manner of its development and the eventual compromise is exactly what we would have expected from a conflict model.[45]

Yet whereas Rex dwelt on 'conflict', the historian must always take account also of 'consensus'. Unlike many other countries, notably the United States, England has never been a society where there was a powerful built-in pressure either in the society or in Parliament for the extension of education. It was a fitting prelude to the story of state intervention that when Roebuck first raised the issue of a grant in 1833 he apologised for taking up the time of the House of Commons on so uninteresting a topic, and it is interesting to note that in 1891 during the debate on free education the House had to be counted to make sure that forty members were present. There have been long periods when little has happened, and these must be explained along with the 'emergencies', 'campaigns' and 'crises' when conflict was always apparent, as it was in 1869 and 1870 and again in 1902. When Butler raised the question of education with Churchill in 1941 he was told by the Prime Minister that instead of thinking of new legislation, which would create a row, he should get on with his main task of getting the schools working as well as possible under all the difficulties of wartime.[46]

MacDonagh's emphasis on cumulative administrative processes of a self-generating kind is directly relevant, therefore, to the historian of education, but attention must be paid also to what created the sense of emergency at particular times, how opinion was mobilized, and what were the practical results. Educational change has come in fits and starts, and we have to look at moments of crisis as well as at administrative processes or social trends. This means going further, of course, than examining particular pieces of legislation, and there is truth in Midwinter's observation that educational history, when it is not written in crude functionalist terms, 'is often studied as a series of legislative enactments, with its students jumping from one Act of Parliament to the next, like mountain goats from peak to peak'. We need amongst other monographs a comprehensive modern study of the activities of the National Education League – explaining clearly why it lost influence as well as why it emerged as a national force. Francis Adams still remains the best source.[47]

Given that England accepted the notion of an educational 'system' imperfectly and falteringly – even Rex's use of the term in relation to the Act of 1902 must be qualified – we have to find a different kind of driving force during many periods of history to that of system-building. The most interesting suggestion for such an alternative was made by John Morley who was profoundly suspicious of 'systems' and at the same time wary about leaving everything to local initiative. As early as 1867 he was writing of the need to develop a 'collective national impulse'; by 1873 he had formulated the idea of reform through the identification of single great 'national issues', among which education was then paramount. His biographer speaks of Morley 'focalising'.[48] It may well be that the interpretation of the history of education in this country during the nineteenth and twentieth centuries would be strengthened if this concept were incorporated within the analysis.

NOTES

1. J.L. Garvin, *The Life of Joseph Chamberlain*, vol.I (1932), 102.
2. See, for example, H.J. Dyos (ed.), *The Study of Urban History* (1968) for the variety of approaches as represented by work in progress.
3. See, for example, the volume of essays which I edited called *Chartist Studies* (1958). Compare S.D. Chapman (ed.), *The History of Working-Class Housing* (1971) which includes essays on housing in London, Glasgow, Leeds, Nottingham, Liverpool, Birmingham, South-East Lancashire and Ebbw Vale.
4. R.F. Berkhofer, *A Behavioral Approach to Historical Analysis* (1969), pp.252–3.
5. See R.W. Fogel and S.L. Engerman (eds.), *The Reinterpretation of American Economic History* (1971); E.A. Wrigley (ed.), *English Historical Demography* (1966).
6. T.S. Kuhn, 'The Function of Measurement in Modern Physical Science' in H. Woolf (ed.), *Quantification: A History of the Meaning of Measurement in the Natural and Social Sciences* (1960), pp.50, 52.
7. Quoted by S. Thernstrom in the book of essays edited by himself and R. Sennett, *Nineteenth-Century Cities* (1969), p.159. For further discussions of quantification, see W.O. Aydelotte, *Quantification in History* (1971) and D.S. Landes and C. Tilly (eds.), *History as a Social Science* (1971).
8. Some of the main aspects and slants of the new social history are set out in the preface and postscript to E.P. Thompson, *The Making of the English Working Class* (Pelican edn, 1968).
9. See, for example, O. MacDonagh, 'The Nineteenth-Century Revolution in Government' in *Historical Journal* (1958), and his reappraisal reappraised by H. Parris in ibid. (1960). There are useful articles on the same theme in *Victorian Studies*, notably V. Cornwell, 'Interpretations of Nineteenth-Century Administration: An Analysis' (1966) and G. Sutherland, 'Recent Trends in Administrative History' (1970).
10. See, for example, L. Stone, 'Literacy and Education in England, 1640–1900' in *Journal of Modern History* (1968) and E.L. Eisenstein, 'Some Conjectures about the Impact of Printing on Western Society and Thought' in *Past and Present* (1969). I have dealt with some of the themes of the 'communications revolution' in a lecture with that title, printed by the University of Leeds (1965).

11. See the very valuable collection of articles edited by M. Ginsberg, *Law and Opinion in England in the Twentieth Century* (1959). For continued reliance on Dicey, despite all that has been written recently, see E.E. Rich, *The Education Act 1870* (1970).
12. The Society for the Study of Labour History was founded in 1960, and it publishes two *Bulletins* each year. There are parallel societies and bulletins in other parts of the world. The Urban History Group came into existence a little later, originating from 'a desire to exchange information on the scope and progress of research and published work'; it publishes an *Urban History Newsletter*. There is a parallel body in the United States.
13. The History of Education Society, which now has 410 members, published its first *Bulletin* in spring 1968. It provides an invaluable record of work in progress.
14. This important essay, originally published in the *Political Quarterly*, was dismissed by a critic as 'pert'. It remains pertinent. It has been reprinted in R. Hinden (ed.), *The Radical Tradition*, (1964), pp.70–81. It traces the history of the ideas of 'status' and 'the career open to the talents' in education.
15. R.H. Tawney, *Equality* (1952 edn.), p.58. The whole of this chapter on 'inequality and social structure' is essential reading. It should be compared with W.G. Runciman, *Relative Deprivation and Social Justice* (1966).
16. J. Fitch, 'Education' in the 'new volumes' of the *Encyclopedia Britannica*, vol.XXVII (1902).
17. See, for example, A. de Tocqueville, *Journeys to England and Ireland* (ed. by J.P. Mayer, 1958), passim.
18. F. Adams, *History of the Elementary School Contest in England* (1882), p.195.
19. See, for example, my article on 'The Background of the Parliamentary Reform Movement in Three English Cities' in the *Cambridge Historical Journal* (1948), and *The Victoria History of the County of Warwick*, vol.VII (1964).
20. One of the most quoted of these is J.H. Bingham's on the Sheffield Board (1949). The centenary of the 1870 Act has led to the unearthing and publication of material about many boards, and it is to be hoped that this work is being collated. For an interesting story which should be compared with the story in neighbouring Sheffield, see *A Survey of Education in Rotherham* (1970). For the rural background in East Yorkshire, see J. Lawson, 'Primary Education in East Yorkshire, 1560–1902', a pamphlet published by the East Yorkshire Local History Society (1959). A 'Table of Yorkshire School Boards' was compiled in 1959. It includes some odd local evidence. Thus, a board was established at Startforth in 1874 and dissolved in 1887/8 on the petition of the ratepayers. At that date it had no school or site, and it was acknowledged by the board that there was sufficient elementary school accommodation in its districts. The best contemporary national source for the work of the boards was the *School Board Chronicle*, and there is a valuable summary of their achievements by Fitch in the *Nineteenth Century* (1902), which was reprinted in the journal of the Social Democratic Federation, the *Social Democrat*. (See B. Simon, *Education and the Labour Movement, 1870–1918* (1965), p.214, and for Fitch's career J. Leese, *Personalities and Power in English Education* (1950), pp.165–71.) There is a useful account of the pattern of activities of the boards in M. Sturt, *The Education of the People* (1967). A recent History of Education Society discussion on the subject is reported in *Bulletin No 3* of the Society (1969), pp.3–6.
21. See, for example, ibid. pp.6–8, for an account of a discussion on the work of the Technical Instruction Committees in the two areas.
22. For a possible approach, see my article 'Social Structure and Politics in Birmingham and Lyons' in the *British Journal of Sociology* (1950).
23. Lytton had chapters on 'the education of the higher classes', 'the state of education among the middling classes' and 'popular education'. His main international comparison was that with Prussia.
24. The phrase 'what may be called the English system' recurs in many later

commentaries. The Robbins Committee on Higher Education used the phrase, 'if it may be called a system'. It is interesting that the parallel article to that of Fitch in the *Encyclopedia Britannica* on the United States was written by Nicholas Murray Butler, President of Columbia University.

25. See, for example, R. Layard et al, *Impact of Robbins* (1969).
26. See M. Blaug, *An Introduction to the Economics of Education* (1971); M.E. Leite, P. Lynch, K. Norris, J. Sheehan and J. Vaizey, *The Economics of Educational Costing*; and an interesting critical review of this approach by T. Barna in *Universities Quarterly* (Summer 1971).
27. See, for example, A. Little and J. Westergaard, 'The Trend of Class Differentials in Educational Opportunity in England and Wales' in the *British Journal of Sociology* (1964). The pioneering work in this field was D. Glass (ed.), *Social Mobility in England* (1954).
28. E.G. West, 'Resource Allocation and Growth in Early Nineteenth-Century British Education' in the *Economic History Review* (1970). See also his article 'Private versus Public Education: A Classical Economic Dispute' in *The Journal of Political Economy* (1964).
29. R. Szreter, 'History and Sociology: Rivals or Partners in the Field of Education?' in *History of Education Society Bulletin* (Spring 1969).
30. See also J. Ryder and H. Silver, *Modern English Society: History and Structure* (1970) which gives education a prominent place in its 'sociological account of some of the more distinctive features of the contemporary English social structure' and its historical base. For an interesting exploratory article, see M. Sanderson, 'Education and the Factory in Industrial Lancashire, 1780–1840' in the *Economic History Review* (1964).
31. D.S. Landes et al, *History as Social Science* (1971), pp.142–3. See also A. Briggs, 'Sociology and History' in A.T. Welford (ed.), *Society, Problems and Methods of Study* (1962), pp.91–9.
32. D. Hopkinson, 'Teachers and the History of Education' in *Trends in Education* (1968).
33. N. Woodard, *Public Schools and the Middle Classes* (1851), quoted in W.L. Burn, *The Age of Equipoise* (1964), p.266.
34. For the Commission, see *inter alia* H. Perkin, *The Origins of Modern English Society* (1969), pp.300–2, and Burn, op. cit., pp.199–201. In both cases the work of the Commission is related to its social as well as to its educational context. See also B. Simon, 'Education: Owen, Mill, Arnold and the Woodard Schools' in *Victorian Studies* (1970).
35. Lytton, op. cit., p.149.
36. H.G. Wells in his *Experiment in Autobiography* (1934), quoted in G.A.N. Lowndes, *The Silent Social Revolution* (1937), p.5.
37. For an interesting, if somewhat one-sided, account of working-class dislike of certain forms of state interventionism, see H. Pelling, 'The Working Class and the Origins of the Welfare State' in *Popular Politics and Society* (1968), pp.1–19.
38. The teachers have been dealt with more adequately than the pupils, but there is more to be said than has already been said by A. Tropp in *The School Teachers* (1957) or in his article on 'The Changing Status of Teachers in England and Wales' in *The Yearbook of Education* (1953). See also R. Bourne and B. Macarthur, *The Struggle for Education, 1870–1970: A Pictorial History*, a by-product of the centenary, and the report of the discussion at a History of Education Society meeting on 'School Boards and their Teachers' in the Society's *Bulletin* (Spring 1969).
39. See the interesting article by R. Johnson on 'Educational Policy and Social Control in Early Victorian England' in *Past and Present* (1970).
40. Quoted in ibid., p.104.
41. R.M. Titmuss, 'Social Administration in a Changing Society' in *Essays on 'The Welfare State'* (1958), p.19.

42. *A Survey of Education in Rotherham*, p.3.
43. Ibid., p.4.
44. See D. Lawton, *Social Class, Language and Education* (1968) and B. Bernstein and D. Henderson, 'Social Class Differences in the Relevance of Language to Socialisation' in *Sociology* (1969).
45. J. Rex, *Key Problems in Sociological Theory* (1962), ch.4.
46. R.A. Butler, *The Art of the Possible* (1971), p.94.
47. The comments on education, brief though they are, in J. Vincent, *The Formation of the Liberal Party* (1966) are particularly useful. He had studied an unpublished Oxford thesis by D. Roland, 'The Struggle for the Elementary Education Act and Its Implementation'.
48. D.A. Hamer, *John Morley* (1968), esp. ch.6, a particularly illuminating analysis.

12

Changing Perspectives in the History of Education

CHARLES WEBSTER

Until recently the major function of the history of education has been to familiarize intending teachers with notable steps in the development of the modern system of public education. This largely uninspired and unedifying exercise, involving as it did the recital of a seemingly endless succession of generally inoperative commissions and many fewer major acts of parliament, has happily come to occupy an increasingly modest place in teacher training, until it is likely to persist merely as a nominal, optional, or ultimately dispensable element. The quality of historical judgment in traditional, linear histories of education, never particularly sound, tends to become progressively weaker the further these works stray back into the past in identifying the sources of the modern educational system. Only rarely have the 'founders' and legislative 'turning points' of any period been able to bear the strain of interpretation traditionally placed upon them. The weakness of this form of the history of education is not simply a matter of academic concern. Because of the neglect of basic issues relating to childhood in history, current discussion of educational problems is necessarily conducted in the absence of a clear historical perspective, although inevitably utilizing historical insights of varying degrees of unreliability.

Paradoxically, the decline in importance of the history of education in vocational training, and its virtual elimination from educational research, has coincided with a revival of interest in the subject among scholars of widely different training and interests. Every year sees the opening up of some new area of investigation by some group or other. Professional historians have played some part in this process, but fortunately it is improbable that education will become the exclusive preserve of the academic historian. There would be little point in

176

rescuing the history of education from a narrow vocational orientation, only to have it evolve into a branch of antiquarianism. This is unlikely to happen providing that the initiative for research remains with commentators whose study of the past is associated with serious interest in the problems of contemporary education. In this context it is significant that a crucial incentive for the ongoing massive re-investigation of the history of American education was provided by anxieties over the formulation of national policy during the 1960s. It is also not coincidental that the recent outburst of interest in the history of English education has occurred at a time of reorganization and controversy. In many areas of education, it is only during the last decade that we have moved beyond the level of knowledge and understanding achieved by the varied but able group of pioneers which included A.E. Dobbs, A.F. Leach, Hastings Rashdall, John Venn, Foster Watson and W.H. Woodward, whose substantial researches were published at the beginning of this century. The most influential figures in this earlier phase were motivated less by antiquarian curiosity, than by an interest in contemporary issues.

Current educational research is able to define many problems which might fruitfully be subjected to historically oriented investigation. The social sciences can furnish methods which may be utilized in the creation of a sound empirical basis for the history of education, as well as a range of interpretative models which could contribute towards the explanation of the process of educational change. While methods of analysis derived from the social sciences have not always been applied to the historical situation with the requisite degree of discrimination, any true understanding of the social systems of the past will necessarily involve the adoption of techniques which are equivalent to those evolved for the investigation of analogous contemporary systems.

The social sciences may thus provide the means by which the history of education emancipates itself from traditional forms of anachronism. But there is also the danger of an emergence of new forms of this failing. Some have already found expression in the distortion of evidence resulting from the search for analogues of situations now topical, and in the construction of latter-day linear histories connected with novel aspects of the modern system of public education. It would not be difficult to produce examples from recent historical writing on such topics as student unrest, or women's education, to illustrate the way in which historical evidence has been marshalled to give an artificial impression of similarity with some modern social phenomenon, the aim often being to generate sympathy for some particular cause. Tendencies of this kind need not be too damaging, provided that they do not lead to another variety of critical orthodoxy. Apologists for different pressure groups are awakening interest in neglected aspects of the history of education. At a more general level Marxist critiques of modern school systems, right wing objections to comprehensive education, and attacks on schooling by architects of alternative culture, have dispelled complacency about entrenched values, and stimulated a new level of critical awareness in the history of the subject. As a consequence, recent writing may be distinctly uneven in quality, and, as in education itself, consensus is discernible on relatively few issues. Nonetheless, there is now a new vitality, spontaneity, and creativity in the field. It is with a view to giving an outlet to the new work in the history of education that the editors of the *Oxford Review of Education* have decided to devote to it a special extended issue of the journal. The authors selected come from many different backgrounds, and no editorial attempt has been made to impose a common approach, or to obtain complete coverage of any specific area. Contributions have been solicited with a view to widening the horizons of the history of education, and to encouraging retrospective reviews by leading authorities on general methodological and historiographical issues. Most of the contributions are drawn from the rapidly expanding and highly relevant fields of research into English education in the nineteenth century. These are complemented by single essays on France and Germany which are indicative of our increasing awareness of continental education. In this, as in so many other fields of research in social history, we are coming to appreciate the degree to which work on France is in advance of that on any other region.

The purpose of this brief introduction is to provide the general background for this collection by indicating some of the main lines of contemporary thinking about the history of education. Consistent with the bias of the collection, most illustrative examples are selected from writings relating to English elementary and popular education, reference being made to developments in France and America whenever appropriate. Intentionally I have confined myself to the discussion of representative contributions produced since 1969, in order to prevent undue repetition of points made in earlier review articles (Talbott, 1970; Sutherland, 1971; Butts, 1974), although there is inevitably a degree of overlap with the forceful and constructive essays by Simon and Silver in the present issue.

One of the most limiting aspects of the history of education has been the assumption that everything of importance could be embraced in an account of the emergence of the state system of schools. From this point of view inordinate importance is attached to the steps whereby government participation in education was secured in the nineteenth century. In the period before 1800 it is supposed that 'the educational system was simple in form' (Musgrave, 1970, p.22), or even that the idea of general education cannot be traced back beyond the last quarter of the eighteenth century (Wardle, 1971a, p.1). General histories of education tend to begin with the late eighteenth century and they carry the implicit assumption that the population at large had only the most limited opportunities for literacy and education before that time. This bias is reinforced by those social scientists who regard education as the prerogative of modern industrialized societies. Hence the general expansion of education, or the wider extension of literacy in England is thought to be concomitant with the industrial revolution. From the educational point of view it is tempting to suppose that English society pre-1780 existed at the 'traditional' or pre-literate level characteristic of underdeveloped countries. Hypotheses which stress this discontinuity have inevitably tended to direct attention away from the period before 1800, and have consequently given English education an extremely truncated chronological perspective.

One of the main factors in breaking down this artificial barrier has been the appreciation that the modern school is only one aspect of the educational mechanism, and that schools themselves can only be properly understood if they are studied as part of the more general framework of education. This broader outlook involves reference to all means employed by the community for the socialization of the younger generation. For historical purposes it has more utility than the narrower definitions of education favoured by contemporary philosophers of education. The value of this conception of education was exhibited more than half a century ago by Durkheim, but it was only after the widespread publication of studies of upbringing by social anthropologists that it became an active influence in the analysis of western education. Schools thereby may be seen as having many different functional roles, and they can take their place alongside the family, the church and other social institutions in determining the educational experiences of each successive generation. The location of educational change becomes not merely a matter of describing the development of one kind of school, but of determining the changing relationships of different kinds of schooling, and the shifting balance in control of education between the parent, pastor, teacher and employer. This approach supplies the basis for the study of education as a continuity, and it provides a particularly sharp incentive to investigate education in the period before the existence of a clearly defined system of state schools.

179

One area of study to benefit in this way is the American colonial situation, which has been treated first by Burstyn impressionistically, and then on a massive scale in the first volume to be completed in Cremin's project to produce a completely new survey of American education (Cremin, 1970). Both of these studies effectively show the manner in which education was conditioned by the religious ethos of the settlers, and educational institutions adapted organically to the needs of the evolving colonies. Cremin's work also highlights the difficulties involved in the integrative approach to the history of education. The more conscientious the attempt to appreciate the complexities of the educational process, the greater the temptation to sweep the net more widely until the history of education becomes an encyclopaedia of social and intellectual history, in which it is almost impossible to obtain any clear focus on the educational experiences of childhood and adolescence.

There is therefore the grave danger that the pendulum may swing too far. For the historian, education as a concept formerly embraced too little; now it is rapidly coming to include too much. Cremin has thus tended to deal with not only higher education, but also general intellectual and cultural history; and he has written almost as much about England as New England, thereby incidentally producing what is probably the most adequate introduction to English education in the pre-industrial period. The monographs by Joan Simon and Kenneth Charlton have effectively updated the work of Foster Watson and corrected Leach's pessimistic attitude towards education during the renaissance and reformation. My own, more recent study of education during the Puritan Revolution has many parallels with Cremin's treatment of the puritan educational programme in New England (Webster, 1975). Both Cremin and myself have been concerned to demonstrate the precise manner in which the protestant social ethic determined the structural framework for education, from birth to maturity. Whereas Troeltsch and Weber dealt with long-term trends stemming from the reformation in Europe, I have been more interested in factors involved in the formulation of social policies during periods of social disruption. I suggest that during such periods a millenarian eschatology becomes an important element in the ideology of assertive groups. The abortive attempt of the puritan reformers to promote a total reconstruction of the educational system stands out as one of the most remarkable cases of discontinuity in English education. Henceforth exercises of this kind were limited to isolated utopian groups.

Our knowledge of pre-industrial English education remains profoundly incomplete. There is nothing to compare with the recent

scientifically precise survey of French education before 1800 (Charlier
et al, 1976). Histories of old schools are no substitute for histories of the
education of the community. The complexity of this task is indicated by
Jordan's work on rural charities, and by some minor surveys which
reveal intense activity in educational philanthropy in the sixteenth
and seventeenth centuries. Indeed it is now becoming questionable
whether the charity school movement of the eighteenth century can be
regarded as little more than the tail end of the movement which was at
its peak between 1550 and 1640. Local studies increasingly support the
contention of Jordan and Stone that a revolutionary expansion in
formal education occurred during this earlier period (Feyerharm,
1976; Smith, 1976). An insight into the elaborate network of local
facilities for education is provided by a study of Cambridgeshire village
communities, which for the first time introduces the wider concept of
education into microcosmic examination of population, economic
conditions, literacy, schooling, and religious practice (Spufford, 1974).
No remarkable findings about literacy have emerged from this work,
but it does indicate the complexity of the pattern of schooling, the high
academic standing of teachers, even in vernacular schools, and a more
impressive level of rational participation in religious affairs on the part
of the lowest orders in society than would be anticipated from the
evidence about diffusion of writing skills. The ability to produce a
legible signature need not necessarily be a sound guide to the level of
rational awareness in either rural communities at the time of the spread
of religious dissent and political unrest before the Puritan Revolution,
or in working-class communities before the renewed expansion of
formal schooling in the nineteenth century. Investigation of social
literacy in industrialized societies – involving reference to the role of
such agencies as ragged schools, public houses, the radical press,
debating societies, circulating libraries, workmen's associations, co-
operative groups, and radical political groups – has been given a strong
impetus by E.P. Thompson's *The Making of the English Working
Class* (1963; revised edn. 1968). The social historian must display
the persistence of an archaeologist in the search into neglected
and often incomplete records relating to a whole spectrum of
ephemeral institutions which are essential for the characterization of
the education and culture of the working-class section of the population
in the nineteenth century (Hollis, 1970; Harrison, 1971; Money, 1971).
There will be some temptation to regard this culture as representative,
whereas it may in fact reflect the situation of a minority of artisans
and labourers. But this ideologically active minority was strategically
placed to counterbalance the influence of the educational agencies

sponsored by the establishment. In this context it is noticeable that a more critical examination is now being made of Sunday schools and Mechanics Institutes, institutions of a more permanent character and large membership, control of which was balanced between different sectional interests. It is no longer possible to adopt a simple view of the educational role of these institutions. Their development was very much dictated by local circumstances, although it is emerging that Mechanics Institutes served the interests of mechanics only to a limited degree, and that Sunday schools evolved to complement the presiding ethos of the factory schools and schools of the voluntary associations.

While the earlier generation of labour historians tended to concentrate on social deprivation, and liberal humanitarian response in the form of the emerging social welfare institutions of the nineteenth century, contemporary social historians are less interested in the development of national education and other agencies. They display a disenchanted attitude towards the humanitarian movement, being concerned more with the characterization of an 'underground' or 'alternative' working-class culture. This shift of emphasis has highlighted enduring class division and economic exploitation. It displaces the acceptance, common to sociologists and conventional historians of education, that social reform involved a process of gradual functional adaptation which served to preserve a balance of interests, or homeostatic relationship, between the various social and political groups. Marxist writing on education has now largely abandoned the explanation of social change according to a simplistic base–superstructure model (a point not appreciated by Vaughan and Archer, 1971), in favour of an interpretation of state apparatus which allows cultural forces like education to occupy a more dynamic role. The educational system is seen as a factor of great importance in constituting the mechanism which, in the course of the nineteenth century, took the place of churches as the dominant instrument of hegemony (Gramsci) or ideological state apparatus (Althusser) serving to promote conformity to the needs of civil society. This position has promoted the view that the school systems evolved in the last century should be regarded as imprisoning the mind of the proletariat (Gramsci, 1965; Broccoli, 1972; Althusser, 1973, 1976; Levitas, 1974; Gluckmann, 1975). A recent general survey of English education which coincides with the above point of view (Shipman, 1971) will be discussed below. This examination of social control, like the work of Althusser, has the disadvantage of being conducted at an extremely generalized level. The idea that 'schooling was repressive for the poor in a social context of repression' (Shipman, p.138) calls for a very much more detailed empirical analysis of the operation of the educational system, before it can be rendered in informative historical terms. Evidence about the course of educational legislation goes only a short way towards providing an insight into the operation of the machinery of social control. Studies undertaken by Johnson and Sutherland have increased our understanding of the ideology of the national educational administration and inspectorate (Johnson, 1970, 1972; Sutherland, 1973). Complementary studies are needed of educational administrations, and particularly of the character of the teaching profession as the instrument responsible for the inculcation of a new code of moral values. We still have a remarkably inadequate knowledge of the experience of children in nineteenth-century schools, but one useful source of evidence is provided by their school books (Goldstrom, 1972). Goldstrom's work may usefully be compared with the study of working-class reading habits by Webb and Altick.

There are innumerable histories of School Boards, and a growing number of local histories of education. However these are inclined to follow conventional lines and for the most part they merely chart the course of development of the local school system, with some regard to local and national political circumstances. Even the more substantial and broadly conceived histories (e.g. Wardle, 1971) tend to be dominated by a description of the orderly development of the various sectors of local education. As in most local studies the post-1870 School Boards are made to emerge with a better record of liberalism than the pre-1870 voluntary associations. On the other hand, as indicated below, the economist E.G. West has argued that the voluntary system had the same order of success as the state system. Social historians would also agree that the similarities of the two systems outweighed their differences, but without ascribing a particularly liberal function to either.

By contrast with those of England, the local histories of American education have reflected to a much greater extent the standpoint of the critics of the indigenous public school system (Katz, 1971; Kaestle, 1973; Schultz, 1973; Graham, 1974). Such authors vary in their bias, but all emphasize the growth of insensitive bureaucratic structures, and the way in which the school system could scarcely avoid becoming the instrument of corporate society. Of the above authors only Katz inclines to adopt an irrevocably pessimistic attitude about the American school, in line with the growing chorus of the deschooling movement. The publications produced by this movement in England have not been historically oriented but, sensing the mood of the times, Wardle (1974) has come forward with a self-consciously anti-

183

deschooling history, which might better serve as a reply to much of the writing on social control. Wardle sees the expansion of the education system in terms of movement towards a liberal and democratic society. In the eighteenth century the philanthropists used education as a 'weapon in the struggle against poverty' (p. 78). Thereafter schools were essentially a means to enlightenment, as a mechanism which opposed 'dangerous or unhealthy movements in popular thinking', or counteracted dominant cultural values (p. 108). In Wardle's view the English school has very rarely reflected the received values of society. The system has therefore served as an antidote to indoctrination. Wardle's attempt to provide an historical apologia for traditional institutions is bound to be widely applauded, but it is doubtful whether he would have been able to state the case in quite such extreme terms had the 'social' intention of his history of Nottingham education been pursued more seriously.

Notwithstanding the widespread use of literacy estimates as an indication of the cultural level of the population, literacy has only a limited value as an indicator of educational achievement. Yet its potentiality for the identification of long-term trends, and detailed regional comparison, make the expedient an alluring temptation to the increasingly quantitatively-minded modern historian. A comprehensive literacy survey for France under the *ancien régime* was produced in the last century by Louis Maggiolo. Recent work on French provincial education has analysed the contribution to literacy of the system of *petites écoles* and *écoles de charité*, and in the course of this work Maggiolo's methods have been criticized and refined (Furet and Sachs, 1974; Charlier *et al*, 1976). It is now realized that estimates of literacy based on the simple enumeration of signatures on marriage licences can be highly misleading (Schofield, 1968).

Historians of English education were for long mysteriously silent on the question of literacy. The first general survey of changes in literacy in England was not attempted until 1969, as a sequel to an investigation of educational expansion in the century before 1640 (Stone, 1969). This work showed little awareness of the methodological difficulties involved in such a survey. Stone simply used marriage licence signatures from relatively small areas in the south of England, supplemented by national statistics from the office of the Registrar General for the period from 1840, as the basis for his conclusions. Some of Stone's brave conjectures may well prove to be correct, especially as the pattern which he describes is not altogether unexpected. A remarkably high level of literacy was attained by 1700 in the course of the 'educational revolution' of the early modern period. This progress

184

was not maintained in England during the next century; with the result that the advantages gained over rival European nations in terms of literacy were largely lost. The recovery which occurred during the nineteenth century seems to have begun well before the 1870 Education Act. It will be interesting to see whether Stone's impressionistic work is confirmed by the much more elaborate survey undertaken by Schofield. Preliminary accounts of this work suggest that remarkably little change occurred in national literacy between 1750 and 1840; the only noticeable perturbation being the closing of the gap between male and female literacy (Schofield, 1970/2; Laqueur, 1974). As in so many cases of general indices, national statistics about marriage licence signatures could serve to obscure pronounced regional differences in the process of educational change. For instance, by contrast with Stone's southern counties, the male literacy rate in different parts of industrial Lancashire fell by more than 20 per cent between 1750 and 1820 to a level of just over 40 per cent; thereafter a slow recovery occurred until in 1850 the rate was virtually the same as a century before. The educational meaning of these statistics is not easy to assess. They may overstate writing ability, but on the other hand they seriously underestimate the level of attainment of the ability to read. It is usually assumed that there is a constant relationship between reading and writing skills, but this may be fallacious; during the industrial revolution, for instance, the gap between them may have opened out owing to the resistance of both Sunday and day school authorities to the teaching of writing.

Recent investigations into changing rates of literacy in industrial Lancashire have served to sharpen the debate on the relationship between education and the industrial revolution, a subject which has for different reasons been regarded as a key issue by sociologists, political scientists, and historians interested in economic change, or in the relationship between science and technology. Each group has tended to approach this problem with its own preconceptions, and there has been a tendency to predetermine solutions by assuming that the historical situation will replicate patterns of social and economic change which are known to be characteristic of the course of industrialization in modern underdeveloped countries. For instance, it is often noted with satisfaction that the industrial revolution in England occurred at a time when literacy rates were at the 40 per cent 'threshold' level established by Bowman and Anderson as a necessary condition for economic emergence. It is less comforting that the requisite level had actually been reached more than a century before, and that the industrialized areas were witnessing a steep *decline* in literacy

185

during the initial phases of the industrial revolution. On the basis of statistics suggesting the divergence of education and industrialization, Sanderson (1968, 1972) suggests that education was disrupted by industrial change to such a degree that it could play little part in promoting social mobility or improvements in industrial efficiency.

An entirely different interpretation of literacy trends is adopted by Laqueur (1974) who sees industrialization as a spur to education and social mobility, and hence as the cause of a reversal in the downward spiral of literacy rates. A much simpler view of this situation is taken by West (1975) who has little taste for detailed local investigations of the kind undertaken by Sanderson and Laqueur. Instead, he mounts a barrage of scraps of numerical data derived from all quarters, to vindicate his view that there is a perfect correlation between the industrial revolution and an 'educational revolution'. West believes that there was an enormous expansion in the quantity and quality of education during the decades before the 1870 Education Act, which, together with public education in general, is seen as something of an anti-climax. West can be ranked as a militant optimist in the cost-of-living debate, and his recent work is part of his continuing onslaught upon the dominant tradition of social history, which adopts a pessimistic view of the social effects of the industrial revolution. If West's exposition were correct, those social historians who have built up such an elaborate picture of the 'Bleak Age' will have been guilty of unscrupulous misrepresentation. To a much greater degree than West would allow, there is a consensus of opinion that the voluntary school system expanded rapidly, with the result that opportunities for formal schooling greatly increased during the first half of the nineteenth century. In this sense education was a beneficiary of the rising industrial system. It is only a disagreement as to the precise nature of this beneficence that places a figure like West at odds with almost all other commentators. Formal primary education before 1850 is increasingly viewed as part of the machinery of social control required for preserving the discipline of the growing labour force. As expressed by the sociologist Shipman, the system of voluntary schools was created in the interests of mobilization and differentiation by the entrepreneurial classes; it was 'part of the total machinery of coercion that was used to limit disturbance and inculcate a new social discipline' (Shipman, 1971, p. 134). Economists have come to adopt a similar point of view, largely abandoning the idea that industrialization initially demanded a large force of literate workers as a manpower requirement (Landes, 1969). Nevertheless, the manufacturers came to appreciate that schooling bred 'attitudes of punctuality, persistence, concentration, obedience',

186

with the result that it could be regarded as a sound investment (Blaug, 1975). Blaug retains a relatively 'optimistic' interpretation of this situation by taking the view that factory owners stimulated education by their willingness to pay educated workers at higher rates. A more complicated and realistic view of this situation can be found in the writings on industrial change of Pollard and Smelser.

There is very little agreement on the role of education as an inducement to social mobility and industrial innovation before 1850. One study has collected a mass of inductive evidence to show that a variety of informal mechanisms operated to ensure the fruitful interchange of ideas between technicians, industrialists and scientists (Musson and Robinson, 1969), while another has conducted a 'crucial experiment' to disprove these relationships, by applying prosopographical analysis to the Manchester Literary and Philosophical Society (Thackray, 1975). Education is mentioned briefly in N. Smelser's *Social Change in the Industrial Revolution* (1959), but it is an implicitly important element in his Parsonian model of the dynamics of family reorganization. This is described in terms of a seven-part sequence of structural differentiation, which is also applied to the organization of industry. In Smelser's view schools emerged as a response to the needs of the new type of working-class family in which there was increasing segregation between the economic roles of children and adults. The specific application to education of the model used by Smelser has been attempted by Musgrave's discussion of educational change from 1860. Musgrave (1970) views each major step in educational legislation as a 'truce situation', involving a redefinition of the situation which indicates a new balance of interests. One further brief study according to the Parsonian action frame reference by Turner (1969) examines the resolution of internal conflicts in the management of local Mechanics Institutes also in terms of a series of truce situations.

A different sociological method has been utilized in a comparative study of educational change in England and France during the first part of the nineteenth century. Here the authors apply Weber's concept of domination and assertion. By contrast with almost all other commentators, they do not accept that industrialization was a major factor in determining the course of educational development in either country. In their view 'there is no direct or mechanistic association between economic development and educational change at the macro-sociological level' (Vaughan and Archer, 1971, p. 227). None of the mechanisms proposed to link education with the economy is thought to have played more than a subsidiary role. Educational change is seen in terms of a conflict between the dominant established church and the assertive middle class for the control of education in each country. The two groups in either case are thought to have had divergent educational aims and interests. In England the educational outlook of the middle classes was determined by an ideology which united the dissenting religious outlook, the principles of classical economics and the tenets of utilitarian ethics. The work of Vaughan and Archer is not without merit. It avoids diffuseness by paying attention to the main characteristics of the school system. There was indeed vigorous competition between the Nonconformist and Anglican school associations for the control of education. Religious and social ideas played a real part in determining the middle-class outlook on schooling. Patterns of education cannot be regarded as simple extrapolations of the economic system.

The authors have thus introduced some important elements into their analyses, but their work is open to certain major objections. In particular, too little care has been taken with the definition of the two competing parties. Almost nothing is said about the social groups backing the Church, whereas it is too readily assumed that the Nonconformists were solidly supported by the middle classes. There is also an element of contradiction introduced in the treatment of industrialization. Although everything is done to minimize the role of this process, the authors find it almost impossible to discuss the motive for educational expansion without reference to preoccupation with the disciplining of the work force. It is altogether unconvincing to regard such factors as concern for the dissemination of the habit of bible-reading as major stimuli to educational expansion. Consequently, this investigation is not altogether successful; but it does demonstrate the especial relevance of Weber's ideas on bureaucracy, religion and status to the explanation of the development of middle-class education in England during the nineteenth century.

Recent sociological approaches to nineteenth-century education have produced disappointingly few insights likely to be of long-term historical interest. Very often they have achieved little more than the translation of conventional wisdom into the wordy terms of Parsonianism. Some of the more ambitious exercises have failed because the application of a model has involved such a degree of simplification that the conclusions generated are incompatible with the historical evidence. Some of the most useful results have emerged from the application of one or other of the theories of social control. Even in the more acceptable cases, sociological methods have been used more for the purposes of interpretation and revaluation than as a means of generating productive historical research. But sociological work need not be conducted at this diffuse level. Educational research has often involved an historical dimension, leading to many valuable studies on problems which have their roots in the nineteenth century. If such specific studies are used as a guideline, the differences between the 'historical' and 'sociological' approaches to the past should gradually disappear.

An increasing amount of work in the history of education is undertaken in the context of research into the history of the family. This is one of the most rapidly expanding areas in the field of modern history. It will not be necessary to comment at length on recent work in this area in view of the perceptive remarks about childhood and adolescence in Joan Simon's essay review (1976). The two main sources for recent work have been the French interest in long-term trends in social history, and the newer largely American fashion for psychohistory. Lastly, the investigation by social anthropologists and sociologists of family life has served to prompt the rather belated drift of Anglo-Saxon historians into the field of family history. It is unfortunate that one of the major recent studies on this subject, by Pinchbeck and Hewitt (1969–73) is disappointingly derivative and uncritical. With respect to interpretations of the origin and evolution of correlated concepts of childhood and schooling, modern work is still little more than a footnote to the achievement of Ariès, whose remarkable book was given fresh prominence by being reissued both in French, with a new preface, and as an English paperback, in 1973. Ariès' work is open to criticism on many specific points, and many of its conclusions apply to France rather than to any other country. But it must be regarded as one of the most original and stimulating studies having reference to education produced during recent decades. The most innovatory sections of Ariès' book relate to the early modern period; his comments about the later history of schooling follow reasonably conventional lines. Much less conventional is the work of the psychohistorians, whose writings are produced under the aegis of Lloyd de Mause, sponsor and editor of *The History of Childhood* (1974) and the *History of Childhood Quarterly* (1973–). Whereas Ariès explains changes in attitudes to childhood in terms of broad cultural shifts, de Mause attempts to define the operation of a process of psychological evolution in which successive generations of parents need to 'regress to the psychic age of their children and work through the anxieties of that age in a better manner the second time they encounter them than they did during their own childhood' (de Mause, 1974, p. 3). In practice this theory emphasizes the element of tension in the parent–child relationship, and

189

much of the work published by this group deals with infanticide or parental maltreatment of children.

Despite their marked diversity of approach, both Ariès and de Mause locate the origins of the 'modern' conception of childhood in the early modern period, with the growth of systematic, deliberate, and sustained age-graded schooling outside the household. The child-oriented approach to schooling of psychohistorians is well illustrated by two articles by Finkelstein (1975, 1976), who deals with education very much in terms of the schools as a convenient vehicle for parents wishing to delegate their traditional educative responsibilities. The tutor and then the teacher were employed to reflect parental values. In de Mausian terms, the 'superstructure of the American public school was built on a foundation of parental anxiety and fear of childhood' (1976, p. 331). Thus the American school is seen as an alliance built up between parents and teachers, not in the interests of children, but out of a fear of the energy and spontaneity of childhood. As Finkelstein's essays indicate, psychological factors tend to fall into the background when detailed problems of social change are discussed. It is unlikely that any one system, or eclectic body of psychological theory, will become the major organizing principle in the history of education. However, the utility of this method has been demonstrated in personal biography, and it could well be applied to further our knowledge of the shaping of personality in the course of collective experience in schools.

This review has examined some of the main approaches currently being adopted to the study of elementary and popular education. The discussion could also have been conducted in terms of recent work on secondary or higher education, or with reference to the studies of Brian Simon and others on the politics of education. All of these subjects have been transformed during the last few years. Elementary education, as the education of the majority of the people, provides a good basis for discussion since it is now, for the first time, attracting the attention it deserves, not only at the level of detailed research, but also in more introductory surveys which are a great improvement on traditional histories of education (Hurt, 1971; Lawson and Silver, 1973).

It remains to be seen whether the revival of the history of education does more than awaken interest in another neglected corner of historical studies. Will policy-makers turn to comparative studies having reference to our own cultural tradition, as readily as they make comparison with contemporary developments elsewhere? Historical reconstruction is likely to be an embarrassment if educational mechanisms are framed in cost–benefit terms, whereas past experience assumes an obviously fundamental importance if education is seen as a means of fostering social cohesion and the critical awareness of the people.

In a political society, decisions are not determined merely by the findings of current psychological, sociological or economic research. Tradition is involved in a forceful yet intangible manner in present-day educational controversy. The grammar schools and universities are defended by reference to long-guarded traditions. Alarm over discipline, literacy, educational standards, or the role of the inspectorate, is fuelled by implicit assumptions about standards earlier achieved. Unfortunately, the historical perspective implied has almost invariably been formed in the absence of any serious regard for the historical evidence. Our impressions of short-term trends are often illusory, and longer-term studies invalidate most of our ideas about continuity and growth. It is only by reference to history that we will understand both the root causes of the present crisis of confidence, and the sources for our inegalitarian and heavily bureaucratized educational system, and it is only by this means that we will be able to retrace the steps by which progress has been made at the cost of insensitivity to the cultural aspirations of the classes which the system was intended to serve. These are lessons which the bureaucrat and the politician are very unlikely to wish to learn.

REFERENCES

Althusser, L. (1973), *Philosophie et philosophie spontanée des savants* (Paris, Maspéro).
Althusser, L. (1976), *Positions (1964–1975)* (Paris, Éditions Sociales).
Ariès, P. (1973), *L'Enfant et la vie familiale sous l'Ancien Régime* (Paris, Libraire Plon).
Blaug, M. (1975), 'The Economics of Education in English Classical Political Economics: A Reassessment'. *In* Skinner, A.S. and Wilson, T. (Eds.), *Essays on Adam Smith*, pp.568–99 (Oxford, Clarendon Press).
Bucci-Glucksman, C. (1975), *Gramsci et l'état* (Paris, Fayard).
Butts, R. Freeman (1974), 'Public education and political community', *History of Education Quarterly*, 14, 2.
Charlier, R., Compère, M.M. and Julia, D. (1976), *L'Éducation en France du XVIIIe siècle* (Paris, CDU & SEDES).
Cremin, L.A. (1970), *American Education: The Colonial Experience 1607–1783* (New York, Harper).
De Mause, L. (1974) (ed.), *The History of Childhood* (New York, Psychohistory Press).
Feyerharm, W.R. (1976), 'The status of the schoolmaster and the continuity of education in Elizabethan East Anglia', *History of Education*, 5, pp.103–16.
Finkelstein, B. (1975), 'Pedagogy as intrusion', *History of Childhood Quarterly*, 2, pp.349–78.
Finkelstein, B. (1976), 'In fear of childhood', *History of Childhood Quarterly*, 3, pp.321–36.
Furet, M. and Sachs, W. (1974), 'La croissance de l'alphabétisation en France XVIIIe–

XIXe siècle', *Annales E.S.C.*, 29, pp.714–37.

Goldstrom, J.M. (1972), *The Social Content of Education 1808–1870: A Study of the Working Class School Reader in England and Ireland* (Shannon, Irish U.P.).

Graham, P.A. (1974), *Community and Class in American Education 1865–1918* (New York, Wiley).

Gramsci, A. (1965), *Lettere dal carcere* (Turin, Einaudi).

Harrison, J.F.C. (1971), *Underground Education in the Nineteenth Century* (Leeds, Leeds U.P.).

Hollis, P. (1970), *The Pauper Press* (London, O.U.P.).

Hurt, J. (1971), *Education in Evolution* (London, Hart-Davis).

Johnson, R. (1970), 'Educational policy and social control in early Victorian England', *Past and Present*, 49, pp.96–100.

Johnson, R. (1972), 'Administrators in Education before 1870: Patronage, Social Position and Role'. *In* Sutherland, G. (ed.), *Studies in the Growth of Nineteenth Century Government*, pp.110–138 (London, Routledge & Kegan Paul).

Kaestle, C.F. (1973), *The Evolution of an Urban School System: New York City, 1750–1850* (Cambridge, Mass., Harvard U.P.).

Katz. M.B., (1971), *Class, Bureaucracy and Schools* (New York, Praeger).

Landes, D. (1969), *The Unbound Prometheus* (Cambridge, C.U.P.).

Laqueur, T.W. (1974), 'Literacy and social mobility in the industrial revolution in England', *Past and Present*, 64, pp.96–107.

Lawson, J. and Silver, H. (1973), *A Social History of Education in England* (London, Methuen).

Levitas, M. (1974), *Marxist Perspectives in the Sociology of Education* (London, Lawrence & Wishart).

Money, J. (1971), 'Taverns, coffee houses and clubs', *Historical Journal*, 14, pp.15–47.

Musgrave, P.W. (1970), ' Model for the Analysis of the Development of the English Educational System from 1860'. *In* Musgrave, P.W. (ed.), *Sociology, History and Education*, pp.15–29 (London, Methuen).

Musson, A.E. and Robinson, E. (1969), *Science and Technology in the Industrial Revolution* (Manchester, Manchester U.P.).

Pinchbeck, I. and Hewitt, M. (1969–1973), *Children in English Society*, 2 vols. (London, Routledge & Kegan Paul).

Sanderson, M. (1968), 'Social change and elementary education in industrial Lancashire 1780–1840', *Northern History*, 3, pp.131–54.

Sanderson, M. (1972), 'Literacy and social mobility in the industrial revolution in England', *Past and Present*, 56, pp.75–104.

Schofield, R.S. (1968), 'The Measurement of Literacy'. *In* Goody, J. (ed.), *Literacy in Traditional Society*, pp.311–25 (Cambridge, C.U.P.).

Schofield, R.S. (1970/2), 'Dimensions of Illiteracy, 1750–1850', *Explorations in Economic History*, pp.437–54.

Schultz, S.K. (1973), *The Culture Factory: Boston Public Schools, 1789–1860* (New York, O.U.P.).

Simon, J. (1976), 'The History of Education in *Past and Present*', *Oxford Review of Education*, 3, pp.71–86.

Smith A. (1976), 'Private schools and schoolmasters in the diocese of Lichfield and Coventry in the seventeenth century', *History of Education*, 5, pp.117–26.

Spufford, M. (1974), *Contrasting Communities: English Villages in the Sixteenth and Seventeenth Centuries* (Cambridge, C.U.P.).

Sutherland, G. (1971), *Elementary Education in the Nineteenth Century* (London, Historical Association).

Sutherland, G. (1973), *Policy-Making in Elementary Education 1870–1895* (London, O.U.P.).

Stone, L. (1969), 'Literacy and Education in England 1640–1900', *Past and Present*, 42, pp.69–139.

Talbott, J. (1971), 'The history of education', *Daedalus*, 200, pp.133–50. (See No. 10 in this volume.)

Thackray, A. (1974), 'Natural knowledge in cultural context: the Manchester model', *The American Historical Review*, 79, pp.672–709.

Turner, C.M. (1969), 'Sociological approaches to the history of education', *British Journal of Educational Studies*, 17, pp.146–65.

Vaughan, M. and Archer, M.S. (1971), *Social Conflict and Educational Change in England and France 1789–1848* (Cambridge, C.U.P.).

Wardle, D. (1971a), *English Popular Education 1780–1970* (Cambridge, C.U.P.).

Wardle, D. (1971b), *Education and Society in Nineteenth Century Nottingham* (Cambridge, C.U.P.).

Wardle, D. (1974), *The Rise of the Schooled Society* (London, Routledge).

Webster, C. (1975), *The Great Instauration: Science, Medicine and Reform 1626–1660* (London, Duckworth).

West, E.G. (1975), *Education and the Industrial Revolution* (London, Batsford).

13

Aspects of Neglect: The Strange Case of Victorian Popular Education

HAROLD SILVER

More has been researched and written about education in Victorian England than in any other period, and the majority of it has been about popular education. Yet we have neglected it. Most of what has been written has in fact disguised our neglect and ignorance of it. This is not just a question of 'gaps' that need to be filled, of historical enterprise in which we have been engaged. Judgements about historical 'neglect', of course, depend on assumptions about what is, could be, or should be known. They entail definitions of the area, purpose and value of study. Such judgements and definitions are ideological statements. My interest in our 'neglect' of Victorian popular education, in the nature of the historical definitions involved, and in related questions of ideology, arises from difficulties in my current research. In making a judgement about the apparently *most* explored area and period of English education, I am inevitably making a judgement about the direction of the history of education – though I am here confining myself to the nineteenth century, and to the education of the poor. I cannot avoid outlining the personal research situation out of which this discussion arises, or the main thrusts of previous investigations in this field. In outlining these situations I cannot avoid discussing the reasons for them, and the theoretical and historiographical issues which they raise.

The themes that have attracted the most attention in Victorian popular education have been those of policy formation and legislation, commissions and committees, the provision, control and administration of education, and the changing shape of different 'levels' of education – elementary and technical, infant and adult, and 'types' of education – board and voluntary. Some attention has been paid to the broader 'context' of educational decisions and functions – notably that of the churches and the radical and labour movements, and the nature and extent of literacy. Studies have been national and (especially in the case of theses and dissertations) local – with a vast amount of (mainly unpublished) work on local school boards and local institutions. The most researched and discussed areas can be summarized as: the school boards, the voluntary school system, and the development of a national system of administration (focusing on Kay-Shuttleworth and the Committee of Council, Robert Lowe and the Revised Code, Forster and the 1870 Education Act, the politics of the school board era and the events leading up to the 1902 Education Act). Attention has also been paid (again, largely in unpublished work) to pressure groups, from the Central Society of Education in the 1830s to the bodies campaigning for public education in the late 1840s and 1850s, the National Education League of the late 1860s, and the socialist organizations of the last decades of the century.[1] It seems a well-surveyed field, and it has produced such publication peaks as Brian Simon's first two volumes of 'Studies in the History of Education' which encompass the Victorian period (1960, 1965), John Harrison's *Learning and Living 1780–1960* (1961), Mabel Tylecote's *The Mechanics' Institutes of Lancashire and Yorkshire before 1851* (1957), David Rubinstein's *School Attendance in London 1870–1904* (1969), Richard Selleck's *The New Education 1870–1914* (1968), and above all – though only marginally concerned with the Victorian period – A.E. Dobbs's pioneering *Education and Social Movements 1700–1850* (1919). All of these successfully explored education in important relationships with social movements, social change, and related ideas and ideals. The period of major contributions stretches from the early wide-ranging histories by Charles Birchenough, J.W. Adamson and Frank Smith in the 1920s and 1930s, to such detailed studies since the 1950s as those of educational policy, politics and administration by Eric Eaglesham, Peter Gosden and Gillian Sutherland, of religion and education by Marjorie Cruickshank and James Murphy, and of school architecture by Malcolm Seaborne.[2] The bibliographies of work published and unpublished are substantial.[3]

My dissatisfaction with the mass of books, articles, theses and dissertations began to take shape during my co-authorship of *A Social History of Education in England*[4] but became explicit after the completion of another book of which I was co-author, *The Education of the Poor*, a history of a Church school for the children of the poor in Kennington, South London.[5] The work on this book eventually raised some awkward questions about this perhaps 'atypical' monitorial school – as it was when it was created in 1824. The school sources revealed a more imaginative and humane approach to children and to school affairs, and stronger school–community links than we had expected, or could explain. The school was as concerned in its early decades with the children's health as it was with their souls, and the school and its managers were the focal point for Lambeth's fight against cholera, bad sanitation and other environmental nuisances. The teachers were competent and the school efficient. From the 1880s boys were winning a stream of scholarships to London's grammar and other schools. A record of humanity, efficiency and – in a variety of ways – innovation seemed to stretch from the 1820s to the twentieth century. There could be reason for thinking that this school, in the 1820s and 1830s, or in the 1880s, was atypical, but if so what was typical? There was no answer to this question (and when the book was completed it became clear that we had ourselves shied away from it) because historians had surprisingly done no research on the monitorial system as it was operated in practice. Only one British historical thesis has been written, so far as I am aware, on monitorial schools (and we had not seen it when we wrote our *Education of the Poor*). J.R. Carr's thesis on certain Lancasterian schools in London, Middlesex and Surrey investigates some of the subtle differences between the financing, management and operation of these schools and concludes that judgements based on local schools are at variance with those derived from a study of the parent body or of its Borough Road school. Many of the schoolteachers (unlike the ones in Kennington) had no local support, but others did. There were differences between Lancaster's claims and the realities. The Lancasterian schools 'were not units of a nationally planned system of providing education for the poor'.[6] The possibilities of this kind of investigation – and the importance of its findings – have gone ignored. There have continued to be abundant statements about the intentions of the founders of the monitorial system, about its stated methods, about its defects, its critics and its demise – but nothing about the detailed operation of monitorial schools, no attempts to match theory with reality. Yet the monitorial system dominated English popular education for half a century. It is arguable that it was the most influential innovation in the history of English education, but the books on the history of educational innovation have used definitions of the term which exclude any consideration of the monitorial system, refuse to handle it with more 'progressive' innovations.[7] The very terms, like 'innovation' and 'progressive' and 'reform', that historians have used have ensured certain kinds of neglect. The historians of nineteenth-century education have presented the monitorial system as a wraith, and discussed it as if it were flesh.

A project on which I had also been working for some time involved an investigation of the concept of 'social science' in the nineteenth century, and particularly the organizations created in Britain and the United States in the second half of the century for the 'promotion of social science'. The National Association for the Promotion of Social Science and its American counterparts had Education Departments which discussed a range of educational issues and campaigned on some of them. No serious attention has been paid to the educational content of these bodies, either in the published or in the thesis literature.[8] The point of central interest that emerged from this and related studies was that little historical attention had been paid to precisely those themes that were of most interest to the NAPSS and people active in it – including, from the mid-1850s to the mid-1880s, the education of factory and workhouse children, ragged and reformatory schools.[9] During this period at least 50,000 children a year were being educated under the poor law. Between the creation of the ragged school movement in the 1840s and 1881, it was estimated, the London schools alone had 'rescued' some 300,000 children.[10] The number of factory children attending school part-time (in factory schools or elsewhere) was something of the order of 40,000 in 1851.[11] The numbers are not inconsiderable. The question is not, however, just one of quantities. When my collaborator and I began work on the history of one workhouse school, for example, we found beyond doubt that in 1838 it was educationally more 'progressive' than we had expected. It had a Glasgow-trained teacher who made it a condition of acceptance of the appointment that the Guardians should purchase various series of reading books, maps, slates, coloured pictures of animals, battledores and shuttlecocks, and gymnastic poles. For this and other reasons we found the standard stereotype of the workhouse school unhelpful. We were faced with questions about what was 'typical' similar to those raised by the monitorial study. Again, almost nothing in the published literature helped to disentangle statements of intention, motive and policy, on the one hand, from the reality on the other hand – though one unpublished thesis, by Alec Ross, had extremely skilfully handled questions of quality and variety in poor law schooling.[12]

Related questions, unanswered and unexplored, abounded – for example about major nineteenth-century controversies and about the work of some crucial figures engaged in these neglected areas – for instance Edwin Chadwick *as educationist*, Leonard Horner and other factory inspectors prominent in educational discussions, Mary

197

Carpenter and others.[13] Vital areas of the history of educational ideas, it became clear, had been ignored – especially where such ideas could be understood only in relation to deeper currents of social thought – Darwinism, and Marx's views on education, for example. Historians of education have in general taken superficial account of the complexities of the history of social ideas of which education is a part, but it should be added that historians of sociology have been equally unable to recognize and assess the role of educational thought. Poor Herbert Spencer. From the standard histories of education it would be difficult to deduce the extent (or even the existence) of his impact on social thought, and from the books on Spencer's sociology it would be difficult to deduce that he wrote anything at all about education![14]

The conclusion, therefore, was that the great majority of what had been written about popular education in the Victorian period offered few or no real clues as to relationships in schools, their role in the community, or as to the social structures and processes, controversies and changing ideas and assumptions, in which education was intricately involved. The canon of published literature and the majority of unpublished research seemed (a) top heavy, in that it was concerned (and even then selectively) with the provision and administration of education; (b) empty, in that it made few serious attempts to look at the content of schooling or other educational processes; (c) one-dimensional, in that it made no attempt to consider the impact of schooling, and responses to it (or even the range of resistances to it); (d) isolated, in that it made no convincing attempt to explore links between school and family, school and work, school and recreation, school and politics, school and community (though some *formal* relationships, notably that between school and church, have, of course, been widely studied); (e) purblind, in that it recognized only limited areas of 'education' as being suitable for investigation.

The underlying pattern that begins to emerge from these judgements is one of neglect of questions relating to educational realities, to the impact of education, to its role in cultural and social processes. The easier route of describing the structure of educational systems, the motives of providers, the intricacies of policies, has been followed. Although it is an easier route, and one which describes changes and developments, it is not one that often arrives at rounded explanations of change – or even at a felt need to offer any. The 'bits' of neglect therefore fit together to form a picture of widespread historical ignorance, 'disguised', I have suggested, by the very bulk of what has been written. Some of these items of neglect can be clustered into groups, for example:

The impact and 'use' of schooling. There is an absence of work on reactions to school experience, on the *use* of basic schooling by largely self-educated working men, and on the important area of:

The relationship between schooling and literacy. Although useful statistical work has been done in this area, there is little systematic analysis (at least for the period after the 1830s) of literacy and reading matter,[15] literacy and participation in social and political movements (e.g. the co-operative movement), literacy and the commercial press from the mid-1840s.

The quality of educational experience. There are no published studies of possible varieties of educational experience in monitorial schools, workhouse schools, factory schools, dame schools[16] – indeed *all* schools.

The role of the school in total social relationships. The half-time system produced tensions between the child's role in the school, as employee and as an important part of the family economy. Teachers had varying roles and statuses in the community. Ragged schools produced controversy about the undermining of the family. Elementary schools often attracted former pupils and others to evening classes (for example, organized science schools), and served as a focus for other 'community' activities. These and other ways in which schools, pupils, teachers, educational activities in general, related to wider areas of social experience have been largely ignored, and what little research has been done on these areas is mainly unpublished.[17]

Educational ideologies. Preoccupation with the provision and administration of the educational system in the narrowest sense has led to a high degree of selectivity in discussions of 'influential' nineteenth-century educationists. Men and women considered central to educational debates in their own time have been omitted from the twentieth-century records partly because they have not left educational 'monuments' in the shape of recognizable twentieth-century institutions. George Combe and James Simpson, important figures in the controversies and campaigns of the middle decades of the nineteenth century have vanished with their phrenology or their secularism; Edwin Chadwick, Mary Carpenter, Louisa Twining, have vanished with their interest in other vanished objects like poor law schools, workhouse schools and ragged schools; William Ellis and William Ballantyne Hodgson have vanished with the Birkbeck schools and the teaching of social science. The *Transactions* of the NAPSS are

199

occasionally raided for bits of data, but the relationships between educational and social ideas and ideologies have been ignored. (In this connection also it should be added that historians of ideas in Victorian England have tended to ignore education.)[18]

This is neither an exhaustive nor a sophisticated categorization. It is enough, however, to suggest a need to examine the prevalent directions of historical attention, and the assumptions they reveal.

In some respects this is a situation similar to that which obtained in American educational historiography at the end of the 1950s. The historians engaged in revising American educational history were concerned initially both with areas of neglect and with distorted perceptions of what had held the centre of the historical stage – the American public or common school. The radicalization of American politics and intellectual life in the 1960s did, of course, draw attention to areas of neglect – the education of the black, the female, the Catholic, and the under-privileged for example – but the neglect was in some respects relative, as there was distinguished work in existence on the history of the education of minorities.[19] The questions to which Bernard Bailyn and Lawrence Cremin drew attention at the beginning of the 1960s, and which in various ways a generation of different kinds of revisionists have pursued since, related most centrally to the way historians had presented the common school.[20] The history of American education, they suggested, had been distorted and truncated by focusing almost exclusively on the growth of the public school as a basic instrument of American liberal, progressive, industrial, democratic development – adjectives which all became focal points of debate in the political controversies of the 1960s. The old story was not adequate, in Bailyn's view, because it read 'present issues and definitions back into the past', and led – amongst other things – to a 'casual, inconsequential treatment of the colonial period'.[21] Narrowness of historical vision had produced falsified history. 'The moral of educational history', wrote Cremin, 'is the common school triumphant' – a triumph which had become not 'merely an article of popular or professional faith; it had become a canon of sound historical scholarship'.[22] The 'revisionist' nineteenth-century historians who followed – for example Michael Katz, Marvin Lazerson, David Tyack, Carl Kaestle and Diane Ravitch – to different extents and in different ways broadened the discussion from institutions to communities, to complex patterns of demographic and urban change, to the historical role of school and other educational enterprises in social and political dynamics.[23] Explorations of the familiar and of the neglected were being conducted, and new insights and judgements being arrived at and debated. New concepts and definitions were involved, and as Bailyn and Cremin in particular indicated, at the heart of the historical problem was the definition of the educational historian's terms of reference. What *was* education, and therefore what *was* the history of education? Cremin has persistently argued that the history of popular education cannot just be the history of schools, since the school is only part of a configuration of educational agencies: 'public schools are only one among several important public institutions that educate the public'. He has argued that education is about 'families, churches, libraries, museums, publishers, benevolent societies, youth groups, agricultural fairs, radio networks, military organizations, and research institutes'.[24] How broad or how narrow educational history can and should be has become part of the unending historiographical debate that characterizes American educational history.

Although there are important differences between the questions asked in the 1960s and 1970s about the history of education in the United States, and those which I am trying to formulate here, there are some important ideological similarities. The pre-1960s history of American popular education, and the contemporary concerns of British historians of popular education, stem from encapsulation in the present. American historians found in the common school a necessary explanation of twentieth-century industrial democracy. British historians have found in the elementary school and its surrounding legislation and policies an explanation of the development of twentieth-century welfare-state democracy. Both obsessive concerns have involved ideological commitments which have prevented important questions from being asked about the past, or – if asked – from being followed through.

In British terms this seems to me to have entailed an acceptance by historians of crude models of social structure and social change. It has meant that at any moment of time only those phenomena which serve to explain what has survived in institutional form have been seen as worthy of attention. Only those structures, events, ideas, campaigns, successes, failures, in Victorian education and society that have meaning in twentieth-century terms have been admitted to the definition of the history of education. An understanding at any depth of the work of George Combe or Edwin Chadwick, an appreciation of the nature and impact of poor law or factory education, a sense of the forgotten controversies which agitated public opinion, an indication of the subtleties of educational and social experience, the relationships between school and wider social and educative agencies, have not been seen as of major importance in justifying twentieth-century models of institutions implicit or explicit in historical research. Failure to pursue such aspects of Victorian education and society has therefore resulted in the imposition of narrow and inappropriate models of social structure, social interaction and social change on nineteenth-century experience. It has resulted in profound distortions of the history of education, of social and cultural realities. It has, incidentally, resulted in some of the best and most useful thesis literature (for example that of W.P. McCann, D.K. Jones, A.M. Ross, J.R. Carr and P.J. Rooke) remaining unpublished – as the references in this paper suggest.

Even when attempts have been made to widen the understanding of Victorian popular education, and to explore some of the conceptual difficulties in our existing historical analysis, they have been half-hearted. One well-known attempt was that of Richard Johnson in 1970 to apply the concept of 'social control' to the work of Kay-Shuttleworth in particular, in an effort to redeploy some familiar historical material. Johnson's article on 'Educational Policy and Social Control in early Victorian England'[25] expressed an awareness of gaps in historical knowledge, including 'the founding and maintenance of schools for the poor in thousands of local communities, the critical subject of an educational history that still largely waits to be written'. It spoke of the 'rather familiar grooves' of educational research. Outlining various possible approaches to explaining the interests of those who helped to provide voluntary popular education, Johnson admitted to selecting the 'more accessible and more traditional' one – 'to scrutinize the social assumptions implicit in a particular measure; to study, in a critical way, declarations of intent in conjunction with an item of educational practice'. Such an attempt removed any value there might have been in using the concept of social control, and Johnson relapsed into an unenterprising analysis, concerned with 'intent', using social control as a uni-directional concept, failing to disentangle intent from practice, and practice from effect (and seemingly unaware of the sociologists' difficulties in establishing meanings for the concept). He remained involved in a discussion not, as he suggested, of authority and power, but of the *intentions* of those in authority in power – which is a starting point for an analysis of real situations, but can ultimately mean – as it did in this case – an evasion of it. There is no point in approaching areas of ignorance with crude analytical concepts and a timid version of 'critical' study. But at least Johnson was making an attempt, and had the courage to admit what he was doing. Most historians who have reached the edges of difficult or embarrassing questions have turned away from them altogether, unwilling or unable to acknowledge and scrutinize their own ideological reluctance.

Embarrassment is perhaps as frequent an obstacle as conceptual crudity. Let me take two examples that have arisen in my recent research. The first is that of attitudes towards punishment in school, which of course suggest wider questions about social and human relationships. To know how far corporal punishment, for instance, was administered in Victorian elementary schools would seem to be at least a useful indication of aspects of the educational process, and of wider cultural questions. We do not know, and we have either pretended that we do, or have not thought it important enough to include among the aspects of education we wish to know. None of the published work on elementary schools confronts the material, asks questions, worries about the phenomenon. The Kennington school I was involved in investigating appears to have been without corporal punishment until probably the 1880s – over half a century after its foundation. Did other monitorial schools use corporal punishment? The National Society's records indicate that the Society discouraged it from the outset. Why? How typical was the Kennington school in resisting it? That the answer is difficult and confusing is clear from the only research done on the subject – a very capable, unpublished thesis by P. J. Rooke in 1962.[26] It emphasizes the enlightened view of punishment held by the founders of the monitorial schools, the nature of the discipline sought in the schools, and the 'rarity' of corporal punishment at institutions like the National Society's school in Baldwin's Gardens. At the same time it shows that corporal punishment was in fact used in many, though by no means all, National schools in the 1840s, though with widely differing degrees of frequency. Rooke begins to raise some important questions – mainly about conflicts of attitude, and about the reasons for 'enlightened' views – but in the tradition of English research lets them drop. The point is that it could be embarrassing to pursue them, because what the standard works offer is a set of stereotypes of the monitorial or later elementary school, which might suffer damage if the realities of the punishment situation were pursued too far. Historians have *assumed* that physical punishment was the rule in the Victorian elementary school – because it was the rule in the grammar and public school. They have not thought it necessary to test, or have preferred not to test, this and many other such assumptions.[27] Some monitorial and other schools, schoolmasters, managers and patrons were more humane than the textbook summaries suggest. Most of the histories in any case summarize what Bell and Lancaster *said* about punishment, without attempting to match a stereotype of a discredited system against evidence that might exist of possible diversities in the schools. Too much attention to the realities of punishment raises the embarrassing spectre of having to ask questions about what we think we know of monitorial and indeed all popular education in the nineteenth century. Why the National Society resisted corporal punishment when the middle-class schools relied on it, is ultimately the same sort of question as whether the monitorial system was an innovation, and how much diversity was possible among schools, teachers, curricula and attitudes to children in Victorian England – all questions to which no answers exist.

The second example of silence which results from embarrassment is Marx. Marx's views on the combination of manual work and school have been highly influential in the twentieth century and are constantly quoted in Soviet, Chinese and other analyses of 'polytechnic' education. I would here like to make three points about Marx's theory and his use of the British half-time system to support his case – a theme which I have begun to explore elsewhere.[28] First, Marx's use of precedent involved reference to Robert Owen's experience and views, which Marx misrepresented, and to evidence in his favour from the factory inspectors – evidence which he misquoted and distorted (as well as ignoring comments hostile to the half-time system by some factory inspectors and their witnesses, and the solid opposition of the school inspectors). Second, his view of the half-time system was cold-shouldered by the socialist movement from the 1880s, which campaigned against the half-time system as a dehumanizing process. Third, Marx's views on education, their relationship to earlier educational ideas and experience, and their position in Marx's overall views about society have not been researched and analysed in any serious manner. There are implicit in these statements so many possible sources of intellectual discomfort that the reasons for the silence about Marx's educational opinions may not be far to seek. If Marx distorted the evidence on which he based his case for a combination of manual labour and school (which he did), his views on education become more dificult to treat sympathetically. If Marx's views on education do not fit easily into modern – or even nineteenth-century – socialist or progressive thinking on education (which they don't) his educational philosophy becomes difficult to handle. Marx's views on education and labour are pivotal to this theme. Historians have therefore either made assumptions about Marx and failed to test them, or they have fled from the embarrassment and omitted the central feature of Marx's educational position.[29]

Instead of serious historical analysis what the field of Victorian popular education seems to me to reveal is a pragmatism and a conceptual crudity that inhibit proper research and analysis. Historians of education are not, of course, the only historians who have avoided risks to their stereotypes from the controversies in sociology, philosophy and the social sciences generally that might challenge their foundations. Work on Victorian education rests on assumptions about society, social structure, social class, social change, economic and urban development, democracy, power and a host of other conceptual tools, rarely exposed to analysis by the historians using them, but subject to profound controversies amongst social scientists. The combination of pragmatism and unexamined concepts and models constitutes a historical ideology, and it is one that can be seen clearly in operation both in the areas of neglect and in the areas of apparently intensive research in the Victorian period. It is not possible here to discuss ideologies or the sociology of knowledge. The 'aspects of neglect' about which I have made judgements point towards such a discussion, however, and a number of summary points need to be made. First, this is not an illusory argument for raising history 'above ideology'. It is an argument for a greater commitment to exploring the assumptions on which historical research rests – a direction which historians of education have been particularly reluctant to take. Second, it is an argument for recognizing that 'gaps' in knowledge, difficulties in locating sources, shortage of evidence and data, may not be 'technical' explanations of silence and neglect – they may be indications of the historian's inbuilt reluctance to test the difficulties, or even the existence of such obstacles. (I cannot, for example, accept that the absence of research on monitorial schools, pupil teachers, factory children, reformatories, poor law schools, school–community relations, or – to take a different kind of example – the educational activities of the Chartist movement,[30] is purely a question of the lack of resources.) Third, it is certainly not an argument for replacing one ideology by another – setting out to prove something different. E.G. West's attempt to show how unnecessary has been state intervention in English education (in *Education and the Industrial Revolution* and elsewhere)[31] is such an exercise in substitution, a kind of protracted polemic based on little or none of the kind of research for which I am arguing. West uses insecure and selected nineteenth-century statistics, for example, without exploring the controversies to which they were subjected *at the time*, their nineteenth-century meanings. What he produces is an ideologically slanted analysis intended to support a thesis about the contemporary state. The trouble with alternative ideologies of this kind is that they touch upon important questions, but are inhibited from sustained or sensitive research or analysis by the ideological passion. A new 'version' of an old argument is produced, instead of basing an argument in and around new insights into historical reality. West's struggles to overturn accepted pictures of educational developments in the nineteenth century remind us that there are important questions to be asked (including about statistics), but by imposing misleading patterns on his sources, and even on his adversaries' 'accepted pictures', he makes it *more* difficult to answer the questions he raises. The intervening ideology prevents any clarification of the relationships of education and society (or economics or politics) in nineteenth-century England.

A fourth and final point is that the ideological framework in which historians establish their definitions dictates the whole nature of the enterprise. Discussions of English education in the middle of the twentieth century have been overwhelmingly about *the system*, about the structure of the system, about access to the system, about the organization of secondary education, about the organization of universities and teacher education and technical education and the binary system, about numbers and ages of transfer and sizes of school, about percentages and finances, about the policies of political parties, about the structure of examinations, about urban aid and priority areas. Involved in all of this are implications about and interests in the role of the state, the balance of national and local government, the roles of professional experts and the lay public, pressure groups and interest groups and decision-making, the power of the exchequer, manpower forecasting and economic efficiency. Also involved are concepts such as those of rights (of children or of parents), democracy and equality (in relation to educational and social mobility), and freedom (to buy private education). That there are widely differing views about all of these does not hide the fact that this kind of political and ideological discussion has been dominant in education, certainly since the 1930s. In looking for historical explanations of this system and all it entails historians have accepted a set of definitions or terms of reference that have produced most, though certainly not all, historical work on Victorian education. The interests of the twentieth century help to explain the silences about the nineteenth. There are, indeed, historians who have asked questions about the educational content or impact of social movements and the press, architecture and publishing, industry and towns. Overall, however, the historian's perspectives have tended to focus his attention on the growth of the system, people who have demonstrably made contributions to the system, processes which are still discernible in the system, social and economic changes easily (if mechanically) applicable to a discussion of the system.

The diversities and conflicts within our own system have not alerted historians enough to the dangers in the kind of pursuit to which they have been most committed. The dangers of seeing local studies purely as an extension or confirmation of national trends have not been detected (as the large number of local studies undertaken by B.Ed. students, with their inevitable first 'background' and 'national' chapters testify).[32] Historians have not seen the school child as also a family child, a street child, a working child, an aspiring child, an encouraged child, a discouraged child, a bewildered child, a child whose social-class, school, urban and other experiences are not necessarily identical to those of similar children elsewhere. The history of 'education' has, certainly in its nineteenth-century format, been of a certain kind of education, one that is divested of such complexities, in which children exist only in a set of conceptual stereotypes, are involved in no relationships, belong only to an 'emergent system', and can by and large be ignored by historians – preferring another discussion of Kay-Shuttleworth and the pupil teacher system or Lowe and the Revised Code (though not a discussion of pupil *teachers* or of the operation of the Revised Code in *practice*).

It is arguable how far historians should extend their definitions to encompass all of Lawrence Cremin's wide sweep of 'configurations'. It is necessary, however, to see education not just 'in context' (with all the lack of relationships that the phrase implies), but in society, as something of society, as forming and being formed by society. It is also necessary to identify educational institutions and processes ('education-bearing phenomena' might be a clumsy way of describing them), workhouses and barracks, churches and factories, pupils' families and community activities, for example, which extend our existing concerns. It is necessary to escape from untested, comfortable assumptions. It is necessary to take difficult paths in research, ones which lead to serious questions about real, complex societies – and which take account of difficulties encountered by social scientists in analysing those complexities. It is necessary to approach educational phenomena with sharper tools of analysis and insight, so as not just to open up questions, but also to be willing to pursue them, whatever the difficulty, the embarrassment, or the discomfort.

NOTES

1. See Jones, D.K. (1965), 'The Lancashire Public School Association, later the National Public School Association' (Sheffield, MA thesis); Toms, V.G. (1972), 'Secular Education in England 1800–1870' (London, Ph.D. thesis); McCann, W.P. (1960), 'Trade Unionist, Co-operative and Socialist Organisations in Relation to Popular Education 1870–1902' (Manchester, Ph.D. thesis).
2. Birchenough, Charles (1927), *History of Elementary Education in England and Wales* (London, University Tutorial Press); Adamson, J.W. (1930), *English Education 1789 to 1902* (Cambridge, Cambridge University Press); Smith, Frank (1931), *A History of English Elementary Education 1760–1902* (London, University of London Press); Eaglesham, E. (1956), *From School Board to Local Authority* (London, Routledge & Kegan Paul); Gosden, P.H.J.H. (1966), *The Development of Educational Administration in England and Wales* (Oxford, Blackwell); Sutherland, Gillian (1973), *Policy-Making in Elementary Education, 1870–1895* (London, Oxford University Press); Cruickshank, Marjorie (1964), *Church and State in English Education 1870 to the Present Day* (London, Macmillan); Murphy, James (1959), *The Religious Problem in English Education* (Liverpool, Liverpool University Press).
3. See, for example, Hurt, J.S. (1975), 'Education and the Working Classes', Society for the Study of Labour History, *Bulletin*, Nos.30, 31; chapter and general bibliographies in Lawson, John and Silver, Harold (1973), *A Social History of Education in England* (London, Methuen).
4. Lawson and Silver, *ibid.*
5. Silver, Pamela and Harold (1974), *The Education of the Poor: The History of a National School 1824–1974* (London, Routledge & Kegan Paul).
6. Carr, John Ralph (1963), 'The Origin, Development and Organization of Certain Lancasterian Schools in London, Middlesex and Surrey, A Comparative Study' (London, MA thesis), pp.41, 423 and *passim*. Two theses being written by sociologists contain original research on monitorial schools. Two relevant American theses, using manuscript sources in the United States, are Wall, Edward Flavin (1966), 'Joseph Lancaster and the Origins of the British and Foreign School Society' (Columbia, Ph.D. thesis), and Rost, Ray C. (1967), 'The Influence of Joseph Lancaster and the Monitorial System on Selected Educational Institutions, 1800–1850' (Rutgers, D.Ed. thesis). None of the standard British histories refer to anything other than the publications of the main protagonists and (after 1839) to the *Minutes* of the Committee of Council.
7. Stewart, W.A.C. and McCann, W.P. (1967), *The Educational Innovators 1750–1880* (London, Macmillan), for example, does not include the monitorial system as an 'innovation'.
8. Bernard, L.L. and Jessie (1943), *Origins of American Sociology; the Social Science Movement in the United States* (New York, Crowell) contains a monumental study of the American Social Studies Association and related movements, but does not discuss its Education Department. There are references, but no serious discussion, in Ritt, Lawrence (1959), 'The Victorian Conscience in Action: The National Association for the Promotion of Social Science' (Colombia, Ph.D. thesis), and Pemble, Robert (1968), 'The National Association for the Promotion of Social Science, 1857–1886: Some Sociological Aspects' (Nottingham, MA thesis).
9. Also secular education, adult education, the teaching of social science and physiology, and many aspects of elementary and grammar school education.
10. Bloomer, R.G. (1967), 'The Ragged School Movement before 1870' (Manchester, M.Ed. thesis), p.103. The main existing work on ragged schools is unpublished. See also Webster, D.H. (1971), 'The Ragged School Movement and the Education of the Poor in the Nineteenth Century' (Leicester, Ph.D. thesis), and Clark, E.A.G.

(1967), 'The Ragged School Union and the Education of the London Poor in the Nineteenth Century' (London, MA thesis).

11. Census of Great Britain, 1851 (1854), *Education in Great Britain*, pp.lxiv–lxvi.

12. Ross, A.M. (1955), 'The Care and Education of Pauper Children in England and Wales, 1834 to 1896' (London, Ph.D. thesis). See also Woods, J.E. (1975), 'The Development of the Education of Pauper Children in Workhouse Schools (1834–1870)' (Leicester, M.Ed. dissertation). The only relevant published works are: Pallister, Ray (1968), 'Workhouse Education in County Durham: 1834–1870', *British Journal of Educational Studies*, XVI, and Duke, Francis (1976), 'Pauper Education', in Derek Fraser (ed.), *The New Poor Law in the Nineteenth Century* (London, Macmillan) – both only marginally concerned with the content and quality of pauper education.

13. A thesis is currently being written on Horner in the United States. Manton, Jo (1976), *Mary Carpenter and the Children of the Streets* (London, Heinemann) is an excellent recent study which elucidates her work, but there is much room for wider explorations of her ideas, relationships and areas of concern.

14. Adamson, *English Education 1789 to 1902* gives a typical summary of Spencer's *Education* without mentioning that he wrote anything else. Andreski, Stanislav (1971), *Herbert Spencer: Structure, Function and Evolution* (London, Michael Joseph) is a sociologist's account which manages to avoid mentioning Spencer's view of education. For an American example of a fuller awareness of Spencer's educational and social impact see Karier, Clarence J. (1967), *Man, Society, and Education* (Glenview, Illinois, Scott, Foresman).

15. There are two valuable studies of the 1830s: Hollis, Patricia (1970), *The Pauper Press: A Study in Working-Class Radicalism of the 1830s* (Oxford, Oxford University Press), and Wiener, Joel H. (1969), *The War of the Unstamped: The Movement to Repeal the British Newspaper Tax, 1830–1836* (New York, Cornell University Press). Two earlier studies made useful beginnings in mapping some of the territory: Webb, R.K. (1955), *The British Working Class Reader 1790–1848* (London, Allen & Unwin), and Altick, Richard D. (1957), *The English Common Reader: A Social History of the Mass Reading Public 1800–1900* (Chicago, Chicago University Press).

16. An important piece of pioneering in this connection was Higginson, J.H. (1939), 'the Dame Schools of Great Britain' (Leeds, MA thesis) – a slim but valuable pointer in a direction others have not followed.

17. Parsons, Cheryl (1975), 'Elementary Education in the Local Community: A Study of Relationships in the Attercliffe Area of Sheffield 1870–1940' (Leicester, M.Ed. thesis) is a perceptive study of school and community in late nineteenth- and twentieth-century Sheffield.

18. For example, Houghton, Walter, E. (1957), *The Victorian Frame of Mind* (New Haven, Yale University Press) barely acknowledges the existence of ideas about popular education. Historians of ideas as social processes, for example Elie Halévy and Raymond Williams, have not made this mistake.

19. Notably Curti, Merle (1935), *The Social Ideas of American Educators* (New York, Scribner's).

20. The two classic statements are Bailyn, Bernard (1960), *Education in the Forming of American Society* (Chapel Hill, University of North Carolina Press), and Cremin, Lawrence (1965), *The Wonderful World of Ellwood Patterson Cubberley* (New York, Teachers College). An excellent outline and discussion of 'revisionist' historiography is Butts, R. Freeman (1974), 'Public Education and Political Community', *History of Education Quarterly*, XIV, 2.

21. Bailyn, *Education in the Forming of American Society*, p.13.

22. Cremin, *The Wonderful World of Ellwood Patterson Cubberley*, p.17.

23. For example, Katz, Michael (1968), *The Irony of Early School Reform* (Cambridge, Mass., Harvard University Press); Lazerson, Marvin (1971), *Origins of the Urban School* (Cambridge, Mass., Harvard University Press); Tyack, David (1974), *The*

One Best System (Cambridge, Mass., Harvard University Press); Kaestle, Carl F. (1973), *The Evolution of an Urban School System* (Cambridge, Mass., Harvard University Press); Ravitch, Diane (1974), *The Great School Wars* (New York, Basic Books).

24. Cremin, Lawrence A. (1976), *Public Education*, p.58 (New York, Basic Books); Cremin, Lawrence A. (1970), *American Education: The Colonial Experience 1607–1783* (New York, Harper & Row), p.11.
25. Johnson, Richard (1970), 'Educational Policy and Social Control in early Victorian England', *Past and Present*, No.49.
26. Rooke, P.J. (1962), 'A Study of Rewards and Punishments in the Elementary Schools of England and Wales, 1800–1893' (London, MA thesis).
27. A recent example is Manton, *Mary Carpenter and the Children of the Streets*, which stresses the dominance of punishment in Victorian schools, but draws its examples from *middle*-class schools, and suggests that 'very few people questioned that it was right, proper, and for the child's own good' (p.3). When Mary Carpenter at mid-century rejects the use of corporal punishment (p.87), the author does not see the discrepancy and the question that need to be investigated.
28. Silver, Harold (1977), 'Ideology and the Factory Child: Attitudes to Half-Time Education', in McCann, Phillip, *Popular Education and Socialization in the Nineteenth Century* (London, Methuen).
29. Two studies that have approached these issues have evaded them: Simon, Brian (1971), 'Karl Marx and Education', in *Intelligence, Psychology and Education: A Marxist Critique* (London, Lawrence & Wishart), and Frow, Edmund and Ruth (1970), *A Survey of the Half-Time System in Education* (Manchester, E.J. Morten).
30. No serious work on Chartism and education has been done since Jones, R.A. (1938), 'Knowledge Chartism' (Birmingham, MA thesis). There is almost nothing on education in the contributions on local history to Briggs, Asa (ed.) (1959), *Chartist Studies* (London, Macmillan). Although there is a section on Chartism and Education in Jones, David (1975), *Chartism and the Chartists* (London, Allen Lane), it serves to underline the paucity of research on the considerable educational activities and impact of the Chartist movement. How such studies might develop is suggested by a chapter on Chartism in Greenwood, Maureen (1973) 'Education and Politics in Leicester 1828–1850' (Leicester, M.Ed. thesis).
31. West, E.G. (1975), *Education and the Industrial Revolution* (London, Batsford).
32. Morris, Norman (1972), 'The Contribution of Local Investigations to Historical Knowledge', in History of Education Society, *Local Studies and the History of Education* (London, Methuen), argues against the value of local studies, mainly by students. Morris also sees local as mainly an extension of national educational analysis – seeing the question purely as one of policy. J.R. Carr's thesis on monitorial schools shows how important local studies, differently conceived, can be (see note 6 above).

14

A Possible Model for the Study of Nineteenth-Century Secondary Education in Europe[1]

LENORE O'BOYLE

An attempt to formulate a framework of analysis applicable to the history of secondary education in nineteenth-century European countries, essentially a process of model-building, involves two stages: first, identification of those elements that must be considered in writing the history of education; second, an hypothesis as to how these elements function in relation to each other in a specific historical context.

The exercise results from a certain bafflement at the present diversity in the educational histories of various countries. Traditional German histories concentrated on educational philosophies; contemporary German studies are largely quasi-Marxist in approach, with their emphasis on education as a means to class domination. English historians have focused on the role of the churches and the growth of state involvement, and have displayed considerable empirical interest in what actually took place in the classroom. They have perhaps placed less weight on explicit class interpretation, but probably only because they have taken it for granted so much. French educational history has stressed political influences, and the uses of the educational system in providing social mobility. The study of education in the United States has been centred on the development of the school system as such, and on the way in which the system has expressed American political and religious values. Recent important work has interpreted America's educational system as one designed to perpetuate racial and class privilege.

Can an approach be found to cut across national differences to obtain valid generalizations? This essay goes about the problem by trying to define common units of analysis – society, social class, occupation, school system – and leads to the conclusion that analysis of nineteenth-century education can profitably be studied in terms of occupational groups. A focus on such large categories as society or social class has an undeniable, but limited, usefulness. Study of the professions brings together individual motive and social need; the professions at once offered certain highly prized rewards of status and power to individuals, and produced elites sufficient to meet society's needs at that time.

The degree of unity that currently exists in the study of nineteenth-century education has resulted from the increasing emphasis on the school system viewed, not in isolation, but in relation to the larger society. This particular delimitation of the subject has been forced upon historians by the fact that the nineteenth century saw the growth of a distinct system of schools existing apart from those older institutions – the family, the workshop – that had till then been sufficient for education. In a real sense, education had been coterminous with society. Apparently the modern industrialized society that began to come into existence in the eighteenth century made demands for knowledge and adaptation to change that could no longer be satisfactorily met through learning by example.[2]

The new system produced an obvious problem of analysis: to determine the precise fashion in which school and society interacted. Assuming that the school to some extent at least served the purposes of society, historians have talked of *socialization*. My dictionary defines the verb *to socialize* as meaning, among other things, 'To fit for companionship with others; make sociable in attitude or manners. To convert or adapt to the needs of society.' The definition has, for our purposes, a regrettable lack of specificity: what, after all, are 'the needs of society'?

One answer that suggests itself immediately is that modern societies need schooling for economic growth, but a connection between economic and educational expansion in the nineteenth century is at best an assumption. The recent work of Peter Lundgren, based on sophisticated statistical methods, concludes that in Germany from 1864 to 1911 very little of the impressive rate of economic growth appears directly attributable to the increase in education.[3] Others have concluded that the most one can say is that education is a necessary, but not sufficient, condition for industrialization.[4]

A kind of reverse argument has also been made. It is frequently assumed, for example, that the continuing predominance of classical education helps to explain the decline of England's economic position in the late nineteenth century. Whether England's economic position was in fact worsening is, however, a matter of dispute.[5] And one might wonder how England in earlier decades, when her technical education was if anything even more deficient, succeeded in gaining world leadership.

To describe 'the needs of society' in general terms is, however, possible. Schools of various kinds have aimed (1) to produce individuals with the kind of character and habits required by a stable society; (2) to fit individuals for performance in the economic system at acceptable levels of competency; and (3) to prepare individuals for a particular social rank or status. Such an answer seems unexceptionable but is undeniably loose. Furthermore it rests on the unspoken assumption that the educational system was, in all important respects, determined by the society, and so by implication denies the possibility that the schools, insofar as they were organizations of professional teachers with their own specialized knowledge, training, and aims, could in fact have pursued goals distinct from and transcending those of any particular society.

The emphasis on socialization also diverts attention from the ways in which the schools reinforced, and perhaps even created, social values and arrangements. Knowledge of nineteenth-century Germany shows how closely the structure of the bureaucracy was aligned with the system of academic degrees, so that the bureaucracy can be viewed as a kind of adjunct of the system of higher education.[6] Similarly, in England civil service reform, under the influence of the universities, was deliberately formulated to ensure a monopoly of high offices to Oxford and Cambridge graduates.[7] Throughout the country one can see a clear tendency to identify types of schools and degrees with corresponding types of occupational opportunities.[8] The universities were often powerful forces in creating the professions, as they won, in part at least, the right to define the course of study, monopolize professional teaching, and establish the claim that only university graduates could be regarded as fully competent practitioners.[9] The vested interests of teachers and other professionals need further investigation.

The very idea of society as actor, creating schools for its own purposes, is questionable. Society is not a homogeneous unit, and it is doubtful that it ever functions as such. Laurence Veysey, on the basis of his study of the university in the United States, concluded that the historian would be better off to avoid the idea of society altogether, both because the concept suggests a misleading degree of integration among the institutions of a society and because it takes attention away

213

from the goals of specific groups, each of which wants different things from the schools.[10]

The problem then is to choose the group or groups within society most relevant to the history of education; one would like to be able to settle on a particular kind of social unit existing in a wide variety of times and settings. The Marxist category of class, defined essentially by economic criteria, remains the most widely accepted unit. The category, however, is so large and so difficult to delimit clearly that many historians consider it useless, and even those who believe it indispensable run into problems trying to analyse how a class acts as a unity. Can one assume that the members of the nineteenth-century middle class shared clear ideas on how schools should operate, and worked together to effect their ideas? This was almost certainly not the case. Even if unified action was in fact possible, what were the mechanisms by which this class translated its will into political decisions? Very often these questions are evaded. In consequence, class theory, as a theory of political domination, frequently assumes what it should demonstrate. As a psychology, moreover, it too often fails to do justice to the complexity of men's motives, and overlooks the extent to which men act from ignorance, habit, or sheer muddleheadedness rather than conscious intent. Furthermore, the quasi-Marxist approach in the history of education has led to a considerable amount of high-minded moralizing, resting on the writer's usually unstated assumption that his own educational standards and social values have an *a priori* validity that only the perverse or corrupt could fail to recognize.

Yet the idea of social class remains useful because, on a general level, it is adequate to the facts. There is a sense in which governments from the eighteenth century on can be recognized as class governments. Modern societies have been based on certain fundamental arrangements regulating the distribution of authority and wealth, and governments (whose primary obligation must always be to maintain law and order) necessarily have been committed to these fundamental arrangements: the wealthy have usually been able to count on political authority for support. Any stable society, moreover, must share some consensus on values, and it is clear that less favoured groups have always, within limits, accepted existing institutions as legitimate. Thus, nineteenth-century English artisans taught the virtues of self-help and hard work in the Sunday schools, while middle-class Germans adopted many of the values of the traditional ruling groups.[11] Such acceptance may or may not be judged deplorable, but it does help to explain the otherwise surprising persistence of elite privilege. For the historian,

214

recognition of government bias and moral consensus permits the adoption of the idea of class domination as the basic starting point for study.

It cannot, however, be much more than that. For if the idea of class proves more useful than that of society, it remains a high-level abstraction. In addition, it tends, as does the idea of society, to focus attention on the groups in control, on those who provided the education rather than those who received it. This has been most true in the study of elementary education. Fortunately, the work of scholars like E.G. West and Thomas Laqueur has substantially modified the picture of the nineteenth-century English working class as the passive recipients of an education defined by church and state schools.[12] New attempts to use information provided by demographers have suggested ways in which lower-class attitudes to education might have been based on rational calculation of economic advantage; perhaps it seemed worthwhile to sacrifice for a child's education only at the point where life expectancy had increased sufficiently.[13] What such historians have done is to break with stereotypes of class domination and to investigate the wishes and initiatives of groups within the working class.

There has always been a greater recognition of distinct elements in the history of secondary education, perhaps because the Marxist two-class model is obviously less appropriate here. Various groups within the middle class have consistently exploited education as a means to upward mobility, with each stratum seeking acceptance by the one immediately above it. In England, sons of rich businessmen attended the public schools, acquired the proper accent and the right acquaintances, adopted a profession, and felt themselves closer to the aristocracy than to the business middle class.[14] In France, governments' well-meaning attempts to provide technical high schools for the lesser middle class were often frustrated by parents' equally well-meaning insistence on sending their sons to the *lycées* to study the classical curriculum, regardless of whether or not there existed sufficient opportunity for advancement in the traditional, prestigious professions.[15] Germany, of course, showed many of the same features. Nowhere is it possible to speak without qualification of a middle-class education. Just as with the workers, the middle class must be broken down into groups defined by different criteria for different purposes – race, ethnic group, generation, sex, occupation, religion, and region.

My own thinking about these problems grew originally around a particular problem, or at least what I then took to be a problem.[16] Why did secondary education in early nineteenth-century Germany turn

215

sharply in a humanist and classical direction, at the very time when the possibilities of large-scale industrialization were becoming visible, and when the study of science, technology, and modern languages might sensibly have been seen as desirable?

One explanation that emerged was the self-interest of the philologists, who seemed, whether consciously or not, to be fighting for a monopoly of teaching posts in the *gymnasia*. The teachers succeeded because humanist education was believed to produce superior men claiming positions of leadership and privilege. Accordingly, such education appealed to the large element within the German middle class that was seeking highly regarded jobs in the government bureaucracy. Far from being dysfunctional for its recipients, it qualified as directly vocational.[17] At the same time, the philologists themselves acquired a new dimension of importance and status because they mediated access to official positions. I found myself dealing with groups within the middle class that were defined largely in terms of occupation and that linked personal desires for worldly status with an occupation structure, entrance into which was made possible by a higher education. Further study also pointed to a very similar pattern in England and France.

Status arising from the exercise of power seemed the crucial factor in choice of occupation. My initial error had been the rather easy assumption that men would be guided by considerations of direct economic advantage and seek to exploit new industrial opportunities. Instead, it appeared that they continued to look for personal satisfaction and social rank within pre-industrial structures and behavioural patterns. Why the traditional professions appeared so attractive was the question that had to be asked, and the explanation seemed to me to be that these occupations gave power over men rather than things, even when, as in the cases of the *gymnasia* professors, it was power once removed. I am not suggesting that economic gain was ever unimportant, or that power over men can ever be sharply separated from power over things; obviously, over time, they tend to coincide. My suggestion is that economic gain does not seem to have been the primary consideration for these groups. Rather, it was viewed as incidental to power, which remained the great source of status. Education came to be seen as a way to gain a kind of quasi-nobility. As the aristocrat enjoyed power merely as an attribute of what he was – which in fact, of course, implied a certain kind of education – so the professional man exercised power by virtue of what he had become through education.[18]

Why was this particular kind of education considered desirable, and what justification is there for describing it as directly vocational?

Supposedly, it was general, esoteric, disinterested, and moral. It was general in that the study of languages (and, secondarily, higher mathematics) was seen as the study of abstract form rather than of a limited segment of reality. Such study trained the mind to handle abstractions and to deal in formal properties, and, accordingly, was believed proper for men destined for positions of authority, which required broad perspectives. Language study, moreover, conceived increasingly as a concentration on form, was valued as a kind of mental calisthenics, the development of mental skills that could supposedly be transferred from one subject to another. The belief rested on rather shaky scientific foundations and so was largely an article of faith, but it served to justify the claim that humanist education was preeminently fitted for future governors and directors of all kinds, men who would be called upon to deal with many kinds of problems and to make decisions with wide applications.

It was an esoteric education, based on study of the literary text and manipulation of verbal and mathematical symbols, and reflecting the enduring belief in the power of language. It was disinterested in that this kind of study seemed at the farthest remove from manual labour and practical techniques, and accordingly, superior. Such an education, in its avoidance of any narrow utilitarianism, appeared to rest on an aristocratic disdain for the petty and ordinary. And, in practical terms, it indicated that a man could count on family resources sufficient to support him through years of education and professional apprenticeship; it thus served as an index to wealth.

Lastly, the education was believed to inculcate a higher morality. Study of the classics was to expose the young to norms of behaviour embodied in a civilization that the philologists judged the highest ever attained by man. Love of the good and the beautiful was to be the result, and moral superiority was to be added to intellectual.[19]

However insubstantial its objective justifications, this kind of education actually did meet the demands of society, and thus can be interpreted as a kind of socialization. Individual motives were consonant with society's needs. This was possible only because the economic and political systems did not as yet demand highly specialized skills. The idea of a general education, writes Sheldon Rothblatt,

... has only been possible for a leisured class and at a stage in the evolution of society when expert knowledge was not necessary for the exercise of political and economic leadership. A leisured class — and it must at the same time supply a political elite — can afford the luxury of an education that emphasizes broad principles of leadership and conduct derived from the reading of a few select texts.[20]

The education sufficed for the great traditional professions: government, law, church, and army.

The history of the professions provides a kind of reverse image of the history of education. The prestige of each profession appears to have been correlated quite precisely with two factors: one, the degree of power exercised over other men; two, the degree to which preparation involved a general education. To see the correlation one need only list nineteenth-century professions in order of prestige, and then examine the sources of their power and the nature of their preparation.[21]

The union of education and occupation is expressed by speaking of the learned professions. These professions formed a hierarchy of status that both paralleled and cut across the hierarchies of birth on the one hand and economic success on the other hand. These ranking systems co-existed and overlapped. Each provided the possibility of a degree of social power over other men. It is obvious, of course, that access to secondary education usually required wealth, so that educational opportunity was in part a function of social class. But the correlation was never exact. Business men of great means might judge higher education irrelevant or even harmful, while government officials on inadequate salaries would sacrifice to give their sons a university training.[22]

The importance of education and occupation as a means of ranking probably varied. It was perhaps most important in Germany. Wolfgang Sauer writes that 'the division between the educated and the uneducated may have developed in the nineteenth century into the true dividing line between the ruling oligarchy and its subjects'. Fritz Ringer's important book suggests the same argument.[23] I wonder, however, if concentration on national histories has not led to somewhat misleading suggestions of national uniqueness.[24] Was the German educational system really so different from that of England or France that it can explain the peculiar character of German development in the modern period? Investigation of national differences is enormously important, and doubtless more difficult than a statement of similarities. My immediate purpose, however, is to clarify general patterns, and the *lycées* and great Paris schools of France and the public schools and two universities of England do seem to have been very similar to the German *gymnasia* and universities in their social effects.

It is apparent that this nineteenth-century pattern could exist only within societies at a certain stage of growth. The countries of Western Europe were in the early stages of industrialization, were pre-democratic in political structure, and had limited educational opportunities.

The stage of economic development dictated the extent of economic activity. Where opportunity was already great, as in England, the need for the traditional education required for the established professions was less, and a higher percentage of men found satisfaction and status in building an enterprise and acquiring wealth. With the growth of the economy, the tension between business and professional men that had always existed became more overt. More questions were asked about the value of classical education, and more demands made for a system based on science and modern languages. In Germany, advocates of the *Realschulen* won greater successes towards the end of the century; in England, more attention was paid to technical education.

A pre-democratic political structure meant that political power was concentrated; the group of people who had to be consulted in making political decisions was small.[25] Education was of prime importance as a means of entry into this political class; the connection accounted for a large measure of education's value. Obviously not all members of the political class shared a higher education, but many did, and this meant that they worked within the understandings of a common culture.[26]

The limited extent of educational opportunity resulted naturally from the economic and political structure. When educational opportunities are few, education becomes what Fred Hirsch has termed a 'positional' as opposed to a 'material' good. In his definition, material goods can be enjoyed by everyone without diminution of any one person's satisfaction, while the value of positional goods depends on being enjoyed by only a restricted number.[27] A society where advanced degrees are common is one in which higher education provides only limited advantages to the individual, even though it may be indispensable. In nineteenth-century Western Europe, higher education must be classified as a positional good.[28]

This model, incidentally, should be applicable, with appropriate modifications, to the countries of Eastern Europe. Although the intelligentsia of these areas are often sharply distinguished from the educated groups of the West, they probably represent rather an extreme case of the Western pattern.

In summary, analyses of educational systems in terms of society's needs or class domination are unsatisfactory. One needs (1) to define smaller, more carefully delimited groups; (2) to explain what such groups wanted for themselves and what society required of them; and (3) to ask how the motives of individuals were reconciled with the larger needs of society. In nineteenth-century Western Europe, occupational units appear to have been most important for the study of middle-class education. Individuals wanted to join the professions because such professions conferred social power and thus social status. A certain kind of general, literary education was seen as necessary, and so can properly be labelled directly vocational. Even though at first glance this education appeared dysfunctional for societies beginning to industrialize, it did in fact produce a leadership elite adequate to the needs of society at this stage of development. Occupation prepared for by education provided a system of social ranking that at once paralleled and overlapped the ranking systems provided by money and/or birth. Conclusions about the relative importance of such ranking systems in different countries would seem to require caution. A corollary of this argument is that nineteenth-century occupations can be ranked according to two criteria: one, their degree of social power; two, the degree to which the preparatory education required for them was general and literary.

I am aware that I have failed to consider questions of major importance. There has been next to no effort to evaluate differences of size, structure, location, political and religious control, or enrolment patterns among different countries. Nor have I attempted to explore historically-conditioned cultural differences. Any full treatment of nineteenth-century education would require discrimination among periods of time in each country. Perhaps equally important would be clarification of differences in content and emphasis among national systems of education: French education stressed different qualities of mind than did German, and philology was not quite the same study in every country.

Some questions, which I have either only mentioned or altogether neglected, seem to me important. One concerns the role of the teachers themselves. This involves both teachers as a professional interest group seeking worldly advancement and teachers as professional men with their own discipline, standards, and aims. The second aspect has been particularly neglected here. What did teachers believe or hope they were doing in the classroom? Did these beliefs and hopes affect society? If so, just how? My analysis, by passing over these questions, implies that what the teachers thought they were doing did not make much difference. Such a conclusion, which rests on ignorance more than anything else, may very well be wrong, and certainly needs testing.[29]

The final two issues are inherently difficult.[30] The first has to do with a basic division within the middle class, namely, the division between what can be termed the traditionalist and the progressive or modernizing mentalities. This distinction cuts across the more obvious one between business and the professions. The desire for a certain type

220

of traditional education may well have been linked more to a conscious determination to preserve a certain way of life than to hope for social status through entry into the professions. Within the professions themselves there were varying degrees of commitment to classical education. Engineers, forming a new profession, had ideas about what constituted useful education that differed from those of a more established professional group, like the lawyers. Even within the older professions – the ministry, law, medicine – different views of curriculum emerged as certain elements were attracted to new kinds of advancing knowledge.

At least as important is the last question: how much stress should be laid on purely intellectual factors in explaining the dominance of traditional education? In the last analysis, is it not likely that many individuals supported such education because it afforded them intellectual and aesthetic enjoyment, stimulated the mind, and encouraged thought about human responsibility and virtue? The model outlined in this paper, while resting on a quite broad definition of vocationalism, does undeniably narrow the possibilities to be considered in a theory of causation.

The difficulty here, and to a certain extent in the traditional/modern contrast, seems to me a technical one: how does one go about studying these problems? Theoretically, one can assume that there is a research design conceivable to investigate any historical question. One would have to find a procedure to isolate and measure this element of personal satisfaction for a large number of people and, as of now, I simply do not know what that procedure would be. I have little doubt that the problem is a significant one.

Thus, the conclusions of this paper must be regarded as tentative and incomplete. The thesis argued may nonetheless be useful as a starting point for future research: nineteenth-century secondary education was designed to respond to society's needs for government by generalists rather than experts, and to satisfy individuals' needs for status by facilitating access to occupations of high prestige.

NOTES

1. This article is substantially the same as a paper read at the 11th annual Duquesne University History Forum held in Pittsburgh, Pa., 20–22 Oct. 1977.
2. For a lucid analysis, see Hartmut Titze, *Die Politisierung der Erziehung: Untersuchungen über die soziale und politische Funktion der Erziehung von der Aufklärung bis zum Hochkapitalismus* (Frankfurt am Main, 1973), pp.11–12.
3. Peter Lundgren, with a contribution by A.P. Thirlwall, 'Educational Expansion

and Economic Growth in Nineteenth-Century Germany: A Quantitative Study', *Schooling and Society*, ed. Lawrence Stone (Baltimore and London, 1976), pp.20–66. Also Christa Berg, 'Volksschule im Abseits von "Industrialisierung" und Fortschritt'. Über den Zusammenhang von Bildung und Industrieentwicklung', *Pädagogische Rundschau*, 28 (1974), 385–406.

4. C. Arnold Anderson and Mary Jean Bowman, 'Education and Economic Modernization in Historical Perspective', *Schooling and Society*, pp.3–19.

5. George Haines IV, *Essays on German Influence upon English Education 1850–1919* (Hamden, Conn., 1969); John Clive, 'British History, 1870–1914. Reconsidered: Recent Trends in the Historiography of the Period', *American Historical Review*, 68 (July 1963), 987–1009; C.H. Wilson, 'Economy and Society in Late Victorian England', *Economic History Review*, 2d. ser., 18 (Aug. 1965), 183–98. Donald N. McCloskey, *Economic Maturity and Entrepreneurial Decline: British Iron and Steel, 1870–1913* (Cambridge, Mass., 1973), vii: '... entrepreneurs in British iron and steel, from whatever perspective they are viewed, performed well.'

6. Ruth Meyer, 'Das Berechtigungswesen in seiner Bedeutung für Schule und Gesellschaft im 19. Jahrhundert', *Zeitschrift für die gesamte Staatswissenschaft*, 124 (1968), 763–76; Detlef Müller, 'Sozialstruktur und Schulsystem. Forschungsbericht über eine mehrdimensionale Analyse des Schulwesens im 19. Jahrhundert, Modellfall Berlin', *Annales cisalpines d'histoire sociale*, Ser. I No.2 (1971), 31–60.

7. An interesting recent treatment is James Winter, *Robert Lowe* (Toronto, 1976), 262–7.

8. E.g., Olive Banks, *Parity and Prestige in English Secondary Education: A Study in Educational Sociology* (London, 1955); R.W. Rich, *The Training of Teachers in England and Wales during the Nineteenth Century* (Cambridge, 1933); *Papers Relating to the Re-Organization of the Civil Service* (London, 1855); Eugen Weber, *Peasants into Frenchmen: The Modernization of Rural France 1870–1914* (Stanford, Cal., 1976), 301–34.

9. Vern L. Bullogh, 'Education and Professionalization: An Historical Example', *History of Education Quarterly*, 10 (Summer 1970), 160–9.

10. Laurence R. Veysey, 'Toward a New Direction in Educational History: Prospect and Retrospect', *History of Education Quarterly*, 9 (Fall 1969), 343–59.

11. Thomas W. Laqueur, *Religion and Respectability: Schools and Working Class Culture 1780–1850* (New Haven. Conn., 1976).

12. E.G. West, *Education and the Industrial Revolution* (New York, 1975).

13. Charles Tilly, 'Population and Pedagogy in France', *History of Education Quarterly*, 13 (Summer 1973), 113–28. E. Weber stresses throughout *Peasants into Frenchmen* the willingness of the peasants to educate themselves once they could see some usefulness in the knowledge offered them.

14. Matthew Arnold, 'Schools and Universities on the Continent', in *The Complete Prose Works of Matthew Arnold*, ed. R.H. Super (Ann Arbor, Mich., 1960–77), IV: 308–9; Rupert Wilkinson, *Gentlemanly Power: British Leadership and the Public School System* (London, 1964); Sheldon Rothblatt, *The Revolution of the Dons: Cambridge and Society in Victorian England* (London, 1968), pp.87–92, 248–73.

15. E.g., *Archives parlementaires de 1787 à 1860: recueil complet des débats législatives et politiques des Chambres françaises*, M. Guizot, Chamber of Deputies, 1 Feb. 1836, 24 March 1837; Robert Anderson, 'Secondary Education in Mid-Nineteenth-Century France: Some Social Aspects', *Past and Present*, 53 (Nov. 1971), 121–46.

16. Lenore O'Boyle, 'Klassische Bildung und soziale Struktur in Deutschland zwischen 1800 und 1848', *Historische Zeitschrift* 207/3 (December 1968), 584–608.

17. Sheldon Rothblatt, *Tradition and Change in English Liberal Education: An Essay in History and Culture* (London, 1976), pp.200–3, makes the point that because a general education may prove useful for a certain occupation does not mean that such an education should be called vocational. But German secondary education was so closely connected with preparation for government position that it is difficult

to see it as anything but vocational. Whether this education was as useful to German society as it was to individuals is certainly open to question. Conceivably other kinds of education might have led to less social conflict and healthier growth.

18. The belief that the German middle class had formed an aristocracy of education existing alongside the aristocracy of birth is a common theme in the writings of 19th-century German liberals. After 1867, a number of these writers argued hopefully that the German government officials in representative assemblies could play a role similar to that of the nobility in the English Parliament.

19. The selfish and even antisocial implications of this ideal have been pointed out by W.H. Bruford, *The German Tradition of Self-Cultivation, 'Bildung' from Humboldt to Thomas Mann* (Cambridge, England, 1975), and in a study of unusual interest, Ralph Fielder, *Die klassische deutsche Bildungsidee* (Weinheim, 1972).

20. Rothblatt, *Tradition and Change*, p.200.

21. A systematic classification of professions correlating prestige, power, and education should be possible. Such a typology would show the correlation to be most exact in the case of the older professions: government, law, clerical, and military. In the 19th century, medicine became established as a profession enjoying comparable rank. New professions, such as engineering, journalism, and teaching, exercised less power, required less education, and were accorded less prestige. In our own time, the definition of a profession has become increasingly problematic, as the word has been extended to a growing number of occupations.

22. Ralf Dahrendorf, *Society and Democracy in Germany* (New York, 1967), argues that the authority structure of a society is the decisive determinant of class formation. Marx did not see that legal ownership of the means of production represents only one special type of authority.

23. Wolfgang Sauer, 'National Socialism: Totalitarianism or Fascism?', *American Historical Review*, 73 (Dec. 1967), 424; Fritz K. Ringer, *The Decline of the German Mandarins: The German Academic Community, 1890–1933* (Cambridge, Mass., 1969). The idea can be found in Friedrich Paulsen, 'Bildung', *Gesammelte pädagogische Abhandlungen*, ed. Eduard Spranger (Stuttgart, 1912), p.126: 'Educated and uneducated, these are the two halves into which society is at present divided. They have gradually caused older divisions to be forgotten.' In this connection see Walter Struve, *Elites against Democracy: Leadership Ideals in Bourgeois Political Thought in Germany, 1890–1933* (Princeton, N.J., 1973).

24. See the very helpful criticism of R.R. Palmer, 'Some Recent Work on Higher Education', *Comparative Studies in Society and History*, 13 (Jan. 1971), 108–15.

25. I adopt this formulation to avoid, in this context, the difficult question of who in truth does exercise political power. It is quite possible that in our present society, for example, important political decisions are actually made by a handful of men, but even if this is so, there remains the necessity of going through the whole elaborate procedure of democratic voting, consultation, lobbying and so forth, with whatever complications and incalculable results that may bring. Far less of this was required in the 19th century. This factor of the size of the elite groups has been curiously neglected. But see J.H. Plumb, *England in the Eighteenth Century* (Penguin Books, 1965), p.34: 'there was one factor of great importance about life both in the town and in the countryside. It arose from the smallness of the population. This meant that it was much easier for those who exercised political power or were born to privilege to know one another quite intimately ... The result was to make politics more personal, intimate, and clannish, and ... the institutions of government were very appropriate to such a world.' Also Noel G. Annan, 'The Intellectual Aristocracy', *Studies in Social History: A Tribute to G.M. Trevelyan*, ed. J.H. Plumb (London, 1955), pp.243–87; Eric J. Hobsbawm, *The Age of Capital* (New York, 1975), pp.244–6.

26. While it hindered political participation by the lower classes, the homogeneity of this class facilitated the political process. As democratic institutions expanded, new men from other backgrounds entered the process. Their unwillingness to accept the

223

existing rules of the political game, and their expression of a new range of demands from previously under-represented groups, meant a sharpened and often disturbing degree of conflict.

27. Fred Hirsch, *Social Limits to Growth* (Cambridge, Mass., 1977).
28. The situation had its value for social stability, since it provided a means of upward mobility first for the lower middle class, later for the peasant and worker. See R. Anderson, 'Secondary Education in Mid-Nineteenth-Century France'; Patrick J. Harrigan, 'The Social Origins, Ambitions, and Occupations of Secondary Students in France during the Second Empire', *Schooling and Society*, 206–35; E. Weber, *Peasants into Frenchmen*, 328: 'But another army was growing, as important as the regular one – the body of public and private employees, access to which was opened by the school certificate, the certificate of elementary studies.' The result was the absorption of some of the more gifted and ambitious into the upper elites, the diminution of class conflict, and the strengthening of the elites themselves. It may also have weakened the elites. The secondary schools did not act only to assimilate new classes to old. Influence was mutual, and the process was more one of accommodation between classes. Certainly this was true in England, and in Germany where the vulgarities and materialism of a new plutocracy probably did more to dilute aristocratic virtues than to strengthen the more admirable of bourgeois traits. In France, the process of accommodation may have been less marked because of the predominance of bourgeois values and the relative insignificance of aristocratic elites as independent social and political factors. French education was decidedly meritocratic, and its successful graduates dominated in all areas, including business. See John A. Armstrong, *The European Administrative Elite* (Princeton, N.J., 1973).
29. For an interesting study of the relationship between the actual classroom situation and the content of education, see Robert Dreeben, *What Is Learned in School* (Reading, Mass., 1968).
30. I am indebted to Professor Peter Stearns for a very helpful extended criticism that raises these points.

15

History as Propaganda: The Strange Uses of the History of Education

ROY LOWE

Most readers will be familiar with the beleaguered position of history of education in teacher-training and in-service courses. At the close of two decades which have seen what is little short of a Renaissance, much of it conceived and carried out within Colleges and Faculties of Education, it is ironic that historians of education should find themselves under renewed attack. If one outcome of this situation is that historians are forced to offer a reasoned justification of their contribution to teacher-training courses, then there may even be grounds to welcome these new challenges, for any historian worth his salt is prepared to rethink and restate his defence of his subject. Yet, in articulating this defence, it is worth reflecting on the causes of these present discontents, and, in particular, on the extent to which historians of education may have themselves to blame for the suspicion in which, by some at least, their teaching is held.

First, though, it is clear that many of the mainsprings of the present attack are extrinsic to the study of the history of education. These same twenty years have seen the rise of new educational 'disciplines', most notably those of curriculum theory and educational administration. The growth of research in these areas, necessarily focused upon more immediate concerns than those of the historian, and seeming to offer the prospect of panaceas to those concerned in the management of schools and colleges, has clearly fanned a popular conception that the older educational disciplines are at best unfashionable and at worst irrelevant. It is perhaps worth commenting that, while these newer fields of study offer valuable insights into the working of educational systems, into relationships within schools and between schools and wider society, their very practice depends upon the deployment of methodologies and approaches drawn from the older educational disciplines – philosophical, historical, sociological and psychological. In brief, without some proper consideration of history of education, there can be no curriculum theory. A further reservation concerns the fact that, in so far as they tend to focus upon the 'phenomenology' of education, upon educational practice, these very disciplines may inadvertently be contributing to the production of 'educational helots'. When future historians come to examine the kinds of 'social control' developed within contemporary teacher-training institutions, they may well conclude that the narrow, 'instrumental' and essentially pragmatic approach of some of the less enlightened devotees of these new sciences is a factor worthy of remark. The failure to ask the basic questions is as venial a sin among contemporary educationists as it was among some of the pioneer historians of education who will be considered later in this article.

A wider cause of the present threat to the standing of history of education lies in the effects of the present economic crisis, which has resulted in popular demands for 'accountability' from all sectors of the educational system, not least the teacher-training institutions. Regrettably this concept of accountability is used to justify the emphasis on practical teaching skills and disciplines which appear to bear more directly upon the classroom situation, at the expense of studies which involve reflection upon the deeper significance of formal education.

In this situation it is all too easy for historians of education to shrug their shoulders, to point out external factors (perhaps temporary) which threaten their position and to assume that their house is in order and that a sufficient defence of their subject has already been made. There have, indeed, been powerful statements of the significance of the history of education for student teachers, most notably by Brian Simon (1966),[1] Brian Holmes (1970),[2] and Malcolm Seaborne (1971)[3]. Recent surveys of the history of education by Brian Simon[4] and W.B. Stephens[5] range over the rich diversity of the work of historians currently writing and reflect the healthy state of research.

But, it must be remembered, too, that some recent statements have expressed unease about the kinds of question which preoccupy historians of education. Harold Silver raised this issue in his contribution to the *Oxford Review of Education*, commenting that

most of what has been written has in fact disguised our neglect and ignorance of it. This is not just a question of gaps ... It is a more basic question of the kind of historical enterprise in which we have been engaged.[6]

226

Only a few months later, he returned to this problem in his inaugural lecture, and amplified the case for historians of education to exercise a greater degree of self-criticality. Beginning from the proposition that all historical knowledge is relative to the position in time of the historian, he argued that much recent work on mid-Victorian education had failed to escape from 'an obsessive concern with what are often the superficialities of the state and its related institutions'. For him, the great danger was the present 'use' of history:

We *use* history to help us to convince and to act all the time. This is right and proper, but it is one use of history, and we may learn little of the past through it, getting partial and faulty messages when we imagine that we have got them whole.[7]

It is impossible so briefly to do justice to the detail and subtlety of his argument, but it is clear that Harold Silver feared an abuse of the past by using it to propagandize contemporary beliefs and practices.

It is my intention to explore briefly this concern with reference to earlier work in the history of education – to what may be loosely termed the 'Whig school' of English historians of education. An investigation into the kinds of propaganda which have been disseminated by earlier historians can give rise to two important questions. First, how far have we in fact moved away from a propagandist tradition during the past twenty years? And secondly, how justified are commentators in questioning the value of the study of history of education if much that has been written smacks of a propagandist function? These questions are of considerable contemporary significance and can only be fully answered by reference to the historiography of English education.

But, as a prior question, it is important to explore exactly what we mean by 'propaganda' and 'propagandist' in the historical context. Are not all historians necessarily subject to bias? Is it possible to draw a line between, on the one hand, 'distortion', which presumably no historian would condone, and 'subjectivity' on the other, which many would see as enlivening and informing an otherwise dull narrative? It was E.H. Carr who wrote:

When you read a work of history, always listen out for the buzzing. If you can detect none, either you are tone deaf or your historian is a dull dog ... By and large the historian will get the kind of facts he wants. History means interpretation.[8]

But this defence of subjectivity on the part of the historian was quickly followed by a clear statement of the scholarly criteria by which all historical writing may be judged. Pleading that historians should seek a balance between the processes of reading and writing, Carr added:

If you try to separate them or to give one priority over the other, you fall into one of two heresies. Either you write scissors-and-paste history without meaning or significance; or you write propaganda or historical fiction, and merely use facts of the past to embroider a kind of writing which has nothing to do with history.[9]

Similarly, David Thomson in *The Aims of History* warned that

the price of effective free-thinking, however, is submission to the disciplines imposed by the principles of the historical method. Investigation and verification of 'facts' are undertakings governed by certain ineluctable rules. To ignore them or to be unskilful in applying them, is to court disaster.[10]

It was the failure of pioneer historians of education to adhere to these 'ineluctable rules' of investigation which led them, in the view of the present author, to offer accounts of the rise of schooling which were, in effect, propaganda, of the type defined by Carr. It is this 'propagandist' use of the history of education which will now be examined more closely.

* * * * *

The earliest historians of education may be said, loosely, to have belonged to one or other of three schools or genres of writing, each with its own vested interests and viewpoint. First came the 'teacher trainers', R.H. Quick, Meiklejohn, S.S. Laurie, Oscar Browning and, at the start of the twentieth century, J.W. Adamson and Foster Watson. A second group, smaller in number, were those 'administrative/legal' authors whose interest in the history of education arose from careers which were concerned with educational reform of one kind or another and which naturally led them into contact with educational source materials. The best-known, and clearly the most influential of them, was A.F. Leach, although R. Fitzgibbon Young, G.A.N. Lowndes, and Michael Sadler (so far as he may be considered an historian of education) may all be bracketed with Leach. Their partiality influenced both the questions which they asked about the rise of popular education and the conclusions they drew. Thirdly, it is possible to discern a group of 'participant historians': figures who were involved in educational innovation and who, often in old age and in response to encouragement, offered memoirs or autobiographies enshrining an idealized image of their earlier endeavours. Albert Mansbridge, Mary Stocks and W.W. Craik are early examples of this school, which persists. Their work helped sustain a 'Whiggish' approach and confirmed the early focus upon formal educational systems. Almost all work in the history of education in England before 1960 can be seen to belong to or draw from one or other of these schools, as does a good deal of more recent work. We will deal with them one by one.

Turning first to the 'teacher trainers', it is clear, with hindsight, that their involvement in the initial training of teachers led each of these historians to offer accounts which glorified the process of teaching, over-emphasized the significance of teachers as transmitters of culture and, by concentrating upon the continuity of educational tradition, effectively established a Whig school which took more than fifty years to supplant.

Foster Watson's defence of the history of education, which appeared in the *Contemporary Review* in 1914, neatly summarized the position which could have been adopted by any of these immediate predecessors: for him the study of the past offered a safeguard against radical change. He pleaded that all educationists should have some acquaintance with history

so that with judgements intelligently and carefully formed, they may enter into the discussions affecting the continuity of national education progress.[11]

For Quick, whose *Essays on Educational Reformers* established the biographical tradition among English historians of education, the evidence of progress was so clear that there was no difficulty in adopting a positivist position:

By considering the great thinkers in chronological order we see that each adds to the treasure which he finds already accumulated, and thus by degrees we are arriving in education, as in most departments of human endeavour, at a science.[12]

Against this background, and the background of 'Whiggish' writing which was generally in vogue among historians, it is hardly surprising that his contemporaries found little difficulty in discerning important educational principles in the lives of great educators and were prepared to use the history of education as a device for communicating these ideals to their breathlessly receptive students. Thus, S.S. Laurie, in a prolix introduction to his life of *Comenius* (1895) debated the nature of Renaissance neo-Platonism and showed himself ready for the extravagant metaphor:

The torch that fell from Ratich's hand was seized, ere it touched the ground, by John Amos Comenius, who became the head, and still continues the head, of the sense-realistic school. His works have a present and practical and not merely an historical and speculative significance.[13]

This preparedness to seek those past examples which might offer some guide to contemporary practice was shared by Oscar Browning, whose

Introduction to the History of Educational Theories emphasized the 'practical use to teachers' of studying the past:

It may show what is the historical ground for retaining existing practices in Education, or for substituting others; and it may, by telling us what great teachers have attempted, and what great thinkers have conceived as possible in this department, stimulate us to complete their work ... The writer has attempted to give an account at once popular and accurate of the main lines of thought which have been followed upon educational subjects, so far as they are important at the present day.[14]

In these terms the earliest of these 'teacher trainers' justified an approach which emphasized the history of ideas, so that their books became almost an introduction to the philosophy of education in an historical context. Thus they set in train that neglect of the study of schooling as a process of which Harold Silver was still able to complain in the mid-1970s.

Perhaps the first historian to sense this neglect and to seek to remedy it was J.W. Adamson, whose work reflected a conscious attempt to relate educational ideologies more closely to the practice of the schoolroom. He professed in his introduction to *Pioneers of Modern Education* (1905) his main theme to be 'the introduction of "modern studies" into the school course', a process which Adamson discerned as taking place during the seventeenth century. Indeed, when Adamson produced in 1920 an introductory pamphlet on the history of education for the Historical Association, he was dismissive of those immediate predecessors with whom I have chosen to bracket him here:

Some have seen its chief purpose in the edification of schoolmasters and schoolmistresses, and have regarded the study as one of exclusively professional interest ... They remained indifferent to the claims of research and even those of revision; they were content to repeat oft-told tales ... In their pages, the 'educators' accomplished or failed to accomplish more or less self-imposed tasks quite apart from the forces and occurrences of the daily life which surrounded them.[15]

He singled out Quick's *Essays* ... as the best such work, though even this

gave some countenance to the confusion existing in many quarters between the history of education and that of opinion about education – in short, between fact and speculation.[16]

Yet a closer examination of Adamson's work suggests that he, too, fell prey to the very practices he condemned. His *Pioneers of Modern Education* appeared at the end of a decade which had witnessed a major debate on the curriculum of the secondary school, culminating in the reassertion of a broad, 'humane' course of studies

R. LOWE

by R.L. Morant. Adamson's book reads almost as an historical vindication of Board of Education policy. By emphasizing the modernizing tendencies of seventeenth century, he is able to play down the impact of industrialization and concomitant demands for the teaching of applied sciences. For Adamson, many of the 'great conceptions' of the early twentieth century are merely restatements of principles which emerged in the seventeenth century. Not least among these conceptions was a view of education which sought a balance between literary and scientific studies, a point which Adamson labours in his conclusion:

> There was nothing in the mental attitude of the early humanists necessarily inimical to whatever advance in knowledge might be achieved ... their training in literary criticism was bound, in the long run, not merely to compel them to recognize modern vernacular literature ... but even to hasten its advent ... In short, the true humanist was not in the nature of things compelled to be a foe to modern studies ... while literary culture is an indispensable element in a truly human education, room must also be found for other disciplines ... expressly intended to help the learner to a mastery of his physical surroundings ... The formation of a curriculum, therefore, becomes a nice adjustment between the legitimate claims of letters, science and certain forms of skill affecting the graces and utilities of life.[17]

This could almost have been commissioned by Morant, whose 1904 Secondary School Regulations attempted exactly the kind of 'nice adjustment' which Adamson thought so desirable.

A similar stance was adopted by Foster Watson who devoted a lifetime's research to the study of the English grammar school. His work reflected a clear belief in the value of the grammar school to national life, both in the past and in the future. For him, the 'culture' of the nation was at its best during periods when it was nurtured by efficient grammar schools, transmitting 'humanism' through the media of Latin and Greek. This analysis enabled him to dismiss the late-seventeenth and eighteenth centuries as periods of national decline, and to have high hopes of the twentieth century with its newly reformed grammar schools:

> The value of the grammar school – in the sense of the classical school – to the community has by no means been superseded ... It continues to stand for an element in the national life, proved by centuries of experience to be of first importance, viz. the training in humanism, the point of contact between past, present and future ... The democratisation of education has laid special emphasis on the necessity of the addition of the limitation 'for chosen pupils only', but the principle of the old grammar schools is as necessary as ever.[18]

In these terms the history of education was used to justify the establishment of a scholarship ladder to preserve the national function

231

of the old grammar schools. If we are to seek the sources of the strength and vitality of 'the grammar school tradition' in twentieth-century England, then the propagandizing of authors such as J.W. Adamson and Foster Watson must not be overlooked.

A second group of authors may be discerned whose initial interest in education was either legal or administrative. Without exception their interpretations of the development of schooling reflected a wish to vindicate their own life's work. A.F. Leach was the first such historian of education, attracted to the study of schooling by his work in the Endowed Schools Department of the Charity Commission, which he joined in 1884. Over a twenty-year period, beginning with his first book in 1896 and ending with *The Schools of Mediaeval England*, which appeared in 1915, he produced an impressive canon of work all of which contributed to 'the Leach thesis', that the English grammar school originated in the mediaeval period and not, as had been previously assumed, at the Reformation. Leach was recognized by his contemporaries as a firebrand. A.L. Poole, editor of the *English Historical Review*, warned A.G. Little to tread warily in reviewing *The Schools of Mediaeval England* since Leach 'though really a very good fellow is a furious controversialist'.[19] Yet this suspicion did not prevent *The Times* from recording in its obituary only a few months later that A.F. Leach had

restored the grammar schools to the place from which they had been unjustly deposed and vindicated for them their true place in English life.[20]

This was a fair summary. If it is remembered that, as a schools' commissioner, Leach was involved in the reform of the town grammar schools offering education to the sons of the middle classes, then one significance of his view of their historical development becomes clearer. As early as 1896 he emphasized that

the Grammar schools which existed during the Middle Ages were not mere monkish schools ... Many of them were the same schools which now live and thrive. All were schools of exactly the same type, and performing exactly the same sort of functions as the Public Schools and Grammar schools of today.[21]

In proclaiming the continuity of the English grammar school, and its benign influence upon the life of the nation, Leach stressed the value of Latin as a living and useful language and argued too that from their inception these schools catered for the middle classes.

The poor spoken of in these old foundations are not the poor in our sense, the destitute poor ... but the poor relations of the upper classes ... It was the middle classes, whether country or town, the younger sons of the nobility and farmers, the lesser landholders, the prosperous tradesmen, who created a demand for education, and furnished the occupants of the Grammar schools.[22]

By the end of his life Leach was linking this defence of the vital functions of the grammar schools with a passionate attack on monasticism. Whether this reflected unease at the route followed by the major public schools during the nineteenth century is unclear, but it certainly reflected well upon the reformed grammar schools:

So long as the monasteries furnished a safe and easy refuge from the struggle for existence, and monasticism forced celibacy upon churchmen ... education made little impression upon society at large. It was in vain for clever boys to be educated and to be promoted to the chief offices of state when they were doomed to die without issue ... The advancement of science and learning comes from a cultured middle class.[23]

While Leach's resuscitation of the mediaeval grammar schools stemmed clearly from his contact with documents relating to their foundations, it did enable him to proffer a condemnation of Edward VI, which, with hindsight, reads more like a congratulatory note of the work of the Charity Commissioners during the 1880s and 1890s than a judgement on the sixteenth century:

As for poor Edward VI, meaning thereby the ruling councillors of his day, he cannot any longer be called the founder of our national system of secondary education. But he, or they, can at least claim the distinction of having had a unique opportunity of reorganizing the whole educational system of a nation from top to bottom, without cost to the nation, and of having thrown it away.[24]

As the twentieth century progressed and the Board of Education committed itself increasingly to a tripartite organization of secondary education, other civil servants devised, in official reports, an account of the history of English education which emphasized the appropriateness of a divided system. R. Fitzgibbon Young was perhaps the most notable, as the author of the historical sections of the 1926 *Hadow Report* and the 1938 *Spens Report*. Young served as secretary of a number of influential Consultative Committee reports during the inter-war years and repeatedly offered accounts of the development of English education which reflected favourably upon Board of Education policies, showing them as the natural outcome of gradual and almost inexorable policies. Thus the advocacy of a break in education at 11+, involving a transfer from primary to senior school, was presented by him in the 1931 Hadow Report as the outcome of a natural evolutionary process, stretching back to the early nineteenth century.[25] But it was in the reports on secondary education that the propagandist function of his 'potted histories' was most clearly discernible. His lengthy historical introduction to *The Education*

233

of the Adolescent (1926) was concluded by a passage in which Young portentously spelt out the lessons of history:

It will be seen from this historical survey that at every stage of the development it has been the general tendency of the national system of elementary education to throw up experiments in post-primary education. Though such experiments have again and again been curtailed or rendered difficult by legislative or administrative action, they have persistently reappeared in various forms. This fact in itself seems to indicate the half-conscious striving of a highly industrialised society to evolve a type of school analogous to and yet distinct from the secondary school, and providing an education designed to fit boys and girls to enter the various branches of industry, commerce, and agriculture at the age of 15.[26]

Twelve years later these ideas were developed in the Spens Report. By 1938, Young was ready to attack Morant's 1904 Secondary School Regulations as a deviation from the true course of educational policy since they

failed to take note of the comparatively rich experience of secondary curricula of a practical and quasi-vocational type which had been evolved in the Higher Grade Schools, the Organised Science Schools and the Technical Day Schools.[27]

This lesson had been reinforced more recently by the appearance of Central Schools in London and Manchester before the First World War, and subsequently by the development of Junior Technical Schools. Against this historical background, the only proper course for the Board of Education was

to foster the development of secondary schools of quasi-vocational type designed to meet the needs of boys and girls who desired to enter industry and commerce at the age of 16 ... The present difficulties in the field of secondary education have arisen largely out of the confusion which began about 1904 between a type of secondary education appropriate to the needs of boys and girls between the ages of 11 to 12 and of 16 to 17 and the traditional academic course orientated towards the universities.[28]

For Young, one of the keys to this reassertion of an earlier policy was the new light thrown upon individual difference by the development of educational psychology. Thus the traditional faculty psychology of the nineteenth century which tacitly assumed that most boys and girls 'developed in much the same way' led to the neglect by both teachers and administrators of individual differences in interests or abilities. The new psychology, resulting from 'practical experience with a constantly increasing body of pupils in secondary schools', was now forcing changes in the organization of the curriculum and its content:

Teachers must be on their guard ... to see that instruction is adapted to the interests and abilities of the pupils.[29]

234

In these terms tripartism was vindicated with reference to the lessons of history as perceived through the looking glass of Board of Education officials. The increasing certainty of psychometrics enabled a growing confidence about the best organization of secondary schooling.

Another pæan of praise for the work of the Board of Education appeared with the publication in 1938 of *The Silent Social Revolution*. G. A. N. Lowndes, writing during 'a lifetime of educational administration', much of it spent within the Board, was to influence a whole generation of students of education, since his book ran to numerous imprints before the appearance of a second edition in 1969. In Lowndes' view the revitalizing and expansion of the educational system in the twentieth century was largely due to the initiative of the Board of Education, which had thus exercised a civilizing influence upon English society. The benign influence of formal education extended to 'the sobriety, orderliness and stability' of the population. Rather ironically, in view of developments during the 1980s, he chose Liverpool to exemplify this, citing the absence of civil disorder during a suspension of policing in 1921.[30] The British war effort of 1914–18 was due in part to the school system sending out 'year by year after 1902 hundreds of thousands of scholars a little better trained, a little more accustomed to leadership, than their prototypes of twenty years before'.[31] This benign influence extended to the inculcation of thrift so that working-class households were now less prone 'to fritter away the balance on perishable extravagances', but instead 'laid out the family income wisely and regarded settled home ownership as a worthy aim'.[32] Sir George Newman, 'author and chief architect' of the school medical service, was singled out for particular praise as one of the founding fathers of an effective preventive health service.[33]

Thus, this second group of historians of education reinforced a popular belief in the beneficent effects of formal education. Their work gained in authority since it derived from a more detailed knowledge of educational statistics – and in Leach's case from a far more intimate study of documentary sources – than was possessed by their near contemporaries writing within the teacher-training institutions.

This relatively uncritical stance, by today's standards at least, was reinforced by a third group of authors, whose main concern seems to have been to cement their own niche in history. Albert Mansbridge was an early example, and helped establish a style which has afflicted the historiography of adult education. Mansbridge's book, *An Adventure in Working Class Education*, which appeared in 1920, gave an idealized account of the origins and significance of the W.E.A., which he portrayed as the outcome of the highest aspirations of organized labour to scholarship. The Association's influence was seen as benign, not least in spreading the gospel of adult education to the dominions and thereby helping to 'build life ... on the large and splendid lines expected by the whole world'.[34] Significantly, Mansbridge glossed over the opposition to the W.E.A. which came from within Ruskin College and the Labour College movement, and which is now seen by historians as evidence of deep tensions within the adult education movement. For Mansbridge this was no more than

opposition from a few persons who declared that the Association was a device to side-track the attention of working men and women from their legitimate movement. It never rose to any great proportions and, generally, those who, from misinformation, had adopted this attitude gave it up when they came into contact with the Association.[35]

Hardly surprisingly, Mary Stocks' account of the first fifty years' work of the W.E.A. followed this interpretation. She portrayed the Association as being committed to 'the constructive task of peaceful penetration' of the universities, which 'could be licked into shape' by these articulate working men.[36] For her, too, the supporters of the Labour College movement lacked this blend of idealism and common-sense. It was in exactly this spirit that Mansbridge's account in 1923 of the rise of the ancient universities culminated in the judgement that

the hope is sure that Oxford and Cambridge will tend more and more to obliterate class distinctions, to remove sectarian animosities, and to unify knowledge.[37]

The counterblast to these rather partial accounts of the growth of adult education in the twentieth century appeared with the publication in 1964 of W. W. Craik's history of the origins and work of the Central Labour College. Just as Mansbridge and Stocks had both been prominent members of the W.E.A., Craik, as a young student at Ruskin College, had helped found the Plebs League and participated in the student unrest which followed attempts by Oxford University to control this branch of the adult education movement. For Craik, this sudden concern of university tutors with the work of Ruskin was no more nor less than a repetition of nineteenth-century attempts to stifle, or at least to 'strait-jacket', indigenous working-class educational activities. Oxford's approaches to Ruskin showed

the University ... trying to make a virtue of necessity. Its helping hand was 'the hand of Esau, but its voice was the voice of Jacob' ... Hence Lord Curzon's preference for 'liberal' over 'utilitarian lines'. It was only cover for an education designed to protect the ruling-class State from being 'disintegrated by the blind impulses of numerical majorities'.[38]

236

These radically differing interpretations not only reflected the political positions of these pioneers of adult education, but helped determine the interpretations of, and even the major issues investigated by, subsequent historians of education. The same problem hangs over the study of the rise of popular schooling, fuelled not only by local sources and official reports, but also by a host of memoirs and histories of individual schools, all to some degree subjective. This fact may enhance the value of such works as sources in their own right for future historians; equally, their very partiality may constrain or cloud the task of contemporary researchers.

In combination these three strands in the writing of history of education in England, all clearly discernible by the early twentieth century, contributed to its relative poverty until recent years. A readiness to propagandize, by imposing present concerns and preoccupations upon the past, led to this field of study developing strange characteristics. Schooling and educational systems were considered largely in isolation, with scant attention being paid to the wider social changes which reverberated upon the schools. The work of A.E. Dobbs stands as the solitary exception to this judgement.[39] The neglect of comparative themes, through which English developments might have been viewed in the wider focus of international trends, can also be traced to this period. The convention that history of education was written by a 'sub-group' of historians also emerged during these early years. This was doubly damaging, since it led to the almost complete neglect by historians of education of developments in the study of social and economic history: at the same time those historians dealing with the 'modernisation' of English society and the rise of industrialisation tended to neglect any consideration of the interaction of formal or informal education with economic growth. In this way the whole fabric of English social history was weakened in the early twentieth century, and it was not until the appearance of historians such as Lawrence Stone and Laslett that this disjunction was clearly seen to be nonsensical.

This lack of criticality has extended to the historiography of English education which has only very recently attracted serious scholarly attention. This is in clear contrast with North America, where, for over twenty years, the fierce and often polemical debate over 'revisionism' has led to close analysis of the implications of earlier work. Indeed, Bernard Bailyn, writing as long ago as 1960 in a brief book which was one of the triggers of the American revisionist movement, summarised the shortcomings, as he perceived them then, of American history of education. His remarks might almost stand as an epitaph of English historians of education prior to that date too:

237

Its leading characteristic is its separateness as a branch of history, its detachment from the main stream of historical research, writing, and teaching ... The development of this historical field took place ... in a special atmosphere of professional purpose. It grew in almost total isolation from the major influences and shaping minds of twentieth century historiography; and its isolation proved to be self-intensifying; the more parochial the subject became, the less capable it was of attracting the kinds of scholars who could give it broad relevance and bring it back into the public domain ... To these writers the past was simply the present writ small. It differed from the present in the magnitudes and arrangement of its elements, not in their character ... In the telescoping and foreshortening of history that resulted, the past could be differentiated from the present mainly by its primitivism, the rudimentary character of the institutions and ideas whose ultimate development the writers were privileged to know so well.[40]

It is surely of significance that, during the 1960s and for much of the 1970s, English historians of education remained silent on the historiography of their subject at precisely the time that a major debate was raging in the United States, the only significant exception being a brief but perceptive contribution to *Blond's Encyclopaedia of Education* by W.H.G. Armytage.[41]

If this was one direct result of 'the English tradition' within the history of education, another was the failure of many more recent authors to break with this propagandist tradition. Thus, some of the most popular post-war authors perpetuated the myths which were first elaborated in the early twentieth century. Curtis, Boultwood, Jarman, A.D.C. Peterson, H.M. Pollard, H.C. Barnard and H.C. Dent can all be identified with one or other of the 'schools' or 'strands' identified earlier in this article; and it was their work which helped mould the attitudes of student teachers and educationists for at least two decades after the Second World War.

The irony confronting historians of education at the present time, seeking to justify their own function, is that, on the one hand, much impressive work has been completed during the most recent twenty years, yet on the other, the continuing threat to history of education as a taught subject in initial-training and in-service courses may reflect suspicion of the earlier 'propagandist' tradition which, although now largely a thing of the past, is all too familiar to many educationists and administrators now in their mid- or late-careers. Brian Simon and W.B. Stephens[42] have made clear the wide variety of approach adopted by recent and contemporary historians of education; and, although not referring directly to this earlier tradition, they make clear, by implication at least, the contrasts between earlier and recent approaches.

Two implications of all this are very clear. First, it behoves historians of education to ensure that their work is not threatened through reference to the shortcomings of an earlier period. One suspicion is that, where the history of education is under threat, its opponents may simply be unaware of the insights to be gained through acquaintance with some of the most recent work. There is, though, a second and wider threat. One lesson which we can learn from the past is that 'progress', however defined, is not necessarily sustained or extended. Just as, at earlier periods, the history of education has subsided to become a relatively trivial and isolated adjunct to social history, such a development is again possible. It would be richly ironic, and a matter for regret, if the History of Education Society, which has done so much to encourage dialogue between historians of differing styles, methodologies and persuasions, should, during a period of economic recession, become the catalyst of a similar divorce. There is much in the present situation which makes such a development possible; increasingly overloaded teaching timetables, difficulties in restocking libraries, the prohibitive cost of attending academic conferences, the need to seek 'attractive' or 'popular' conference themes. In the contemporary crisis, perhaps the best defence which historians of education can make of their work is to seek to ensure that they never become the victim of some future critic, pen dipped in vitriol, who may accuse them of perpetrating their own particular versions of propaganda.

NOTES

1. B. Simon, 'The history of education', in J.W. Tibble (ed.), *The Study of Education* (1966), pp.91–131. See No.5 in this volume.
2. B. Holmes, 'The contribution of history to the science of education', in P. Nash (ed.), *History of Education* (1970), pp.308–31.
3. M.V.J. Seaborne, 'The history of education', in J.W. Tibble (ed.), *An Introduction to the Study of Education* (1971), pp.65–79.
4. B. Simon, 'The history of education in the 1980s', *British Journal of Educational Studies*, 30, 1 (Feb. 1982), 85–96.
5. W.B. Stephens, 'Recent trends in the history of education in England to 1900', *Education Research and Perspectives*, 8, 1 (June 1981), 3–15.
6. H. Silver, 'Aspects of neglect: the strange case of nineteenth century education', *Oxford Review of Education*, 3, 1 (1977), 57–69. See No.13 in this volume.
7. H. Silver, *Nothing but the present, or nothing but the past?* Inaugural lecture, Chelsea College, University of London (1977).
8. E.H. Carr, *What is history?* (Pelican edition, 1964), p.23.
9. *Ibid.*, p.29.
10. D. Thomson, *The Aims of History* (1969), p.35.
11. F. Watson, 'The study of the history of education', *Contemporary Review*, 105 (1914), 82–91. See No.1 in this volume.

12. R.H. Quick, *Essays on educational reformers* (2nd edition 1898), p.505.
13. S.S. Laurie, *Comenius* (1895), p.31.
14. O. Browning, *Introduction to the history of educational theories* (1881), preface.
15. J.W. Adamson, *A guide to the history of education*, Historical Association, Helps for students of history, 24 (1970), 3–4.
16. *Ibid.*, 4.
17. J.W. Adamson, *Pioneers of Modern Education* (1905), pp.268–9.
18. F. Watson, *The Old Grammar Schools* (1916), pp.141–2.
19. P. Wallis, 'Leach; past, present and future', *British Journal of Educational Studies*, 12 (1963–4), 184.
20. *Times* (21 Sept. 1915).
21. A.F. Leach, *English Schools at the Reformation* (1896), p.6.
22. *Ibid.*, p.109.
23. A.F. Leach, *The Schools of Mediaeval England* (1915), p.331.
24. *English Schools at the Reformation*, p.122.
25. Board of Education, *Report of the Consultative Committee on the Primary School* (1931), Chapter 1.
26. Board of Education, *The Education of the Adolescent: report of the Consultative Committee* (1926), pp.34–5.
27. Board of Education, *Secondary Education: report of the Consultative Committee* (1938), p.66.
28. *Ibid.*, pp.72–3.
29. *Ibid.*, pp.77–8.
30. G.D.N. Lowndes, *The Silent Social Revolution* (1937), p.240.
31. *Ibid.*, p.241.
32. *Ibid.*, p.244.
33. *Ibid.*, p.225.
34. A. Mansbridge, *An Adventure in Working Class Education* (1920), p.53.
35. *Ibid.*, p.82.
36. M. Stocks, *The W.E.A.: the first fifty years* (1953), p.51.
37. A. Mansbridge, *The Older Universities of England* (1923), p.285.
38. W.W. Craik, *Central Labour College* (1964), p.56.
39. A.E. Dobbs, *Education and Social Movements* (1919).
40. B. Bailyn, *Education in the Forming of American Society* (1960), pp.5–12.
41. W.H.G. Armytage, 'Historiography of Education', in E. Blishen (ed.), *Blond's Encyclopaedia of Education* (1969), pp.345–7.
42. See notes 4 and 5 above.